SHOW
TIME

SHOW TIME

Inside the Lakers' Breakthrough Season

BY COACH
PAT RILEY

WARNER BOOKS

A Warner Communications Company

Warner Books, Inc., 666 Fifth Avenue, New York, NY 10103

 A Warner Communications Company

Printed in the United States of America
First printing:April 1988
10 9 8 7 6 5 4 3 2 1
Library of Congress Cataloging-in-Publication Data

Riley, Pat.
    Show time.
    1. Los Angeles Lakers (Basketball team)   I. Title.
GV885.52.L67R55   1988   796.32'364'0979494   87-40417
ISBN 0-446-51427-6

Book design: H. Roberts

To Chris and James Patrick, for all the triple kisses on the way to the game. For being the reason why this is all possible.

To our families, the Rodstroms and the Rileys, for getting this whole thing going.

Acknowledgments

To Bill Bertka and Randy Pfund. Your constant support has made me grow. To Chick Hearn, who, at three crucial times in my life, encouraged me to move forward. Thank you. To Jerry West, who simply said, "Yes . . . Take the job."

To Jerry Buss for agreeing.

To Angela Worthy, Wanda Cooper, Linda Rambis, Anita Scott, and Pam Matthews, whose undying support and loyalty to their Laker husbands made my job so much easier. Just make sure you check with me before you make another road trip.

To Claire Rothman for her ever present smile—win, lose, or draw. To Josh Rosenfeld for his professionalism, and for always keeping the media two inches away. To Bob Steiner for keeping Josh on his toes. To Billy Desser for creating video images that remind our players exactly what it looks like to be successful. To Rick Weinstein for the invaluable computer data and effort charts.

To Byron Laursen for his tireless assistance in the writing of this book.

To Richard Pine and Arthur Pine Associates for their determined work in representing this book.

To Gary Vitti for keeping the Lakers healthy and keeping me sane. To Rudy Garciduenas, our equipment manager, for being Rudy. To Mary Lou Liebich for taking care of my basketball life, and to Tania Hasbrouck for being right behind her. To Lon Rosen for creative team pictures and for always getting us to the parade on time. To Lou Baumeister for understanding why it took me two years to file an expense report. To M. K. The numbers haven't always been right on, but the letters have been meaningful.

To all those people who said we were over the hill and couldn't get the job done. If this is old age, give me more.

To all the Laker players, who believed in the team's greatness, who worked and sacrificed and proved it to the world. Now, fellas, we have to do it again.

Prologue

Teamwork is the essence of life. It makes possible everything from moonshots to the building of cities to the renewal of life. And a good team multiplies the potential of everyone on it, whether the team consists of a family, a school, a business, or an NBA squad.

The key to teamwork is to learn a role, accept that role, and strive to become excellent playing it. "Act well your part," Shakespeare wrote. "Therein lies the glory." The Lakers understand the importance of team roles: floor leaders to guide the team strategically, wingmen and trailers to make our fast break click, aggressive rebounders to deliver the ball to our best shooters, and solid, patient reserves to keep control of the game when the starters need rest.

The coach has a role too: to organize and direct, to create an environment where talent can flourish, to do everything possible to enable the team to win.

My role as author of this book is to enable you to discover the teamwork that underlies the Show Time image, to bring you into the inner circle of our team to see the Lakers through my eyes, and to share the lessons of our championship season.

The Show Time image is a blessing and a curse. We have brought excitement to the game, constantly running, scoring explosively, elevating the transition game to an art. Some fans—and sometimes even the media—are so fascinated with the skyhooks, fast breaks, thread-the-needle no-look passes, slam dunks, and high fives that they imagine it just comes naturally. Except for the Lakers' inner circle, few people realize that, beneath the surface glitter, the players bring a fanatical depth of preparation to every game. Their apparently spontaneous creativity and effortless innovation are actually the product of hundreds and hundreds of hours of hard practice sessions. And with that devotion to hard work the Lakers have made a covenant with each other to put aside selfishness so that the *team* can achieve its goals, saying, "Whatever it takes for the team to win, I'll do it." During a game, when set patterns suddenly flow into creative, split-second decisions, players instinctively do what's best for the team. They function as effectively on the spiritual level as they do on the physical. They've each built mental toughness equal to their God-given talents. That's what allows them to break through their individual limitations to reach their potential as a team. That's why the Lakers are a breakthrough team.

For some fans, Show Time triggers thoughts like these: "Yeah, that's the Lakers. Talent to burn. The coach rolls the balls out and turns them loose to run and gun. A finesse team, but can't take it when it gets tough. They win more than they should." Laker opponents are a different case. When they win, it's because they're determined, hustling, and hardworking. They scrap for every single basket, every rebound, every victory. They win because of character. Not like the La La Land Lakers with their movie-star friends and fragile egos.

The Lakers have been called everything from "best in the history of the game" to "over the hill." We're so rich in talent, so entertaining to watch, that the celebrities who pack our courtside seats sometimes go unnoticed. Some rivals hate us so much that their fans get drunk, violent, and abusive when we come to town. Others show so much respect that our stars are greeted as warmly as their own. David Halberstam, the noted author, expressed a belief that the Lakers represent "basketball as it will be played in the next century." Other writers say we're pathetic unless everything goes our way. Most sports journalists picked the Lakers as the best team in the league as the '87–'88 season began. A year ago, most said we were in decline —maybe third or fourth in the West, but no match for any Eastern power.

As a constant witness to the dedication and growth of my players, I'm tired of hearing such criticism. But after our quick exit in the '85–'86 playoffs, I heard it more than ever; people were already measuring us for coffins. We needed an attitude breakthrough after that loss, and we got it when all the players committed themselves to go all out for a Career Best Effort in '86–'87.

There are significant moments in every person's life—and in every team's life—when breakthroughs occur. If you have a positive attitude and constantly strive to give your best effort, eventually you will overcome your immediate problems and find that you are ready for greater challenges. That's what this team is all about. We had a tremendous breakthrough when we won the '84–'85 championship on the parquet floor of Boston Garden. We had an emotional breakthrough in February '87 after a hard loss, when we woke up and realized that we needed to reaffirm our commitment to strive for that Career Best mentality. We've broken through situations of jealousy and misunderstanding that could have torn the team apart. We've broken through the attitude that our glory days are over. We're fighting this year to break through the belief that no team can stay hungry enough to win back-to-back titles. The Lakers understand the importance of a breakthrough mentality.

I made a conscious decision to put myself on the line for the upcoming season. While I was still soaked in champagne from head to shoes after our Game Six victory over Boston last June, reporters whipped out their notepads and extended their microphones to ask me if the Lakers could possibly win two championships in a row. I looked right at them and answered, "I guarantee you we're going to repeat next year!"

My players thought I was a little crazy. One said, "Well, Coach might have had a little too much champagne when you asked him that." But Bill Bertka, my first assistant coach, gave me a wily look from the corner of his eye that said, "I see what you're doing." My statement was well thought out. I wrote it, and I spent time staring at the words, a week before we took the trophy. I went out on that limb because we have gotten to a point in maturity, in talent, and in emotional commitment where we have a terrific chance of winning consecutive championships. If there's ever a time when the Lakers are going to come forward and redefine the image of Show Time, this is their year. It will be our next major breakthrough.

I'll guarantee something else. Read this book and you'll really know what Show Time means. In the events of one very special season, you'll get an insider's view of all sides of the Show Time image, front and back and top and bottom. Get ready for a breakthrough.

This Magic
Moment

There are two possible states of being in the NBA: winning and misery. Winning also breaks into two categories: savoring victory, and being too damn tired to savor victory. After a pressure-cooker final series and after the parades and the celebrations and the champagne, my wife Chris and I plowed into all the neglected details that had piled up in our home.

Our lives always go on hold over the two months of the playoffs. We shut out the whole world. All our energy is focused on the Lakers. We had a two-foot stack of mail: letters from friends, almost apologetic about staying in touch during our craziest time of the year, bills and relationships stamped "Past Due."

Both of us were still running on playoff energy. I'd get up at six in the morning and start looking for the videotape of last night's game. Then I'd remember . . . "I don't have to do this for four more months." When we opened up the paper there was no longer any

Laker news, no more NBA stories. It was time for us to cool out, to find an island and fall asleep.

Mychal Thompson had talked endlessly about the Bahamas, his home turf, from the day he joined the Lakers. He kept saying how great it was there, how the Bahamian people have adopted us as their own team. During the playoffs, watching one of the games on TV, I saw Mychal in a commercial. The Caribbean answer to Paul Hogan—selling the Bahamas in a colorful shirt while beautiful Bahamian women were frolicking on the sand. He had always said, "I'm going to be prime minister of the Bahamas someday. If you ever go down to the Bahamas, just mention my name. They'll treat you red-carpet royally."

He was right!

We had decided to visit and called Mychal. One day later, a guy calling himself Cap Smith was on the line, saying, "Well, how ya doin'?" in a thick Bahamian accent. "Mychal asked me to call ya."

Cap Smith is with their Ministry of Tourism. One phone call from Mychal and Cap took care of all our arrangements. The people of the Bahamas take hospitality the way I want the Lakers to take basketball: seriously, but with a great sense of fun.

Later on I tried to call Cap at his office and he wasn't in. I told the secretary, "Well, give me his home number." She said, "He doesn't have a telephone at home."

We left a few days early and went to Atlanta. Mike Fratello, the coach of the Atlanta Hawks, heads up a special charity for accident-trauma victims. Chris and I had agreed to stop in at his fundraising dinner.

During the dinner, Mike's wife took Chris aside and said, "Chris, *now* we understand what pressure you're under. Just a little. We got our first taste this year of being expected to win all the time."

Another coach's wife entered the conversation. She could not fathom the idea. Winning all the time was their greatest wish in life. But until you're very close to it, until you've walked in those shoes, it's very difficult to understand the pressure. Losing is misery. Winning is exhilaration. But once you've become a winner, you're expected to produce excellence every time.

Well, the only excellence we had to exhibit for the next week was our talent for relaxing on a sunny beach in paradise.

Mychal's parents met us at the bottom of the airplane's steps, beaming with pride. Everything was set up. Our luggage was taken from our hands. Customs waved us right through. We walked straight into a brand-new Daimler limousine, courtesy of the Ministry of Tourism. We were the first guests to ride in it.

They carted us off in style to the Ocean Club on Paradise Island, Nassau. They explained the rules of the Bahamas: they don't allow you to do anything else but lie down on the sand, put your head back, and relax. We followed the rules.

The Ocean Club used to be Huntington Hartford's Bahamian getaway. He had a main house, "The Manor," and four villas for his guests. All the buildings have deep Moorish arches and thick stucco walls. Dion Strachan, the manager, is a hands-on type. If something needed doing, Dion took care of it personally. He set us up in one of the villas and told us the lore of the Ocean Club, like how the Shah of Iran spent four months of his exile there, with guards and machine guns hidden underneath the sand.

Friday, the day we arrived, we set up an understanding with Matthew and his buddy, the young guys who took care of the cabana gear. We said, "See that area down there, beyond the crowd? Right under that big tree? Every day just have two chairs there, an umbrella, and two rafts. And a couple of piña coladas at noon. We will definitely make it worth your while."

Matthew and his partner took care of those daily requirements. And that's where we spent eight of the sweetest and laziest days of our lives.

Sunday afternoon at about three Chris and I debated which one of us had enough energy to move our chairs into a good position for the late-afternoon rays. We would converse awhile, then sleep, then read books and play cassettes. I had the new John Gregory Dunne novel, *The Red, White, and Blue.* Chris was reading *Men Who Hate Women and the Women Who Love Them,* which fueled some heated discussions. And we were listening to my Bahamas Tape, which I had put together the night before we left: Whitney Houston, Kenny G. and Anita Baker. All their ballads on one side, all their fast stuff on the other. Truly a tape my players could appreciate. And one of them did.

I looked down the beach. There was a figure walking in our direction, maybe eight hundred yards away. I took off my glasses and squinted. This was a big guy. But most of the Bahamian men are tall; it could have been anybody.

This guy ran out into the surf to shake somebody's hand. Then he walked up the sand to slap five with somebody else and do a little pirouette. He kept walking our way until I could see that he was wearing a big, loose, gray T-shirt and a little red bikini bathing suit.

"Chris," I said, "see that guy? Look familiar to you?"

"Where? Who?"

"The guy walking down the beach, looking like he's having a good time."

He was getting closer and you could begin to see some distinctive body language. His steps were short, finely balanced. It almost looked as if he were being pulled ahead, stride by stride, with invisible cords tied at the point of each shoulder. It was someone moving with the style and ease of a great athlete, knowing all his physical components were working in perfect unison.

"That's Magic!" she said. "That's Earvin!"

I scrambled out of my canvas beach chair—the fastest I'd moved in days . . . in years. I ran down the high side of the beach in his direction about fifty yards and hid behind an umbrella. As Earvin passed by, I yelled, "Hey, Buck!" That's another nickname of his. It goes back to his rookie year, when he came into the league and surprised everybody with his energy. We called him "the young buck." Nobody uses that name except people on the team.

He stopped in his tracks and looked around. I shouted again, "Hey, Buck!" Then he caught whose voice it was. He still didn't see me, but he knew. Earvin put his head down and shook it from side to side, holding back a grin. When I walked up, he grabbed me and we embraced. "Somebody told me the coach was here," he said. "They said the coach was down in the Bahamas."

He had just flown in from Lansing, Michigan, his hometown, after conducting a week-long basketball camp for 350 kids. Between that and our victory in Game Six had come several parties, a series of promotional appearances, and a spot on the Johnny Carson show. This was his first walk on the beach, his first few hours on the island. This fellow that everyone thinks of as a big social lion, single, always available, ready to party, was going to take a walk on the sand and sit down alone to watch the sunset. Then he was headed back to his hotel room, where he would order from room service, tune in *Murder, She Wrote*, and drop off to sleep. Instead, he runs into Coach. Life isn't always fair.

"This is the first day I've had to relax," Earvin said. "The first time I've been able to stop and think about what we did this year."

"Come on over and sit down," I said. "Wanna start with a strawberry daiquiri or a piña colada?" Matthew hustled up another chair. We all shifted into a perfect line with where the sun was going to set. The three of us spent the rest of the afternoon having a great, long talk. People would come up, maybe two out of every three that passed by, and approach us to talk or get an autograph. Earvin was polite, as he always is, but he would just say hello and stretch out his hand in a gesture that was halfway between a friendly wave and a running back's stiff-arm. He'd say, "I'm on vacation now. You have a good one, now. Me and Riles need to relax."

"Well, we didn't have to worry much about fans last year, did we?" I said.

He smiled and said, "Yeah, I remember how it was last year. Our problem was watching the Finals in our living rooms instead of being there. That was painful."

It was also unusual. Since Earvin Johnson's arrival in 1979, the Lakers had made eight straight trips to the playoffs and *six* trips to the Finals.

In the '78–'79 season, just before Magic came on board, we were the third-place team in our division. We got blown out of the second playoff round by the Sonics, 4–1.

When Earvin joined the team, he was like a brand-new product. Patent pending. Nobody knew what the hell he was going to do. Nobody figured the Lakers to do much more that season than they had done in the previous six. It was what I call an innocent climb. There was no expectation of winning a championship. It was just a team. New coaches in Jack McKinney and Paul Westhead and the usual great players. Somewhere along the line, most people figured, the Lakers would probably find a way to screw up again.

Then *VROOOOM.* Sixty wins against 22 losses, one game shy of the best record in the NBA that year. Kareem held his usual high standards, nearly 25 points a game. Jamaal Wilkes picked up his average to an even 20. Norm Nixon and Jim Chones, along with Earvin, averaged in healthy double figures. Then a bicycling accident put McKinney in the hospital; Westhead took over and brought an ex-player named Riley out of the broadcast booth to assist. We went 4–1 over Phoenix in the semis, 4–1 over Seattle, the defending champs, in the Western Conference Finals.

We went up 3–2 against Philadelphia in the Finals. Kareem, the heart of our attack, sprained an ankle and couldn't play in Game Six.

The Sixers figured they're in clover. But Earvin Johnson, twenty years old, came out to handle the opening tip-off, filled in at center on offense, then switched from center to guard and forward and back to center. It threw total confusion into the Sixers and we smacked them 123 to 107. Earvin scored an amazing 42 points, grabbed 15 rebounds, and had 7 assists. One year after leading Michigan State to a national collegiate championship, Earvin had keyed an NBA championship for the Lakers.

"That first championship got people to pay attention," I told Earvin.

"I know," he said. "We won that championship, but we weren't a championship team."

I knew exactly what he was talking about. I stood up and mimicked walking through the locker room door as I had once before on a very disappointing day. Earvin nodded. "Yeah," he said, "I remember. I'll never forget it."

Dissension tore up the Lakers in the year following that championship. Success is often the first step toward disaster. I call it "the disease of more." People start thinking, "I'm really the key ingredient. It was my quality minutes off the bench," or "It was my brilliant coaching decisions," or "It was my outstanding defense." People who were quiet during the lean years suddenly want more money, more playing time, more recognition. And they get aggressive and jealous about pulling in their "more."

All due rewards will eventually arrive for players who can keep their focus on playing at top ability. But the disease of more takes away their perspective.

Tremendous attention was focused on Magic Johnson, this new phenomenon, when the next season got underway. Then he tore up his knee and missed 45 games. The rest of the team had to pull the weight. The funny thing is, they did a great job and no one else seemed to notice. Even without Earvin they rallied to a 28 and 17 record. They were getting stronger with every game.

When Magic finally returned, the press and the fans treated it like the Second Coming. There must have been fifty photographers crouching down and elbowing for a shot when he was introduced to the crowd. By the time we got to the playoffs, the jealousy became intense. Players were taking little digs at each other via the sports columnists. Suddenly we had a big talker known as "Unnamed Source" on the roster. Unnamed Source told reporters that Earvin believed his teammates resented his success.

We finished the regular season three games behind Phoenix and had to get by Houston in a best-of-three series. Houston took the first game at the Forum, and we got even at one game apiece with a great effort on their home court. The decisive game was to be played on a Sunday afternoon in L.A.

I walked into our locker room five minutes before our team meeting for the final game of the series. What I saw when the door swung open was a total breakdown of the team. Magic stood on one side, pleading, "I didn't really say any of those things in the paper."

A couple of other players faced him from the other side of the room. They yelled back vehemently, "If it wasn't true, they wouldn't have printed it!"

Some of the rookies were actually trembling. Kareem Abdul-Jabbar and Jamaal Wilkes looked over the scene with pained, distant expressions, as if to say, "I can't believe this shit I'm hearing!"

The game went down to the wire. We had possession late in the fourth quarter. Down by one. Earvin drove the lane hoping to make the winning shot. He threw up an airball instead.

"Yeah," he said, "that situation cost us our title. If we only knew then what we know now. But I guess that's what they call growing pains."

"That was just a little family dispute," I said. "We didn't know how to handle it at that time. But we've sure as hell worked on it."

We learned from that experience how to keep the team together, how to confront the disease of more. We were stripped of our championship role, and not for the last time. But our awareness was developing. By the next season, '81–'82, in spite of some turmoil that resulted in a head-coaching change, we won the championship back. I had stepped in as interim coach while they searched for someone permanent. Bill Bertka came in as assistant coach, giving me one of the most complete and experienced guys in the NBA and a mentor. Kurt Rambis arrived, with all his fire. Michael Cooper blossomed. Bob McAdoo arrived from New Jersey for a second-round draft choice and cash. He turned out to be the secret ingredient in winning the title.

We talked about the next year, '82–'83. How injuries knocked us out of the Finals. James Worthy, our best rookie, named to the NBA All-Rookie team and a future All-Star, broke his leg in the last week of the regular season. McAdoo, a former All-Star and three-time league scoring champ, went down with a torn hamstring. Norm Nixon, a six-year backcourt vet who was on the league All-Rookie team his first year and who averaged around 17 points a game, was out with a shoulder separation. Then in '83–'84, we were the best, but the best team didn't win. We made a gift of that series to Boston. It was exactly as the press described it. We choked; all of us. And we had to live with that all summer long.

Earvin said, "Yeah," and talked about all the free throws he had missed in the Finals. And how he could not get a shot off, with eight seconds to go in Game Two. I had told him to control the ball, then feed Kareem at the last possible second. "I waited too long to execute the play," Earvin said. He could just as easily have told reporters, "Coach told me to freeze the ball. Coach should have given me a second option." But we were a better team by then. We learned from that locker room scene. You don't hear anyone in the Lakers' inner circle accusing their teammates anymore. "Unnamed Source" hasn't produced a quote in years.

It may frustrate the beat writers sometimes, because there's nothing like a dissension angle to get your story noticed, but the Lakers have become a tight family. There's still plenty of ego in the system. You can't expect such talented, accomplished people—the staff as well as the players—to be anything but strong-willed. But over the years of this team's development, the atmosphere of trust and mutual support became a top priority. That's when our growth and our character really became substantial. That's when we became a championship team.

"Yeah," Earvin said, "they called us chokers. They called us the L.A. Fakers. They rubbed the salt in." He let a smile cross his face. "We put it together the next year, though, didn't we?"

On Memorial Day of 1985, the first game of the Finals, we looked like the chokers everyone had been calling us. Boston pinned our ears back, 148 to 114. The famous Memorial Day Massacre.

We met for a game-reviewing session the next morning. I walked into the room and found Kareem Abdul-Jabbar sitting up front. He got right where he could take his criticism full in the face. I let fly. I stopped the tape at every bad spot, backed it up and played it over again. James Worthy sat in the back row. He couldn't believe how the team captain, the greatest basketball player of all time, absorbed every harsh word and looked straight back at me and said, "You're right."

I went all the way around the room. I nailed everybody. I told one guy to stop feeling sorry for himself. I told another one that if he was going to let tough play by the Celtics take him out of the game, I might as well take him out myself and save them the trouble. I told another one that he didn't have to shoot every damn time he came down the court, that it was sometimes okay to pass the ball. Finally, I came back to the captain and I asked him simply and directly, "Kareem . . . what do you want to do?" Kareem said, "Let's just go to work."

I couldn't have been happier. For the next two and a half days the Lakers practiced harder than I'd ever seen them before. They were out to purge themselves. If I didn't drive them hard enough, they said they wanted to go harder. We hit the transition drills, we hammered on getting the big men back quicker while the first line of our defense, the guards, held the attack. I worried that Kareem would run himself into exhaustion, but he just wouldn't stop.

Thursday, May 30th, we boarded the team bus for Game Two. For three days I had struggled over what message to give them for the game. Chris had helped me. We looked to the Bible, to works of inspirational literature, everywhere.

Kareem came up the steps of the bus and asked me if his dad, Big Al, could ride along. I was surprised. We had made a big point that the bus would be 12 players and three coaches. No one else. But I could see a need in his eyes. He was about to face one of the biggest tests of his career. It was important to be with his father. I said, "Fine." Here were these two men sitting together. One big and the other a giant. I knew that they had had their share of father-and-son difficulty in earlier years. But that day they were feeling the importance of their mutual bond. They inspired me to throw away my prepared speech.

Watching them together made me think about fathers and sons. I thought about my father, Lee Riley. He played and coached some pro baseball and scuffled hard to keep his ambitions alive. He wasn't always an open and talkative guy, but he always seemed to be there when it counted. He was at my wedding in 1970. I was then on my way to the Portland Trailblazers from the San Diego Rockets. Three years after being a first-round draft pick, I had seen my playing time cut nearly two thirds. San Diego didn't bother to protect me from the expansion draft. About all I had in the world was a plastic plant, a stack of Motown records and a new bride. It was a scary, exciting, unsettled time.

We were seeing my parents off after the reception. As he was pulling away, my father stuck his head out the window of the car. It was a red 1965 Chevrolet Caprice with primer spots on the fenders. He looked at me and said, "Just remember what I always taught you. Somewhere, someplace, sometime, you're going to have to plant your feet, make a stand, and kick some ass. And when that time comes, you do it."

Those were his last words to me. That was the last time I ever saw him. He died of a heart attack shortly afterward. I thought about him when I looked at Kareem and Big Al.

Three minutes before we were to hit the parquet floor in Game Two I shared some of those thoughts. I talked about motivation. How they couldn't depend on me to provide it. How every time your back is against the wall, there is only one person that can help. "And that's you," I said. "It has to come from inside." I talked about all the voices we've heard from those who cared about us in the past: coaches, mothers, fathers, teachers. I said, "What I want you to do is close your eyes. Rewind the tape. Listen. When your back is against the wall, that's the time to recall those voices." I told them what my father had told me and that became our battle cry. This was the place and the time. We had to make that stand.

We did it that day. We beat Boston 109–102 and took the series back to L.A., where we won two out of three on our court. Then we beat Boston on their own floor in the sixth game, 111–100. In two weeks we climbed from one of our lowest valleys to our highest peak.

The sun was getting low, off toward Florida. I hit Earvin with a direct question. "What did you think about your performance last year, in the Houston series? If you had to focus on one main problem, what was it?"

He shook his head and said, "I didn't rebound enough."

"Nah," I said. "You tried to pick up the team and carry it, but we weren't ready for that kind of leadership. And you weren't really ready either. You can't just take the reins. They have to be handed to you.

"This year, when you took over in the third quarter of the last playoff game, or when you took over any game, the team was conditioned to your taking over. They were in position to rebound. They were in position to get a pass for a better shot. They were in better position because they knew what you were going to do.

"The whole difference between this year and last was your mental and physical conditioning as an offensive player. If we had had the same attitude and preparation last year against Houston, we would've won. It took a year for you to come to peace with your role as a leader in the NBA, as a leader on the team. It's taken all these eight years to get there."

"That's why this is the best of times," Chris said. "It doesn't matter what comes at you now. You've learned to deal with pressure from the players, from the media, from the fans. You've come to grips with the loneliness and waiting and being misunderstood. That's the life of a superstar."

We chewed over the entire playoff experience. James Worthy and Byron Scott getting us off to a fast start. Doug Moe, the coach of Denver, saying our defense was so tight that we didn't give them "room to sweat." Michael Cooper setting a record for 3-point shots. A.C. Green, his second year on the team, leading us in rebounds. Mychal Thompson making the play that set up our Game Four win over Boston on their home court, our most important win of the whole year.

"It all came from different areas," Earvin said. "We were gettin' it here and there, here and there. They didn't know which way to go against us. Or who to really try to stop. That's what made this championship so special. Everybody had a hand in it."

We were savoring the late rays by then, smiling at how pretty it was, smiling at how great it felt to be world champs. I thought about Kareem and all he'd gone through over all his seasons. How he never lightened up all year long, until he came out in the final minutes of the very last game. He shook hands and paid respects to K.C. Jones and the rest of the Celtics. He smiled like I've never seen him smile before.

"It wasn't all good times, Riles," Earvin reminded me. I turned my head to read the expression on his face. I saw some humor in it, but he wasn't smiling. His head was tilted toward me and both his eyebrows were arched as high as he could make them go. "You remember Salt Lake City, don't you? Last February?"

Ice and Salt

Sometimes the breakthroughs aren't the pretty moments. Sometimes losing is more constructive than winning.

February was a prosperous month for us. We had ten victories altogether for the month. We ran off 29 points against the Sacramento Kings before they were able to score a single point. We came from 17 down to beat the Celtics. That was the Laker debut of Mychal Thompson, on national television. With twenty-five games left in the season, we had the best record in the NBA—two games ahead of Boston. We had finally acquired a top-quality reserve center. We led the Pacific Division by 8½, the Western Conference by 6½. We won six straight, nine out of the last ten.

Our record was almost perfect. But something alarming was going on. Even though we were winning, our effort numbers were on the way down.

When you play lousy and you win, you lose perspective. You start believing that lack of effort doesn't matter. Other teams are intimidated by your record. Momentum is on your side. Then playing lousy becomes part of your style and your psyche. You set yourself up to get beat and demoralized someplace down the road.

Lose a game and you might stop, check out the problem, and come back with a sharper attitude. You'd become stimulated. We kept winning and we eased back, dangerously.

My coaching notes for the games of February are full of warnings: "Played tired early in game . . . Came out after half in a walk. Never pushed until late in 3rd quarter." "Played with very little fire—FLAT . . . Let them come back three times." "On free throws we walk away from misses . . ."

Half a week before a February 28th game with Utah, we played Phoenix on consecutive nights in a home-and-home series. Earvin missed both games with Achilles tendinitis. Without him, the team scored under 100 points each time. Even though we won, my coaching antenna was pulling in a message I didn't like.

January and February are always watch-out months. The flights seem longer, the practices seem tougher. Everybody's tired. They call it the Dog Days of the NBA. A leading contender can get burned during the Dog Days—it happens every year. You start finding ways to save your strength. You don't see any damage right away, and players tell themselves they can always turn their effort back on when it's needed.

Then you lose one and you think, "Aw, it's the Dog Days. It's okay." Bullshit! It's not okay.

Then you lose a pair, then three out of five. In the space of a week and a half you can slip a notch in the standings. Then the team gets nervous. They start playing not to lose instead of playing to win. There's a world of difference between the two.

Of all games, basketball is one in which you can never show weaknesses. At the NBA level, everyone knows how to spot and exploit them. Watch what happens when a rookie comes in the game. Watch what happens when a key player gets into foul trouble. The opponent goes right at them. They say sharks can smell eight parts of blood in a million parts of water. An NBA veteran senses that playing-not-to-lose posture just as readily. The results are exactly the same.

I wanted the players to break through that Dog Days attitude. If some teams were going to relax, why shouldn't we use the opportunity to open up a bigger gap between ourselves and the rest of the pack? We needed every advantage this year.

The February 28th game was one of the most significant of the year to me. Utah was growing confident they could beat the Lakers. We had to drive that idea out of their heads. The Salt Palace was always a tough arena for us. We had dropped a game there in early January, 107–101. We had to prove we could win on their home court.

After February 28th our schedule would turn soft, with eight out of the next nine games at home. We'd be able to take things easier, which I kept trying to communicate to the team. We played Golden State at home the night before the Utah game. Those two teams had beaten us a combined three times already. We just had to maintain our focus past Golden State and Utah.

Historically, we had never pushed hard at the goal of having the best record in the NBA. Perhaps we believed we didn't need the home court advantage to win a playoff series, that stretching ourselves to achieve the best record would leave the team psychologically spent for the playoffs. This year had to be different. These beliefs had been coming around to bite us on the ass.

We got past the Golden State hurdle. Kareem put together one of his great efforts—84% shooting from the floor, 30 points and 8 rebounds. Earvin came back from a two-game Phoenix layoff with another triple-double performance. We won the game 121–109, but I wrote in my postgame notes: "Can't play soft—must be quick and active." Even though Earvin had returned to the lineup, he showed tremendous fatigue. We just needed one more performance at the big-game effort level. Then we could afford some rest.

After we got off the plane in Salt Lake City, I decided to call a short practice. I could see that we were on our way to getting our asses whipped. At ten in the morning, riding in the bus to our hotel, I motioned to Gary Vitti, the team trainer. I said, "Tell all the players to check in, toss down their luggage, put on some sweats, and walk over to the Salt Palace."

The hotel where we stay in Salt Lake City is right across the street from their arena. No long bus rides, just a short walk across the street. I only wanted the team to practice free throws. Do some shooting. Walk through the game plan. Get a feeling of the rims and go home. Thirty minutes at the most.

Vitti spread the word. An incredible quiet came over the bus. I was gunning to evoke an attitude like, "Yeah, let's get this game plan down solid! Let's shoot a little and get the touch. Let's kick their ass tonight!" Instead the attitude was, "Damn it. Coach is crazy. He's gonna take us over there and practice us hard."

The shootaround was like pulling teeth. They'd do exactly what they were told, but nothing more. Then they'd take a sullen stance. Arms folded. Weight shifted over to one leg. Heads dropped, looking at me through their eyebrows. Indifference. They looked like kids being made to stand in the principal's office.

We went back to the hotel and we ate and slept. When time came for our regular pregame talk and video session and blackboard work, I still had hopes of sensing a big-game feeling in the team.

The Jazz are one of our toughest matchups. On our last trip to Salt Lake City, Utah had embarrassed us. Their center, Mark Eaton, stands 7'3" and weighs 280 pounds. That makes it tough to shoot from the low post. Karl Malone, who was in his second season after making the All-Rookie team, is the kind of hard-banging physical player who can really disrupt our offense—unless we come back just as hard. Salt Lake City sits about one mile up in the Rockies, which is an additional factor. The Lakers are used to oxygen-rich sea-level air.

The local papers made a big issue about how the Jazz were primed to take us out of the Western Conference race. I pointed this out to the team. Then I went through our objectives again: "We take care of this and we've got eight of nine at home. This is our chance to extend past Boston. This is our chance to shut Utah's mouth. This is our chance to feel good about ourselves, to break through this Dog Day thinking. We could put ourselves in a position to do something good . . . maybe great."

I looked in their eyes. All I saw was, "What else do you want from us, Coach? We've won six in a row already. Isn't that enough for you?"

We hit the floor with that attitude. At the four-minute mark I called time out and raised hell. We were behind 11 to 3. After eight minutes I started to break up the starting lineup. We only shot 32% in the first quarter, but Mychal Thompson played great. Cooper ignited us a little bit. Kurt played hard.

It became a nip-and-tuck game in the second quarter and we went up one basket at the half.

The Jazz pulled out to a five-point lead early in the third period. It was eleven points by the start of the fourth quarter. We got a last-period rally going. A fifteen-footer by Billy Thompson. A basket plus a foul shot from Mychal. A Kareem hook and a 3-pointer from Cooper. We were within three. Back on the seesaw. This was the

point in the game to call up the energy they'd been saving. But the
Jazz weren't showing any convenient weaknesses to exploit. It seemed
that this was an okay game to lose. You've got to lose a few, right?
Why not this one? It's sure going to be a bitch to try to win it now.

I could see the fruits of our attitude problem in front of my eyes.
We stopped making an effort to do anything. We didn't play defense.
We didn't make the offense work. Our execution was horrible, our
passing decisions out of the break were not intelligent. I started thinking they didn't want to win. Maybe they had to show me that it
didn't do any good to push them. Sometimes I think those thoughts.

We lost the game, 107–100.

The first thing I noticed when I entered our locker room was a
couple of plastic bags full of half-melted ice, sitting on the floor. I
let them lay there. I circled the room. I waited for the whole team
to get settled, collect themselves and feel the loss. Then I gave them
a burst of Temporary Insanity.

"We quit!" I yelled at the team. "We just fucking quit!" For
eight minutes I ripped into them about their lack of fire and effort.
I hadn't been so angry since the Memorial Day Massacre. The reporters could hear me word-for-word all the way out in the hall.

This time I didn't hammer on any one player. I hammered on
the Dog Days mentality: the notion that you can turn your winning
attitude off and on when you think you need it. I wanted to uproot
that idea and throw it out of the team once and for all.

I yelled, "We didn't respond on effort plays. We didn't go after
the long rebounds and the loose balls. We didn't work with every
possession like we wanted it. I couldn't tell if we cared whether we
won or not. This is the same bullshit attitude that got us beat by
Houston last year. And I'll be goddamned if I'll allow it now!"

I stopped talking. I refocused on the ice bags. They were straight
in my path to the locker room door.

I kicked them hard, field goal style, and followed all the way
through. Cubes and water sprayed all over the room like shotgun
pellets. Randy Pfund, my assistant coach, was standing by the door-
way with his arms folded. He got soaked worse than anybody. I
tried to mumble "I'm sorry" out of the corner of my mouth as I
walked by, but I kept looking straight ahead.

It was totally quiet. I knew I left behind a roomful of blank
faces. I turned and walked out the door, past all the writers. I thought,
"Now what? How much damage have I done?"

Rocket Launch

Any time you win a champi-
onship, there's a ring ceremony in front of your home crowd early
in the next season. The celebration for our '84–'85 title was held
before a game against the Cleveland Cavaliers on November 4th,
1985. The fifth game of the new season. We had swept the first four.

The championship rings were beautiful: a thick gold band, a
black field, a diamond basketball entering a rim and net of pavé
diamonds. One at a time, each fellow got to walk in front of the
sold-out Forum crowd and accept his ring at the microphone. The
fans whistled and clapped and yelled in admiration.

Cleveland, a team struggling at the bottom of its division,
then proceeded to kick our championship ass. This was the second
time I had seen the same thing happen. Golden State whipped us in
November of 1982, right after we accepted our championship rings
for '81–'82. The visiting team sits there for 20 minutes watching you

get your strokes. It makes them hungry as hell to take it all away from you.

I started talking motivation to the team at our next practice. I said, "We didn't look committed. We haven't looked committed yet this year. Not in training camp. Not in exhibition. Not even in the games we won. We looked complacent. What is it going to take to regain that commitment?"

Kareem said, "Coach, how do you expect us to top last year?"

He had a point. How do you top beating the Boston Celtics in Boston Garden? How do you top bouncing back from the Memorial Day Massacre, winning three in a row, then taking the decisive win on that ugly parquet floor, right in the face of all that "Boston Mystique"?

The obvious answer is this: You drive ahead, become the first team since 1969 to win two championships in a row. And we were very focused on that goal. Kareem was one of the guys you would see wearing the custom-printed T-shirts in practice, white with big black letters across the shoulder blades, saying BACK TO BACK. But there is a difference between being the hunter and the hunted. From moment to moment it's subtle, like the difference between playing to win and playing not to get beaten. Over the course of a whole season and the playoffs, a hundred or so games, the difference between hunter and hunted can become immense. There's always a chance you'll forget how much better winning is than misery, and how much effort it takes to sustain a championship level of play. It takes hard work, psychologically, to overcome that mind-set. Kareem's comment, and the Cleveland performance, told me the Lakers were vulnerable.

In the early going of the '85–'86 season we cranked off 29 wins against 5 losses. We were making a serious run at the '71–'72 Lakers' record of 69 and 13, which remains the best record in league history. *Sports Illustrated* hazarded a guess that the '85–'86 Lakers might be the best team in the entire history of the professional game.

As soon as that article came out, we lost three in a row. We hit the Dog Days early. For a while after Christmas we won just slightly more than half of our games. We eventually righted course and finished at a respectable 62 and 20 for the regular season. Boston finished 67 and 15.

To advance in the playoffs and win the right to face Boston in the Finals again, we had to beat every NBA squad in the state of

Texas . . . first the San Antonio Spurs, then the Dallas Mavericks, and then the Houston Rockets.

The Spurs series brought out our best. We took the first game by a forty-seven point margin. Over the three-game series we averaged 127 points to their 92. There had been a belief that we could turn on our power at the key moment. This series made it look as if the theory were right. Didn't we pull out of the Dog Days slump to finish the season strong? Didn't we look awesome now?

Dallas made things tougher. They scored in incredible flurries. Mark Aguirre had the hot hand from outside. We went out to challenge his shots and our defense loosened up underneath for their guards. We won the opening pair of games in Los Angeles and lost the next two in Dallas for a two-two tie. The series returned to the Forum. We took Game Five by a slender 116–113. They contested us all the way. Then we went down to Dallas and got the job done in Game Six, 120–107.

The "I'll have it when I need it" theory was validated again, but just barely. Dallas served notice. They were an emerging Western Conference powerhouse. But we were through with them for the year. Now all that stood between us and the Celtics was the Houston franchise.

We had beaten Houston convincingly in five out of six regular season games. The Rockets had serious potential, but they always found a way to negate themselves for a few crucial minutes. We would usually play head-to-head for a couple of quarters, then we'd put the game out of reach. The Twin Towers attack, coordinating Ralph Sampson and Akeem Olajuwon, was still uneven. Their guards were prone to cold-shooting streaks, especially in the second half.

One time, on a game day in midseason, the Houston papers printed the news that the Rockets were about to play "the most important game in the history of the franchise." This had to be the game, they told the community, in which Houston made its ultimate grab for greatness. That turned out to be the night Kareem socked the Twin Towers for 42 points. It was one of our most definitive wins of the year.

The first playoff meeting with Houston turned into a comfortable 119–107 win. Our fast break looked unstoppable. Houston's shooting from the guard position went south and we controlled the game. I gave everyone Sunday off. "Go to the beach," I said.

On Monday we held one of the worst practices I've ever seen.

Mentally, everyone was still out on the beach treating their sore, tired muscles to the rays. We half-stepped through our drills. There was no sign of urgency. Houston was going to lay down for us and we might as well save some juice for Boston.

Tuesday's workout was slightly worse. The players saw it. I could sense they wanted to kick themselves out of their mood, but they couldn't quite find the motivation.

Game Two started weird. It took four minutes for the score to reach 4 to 2, Lakers' advantage. We had them 25 to 18 at the quarter and led by 14 in the second. Then we started to slide.

Their outside shooters found the range: 24 points for Lewis Lloyd, 16 for Rodney McCray, 14 for Mitchell Wiggins. The Twin Towers suddenly synchronized. Sampson racked up 24 points and 13 rebounds. Olajuwon had nearly identical numbers: 22 points and 13 boards. They absolutely whipped us on the boards, 51–36, and shot-blocked us into oblivion. That game ended 112–102 in their favor. Just as with Dallas, we were now in an evened-up series. We had to reach for our reserve power.

Game Three was in Houston. If we thought the Mavericks were a team beginning to come of age, the Rockets were suddenly a full-force, high-impact presence. In the heat of the playoffs, they were responding with their greatest performances. They were meshing. Akeem scored 40 and grabbed most of their 20 offensive rebounds.

Just before the half, James Worthy collided with their 6'10", 235-pound reserve center, Jim Petersen. Gary Vitti rushed out. James always plays fearlessly. Because of his tremendous quickness, he's usually ahead of the pack and out of danger—though not always. He broke a leg once, at the end of his rookie season, when he took a sideways hit sailing to the basket. When Gary reached him, James was motionless on the floor, screaming, "Gary! My neck! Broke my neck!" I was right there. Gary put a firm hand on James's forehead to prevent any motion that might sever something within the spinal cord. "Pat," he said, looking at my shoetops, "go get the doctor."

We were out on that court a long time before the doctor decided it was safe to even move James. He came back to play in the second half, but he didn't score again for the rest of the game. By that evening he was unable to turn his head.

With five and a half minutes to play we were still ahead. The Rockets then outscored us with a 14 to 4 run. They took control and they took the game, 117–109. With another home game twenty-four hours away, Houston had the Lakers down 2 to 1 in the series. One more win would put them within striking distance.

Houston was all determination now. In the next game Robert Reid scored 23 outside while Akeem got 35 inside. We stayed in contention until the last minutes. It could have gone either way, depending on who played with the most heart and who got the best breaks in the final few minutes. We fell 105 to 95, and the Rockets led the series 3–1.

Game Five was back in the Forum. That gave us some comfort. We were up 7 points at the half and we held the lead all the way into the late fourth quarter. Akeem gave another awesome performance, spinning left and right off the low post defenders, popping short jumpers and quick stuff shots. Then he and Mitch Kupchak tussled for position late in the game. They both started throwing blows. The officials kicked both the big men out.

Five minutes left. We were ahead 103–99 and their spark plug was gone. We could take the game.

Then Sampson emerged. He switched from forward to center. That has always been his natural position. His best years in the league, as a rookie and as a second year player, were at the center position. He found an extra jolt of vitality and kept the Rockets within reaching distance until the last minute. With 37 seconds left in the game, Earvin hit a baseline jumper and we were up by three. All that was left was to play smart defense. From that point we could rally our forces to retake control of the series. Go strong into Houston for Game Six. Win Game Seven at home and cinch our rightful position as best in the Western Conference. Game Seven would be played on the eve of Memorial Day. One year after our great come-from-behind showing against Boston. The back-to-back drive was still alive.

Coming out of a time-out, the Rockets set up a 3-pointer for Reid. His shot was from 22 feet out. It caromed off the rim, went into James Worthy's hands, then somehow slipped out of his grasp. Mitchell Wiggins snagged the loose ball. It went back out to Reid again in 22-foot range. I knew he wasn't going to miss this one. Reid tied the score at 112.

We played for a final shot and missed the attempt. It looked as if the game would have to be decided in overtime. Houston called time out with one second left. McCray, their small forward, looped the ball in from out of bounds at midcourt, and I could see Sampson going up for it and twisting in the air. Kareem was up close on him, ready to deny the shot. Ralph knew that, and he knew that the buzzer would sound before his feet could touch the floor. He had nothing to lose. He continued his twisting motion and flipped the ball, almost nonchalantly, toward the basket. He was playing out that fraction of a second in the only way possible. Afterwards, he smiled and called it "a funky shot." The ball went up in a soft arch. Good backspin. I could see it was going to land a few inches short.

Ralph's attempt caught the rim and bounced straight up, almost to the top of the backboard. All the spin had been absorbed when it hit the rim. The ball slowed until you could see the grain and the seams. Then it ripped straight through the net like a cannonball.

The Lakers were done for, 114–112. The "best team in the history of the game" had just gotten stuffed in four straight games. Bill Fitch, Houston's coach, gave me a pat on the back as we walked to the dressing rooms. He said, "That's a tough way to lose it."

All summer long reporters, people in restaurants, and people in movie lines asked me, "What did you think of Ralph Sampson's shot?"

I always gave them the same answer: "It stimulated me."

Pressure Drop

At the drop of Ralph Sampson's impromptu shot on May 21st, 1986, the future of the Lakers was up for grabs—or so it seemed.

The sportswriters already had their Laker postmortems half completed when Ralph's shot dropped—just as they keep updated obituaries on file for well-known people, ready for a final sentence or two at the stroke of death. The moment we were dethroned, I started asking myself questions. Why did we suddenly fall short? Could we have done anything about it?

When Sampson took his shot, Michael Cooper thought, "Oh, my God. We've lost." He pressed his body against the man he was defending, staking out the best rebounding turf near the basket. When the ball dropped straight through, Coop involuntarily relaxed. He slumped to the floor and stretched out full length with his arms spread—an expression of ultimate loss and puzzlement. He looked like a scarecrow that had been blown over. The TV cameraman ran up and pointed his lens at Coop. His whole body language was a pleading question: What had happened to us this year? He remembers saying inside his head, "I'm ready to play for next year. This will never happen to us again. We'll never put ourselves in this position again—to lose like this."

All I can remember about the moment is that I started walking. For the first several seconds I was in a vacuum, a timeless space. I can't recall whether I even responded to Bill Fitch when he offered a kind word. I just walked on through the crowd, down the corridor, and into our empty locker room. My first conscious thought was, "Try to show some class, some dignity, some control." I knew the team was hurting bad.

My cubicle is in a corner of the locker room. It's across the width of the room from the entrance and across the length of the room from the showers and the training room. It's an observation post. I stood there and removed my coat. I shook my head. I put the coat on a hook and turned to look at each of the players as they walked in and went to their own cubicles. It was an intent stare, but not a malicious one. Whatever I could learn from their faces, I wanted to know.

Everyone came in quiet. Most sat in front of their lockers, pressed their elbows against their knees, and let their neck and shoulder muscles go slack. Some began slowly to undress. Most of them stared vacantly at the floor.

Earvin Johnson was, to my memory, the only one standing. His left hand was on his hip. The right was in a fist. He leaned against his cubicle and pressed his fist against the post with his forehead.

Kareem sat down and untied his shoes. He tossed them into his gym bag. He undressed quickly and mechanically, staring, never even looking at what he was taking off. He was working, carrying through. It was hard to tell what he was thinking. But you could see a troubled feeling in his eyes. He threw his laundry into the canvas bin and started for the showers.

That's when I stopped everybody and said, "Okay, let's all sit down together."

I let the mood hang silently in the room for about five minutes. What was I going to say to them? Should I say, "We had a great season, guys"? Should I tell them, "I'm proud of you"? They had just absorbed one of the biggest disappointments of their lives. They didn't want to hear any happy bullshit. Platitudes never sound good to an ex-champ. There was only one common emotion in the room and it was misery.

All I could do was remind them of something we had learned from our seven years together in the trenches. It may not have seemed like much comfort, but it was the only peg we had to hold on to for the moment. I said, "It doesn't matter what happens to us. All that's important is how we're going to deal with it. What we've got to do is grow from this, come back from it." I told them I loved them for who they were and not how they played.

I didn't criticize them. I didn't yell at anyone for his play. I just said we had to deal with facts. Things didn't turn out the way we had planned. But we had to go on.

For a long time nobody said a word. Then Mitch Kupchak spoke up. Kup is one of the hardest-striving guys who ever played: a former first-round draft pick and All-Rookie-team selection, on world championship teams in two cities, a ferocious athlete who had had his potential limited by injuries and pain. Gary Vitti used to tell me that it was a remarkable act of courage and defiance every time Kup laced on his shoes and came to practice. This turned out to be his last game as a pro, because of those injuries. He had battled so hard for position against Akeem Olajuwon that they both got ejected. He had literally gone down swinging. Kup said, "Pat, we worked hard. We had our chances. We didn't give up. We battled them down to the wire."

There was a little more silence. Nothing could be added. They trooped off to their postgame showers, dressed, made talk with the reporters, and walked into the darkness of an L.A. night knowing only one thing. It was over.

Yelling and criticizing had already been tried. At our last practice, when we stood three games down and the team was still uninspired and half-stepping its way through the drills and preparation, I tried to get their attention, sting them a little. Getting angry is always a last resort for me. I've always been known as a tolerant tyrant. There are times when it works beautifully, but you can't afford to wear it out. You have to pick those spots wisely.

Sometimes the players know and accept the fact that they need strong medicine. The year before, following the Memorial Day Massacre, some of them were mad at me for not doing it sooner.

But this time, in the dying moments of the Houston series, they just looked tired and empty. They stood there in the gym and stared straight ahead, listening to every word and never making a sound. They were like robots standing behind Plexiglas shields. When the tirade was over, they requested a few minutes of their own for a team meeting. They went into a corner and spent a quarter of an hour talking among themselves.

The year before there was no team meeting. There was only an attitude of "All right! Let's go to work." The Dallas series was tougher than anyone had expected it to be. Then Houston appeared. This was the team we always destroyed. This year the attitude was that we deserved, and were going to get, some respite.

Houston beat us in every situation. Where they used to fold, we were the ones that folded. It was the coming-of-age scenario Houston fans had been demanding. Akeem Olajuwon was treacherous and unstoppable. Ralph Sampson had his soft touch working from midrange and his intimidating height inside. Robert Reid kept hitting the long shots that forced our defense to extend and kept their low-post play fluid. In any minor skirmish, any potential turning point, the Rockets had an extra measure of hustle. They had been hungry all season long. Now they were taking charge. Meanwhile, most of the Lakers had horrible games. In a week plus one day, Houston flushed us out. That's how fast it happened. We got the respite we had been looking for—a whole summer's worth.

Eventually we had to let the press enter our locker room. I stood up with my back to my locker, answering until all questions were exhausted for the night. Finally I heard myself saying, "Anything else, fellas? Okay? That's it. See you next year." Oddly enough, something about being there in the locker room made me feel safe. Safe in our little haven.

Dr. Jerry Buss, the Lakers' owner, had come through the room earlier with a smile on his face. He looked optimistic. The pain was well hidden. He greeted the writers and went from cubicle to cubicle, shaking each player's hand. He had some good banter for everybody. The most serious thing I heard him say was, "Hey, we just didn't get the job done this year."

An hour later nearly everyone had cleared out. Buss and I were with Gary Vitti in the training room, which is a nerve center for the team. Gary, the best trainer in the NBA, knows the mechanics of the human body like an engineer. He takes exceptional care of injuries, and more importantly, he gets every player working on special conditioning programs to prevent further problems. The players call me The Big Kahuna, so Vitti is The Little Kahuna. When you're hurting, you go to The Little Kahuna's magic room and you get better. Maybe that's what Jerry Buss and I were doing there.

Gary was just putting away his tape and bandages and getting ready to go. Ron Wilder, an assistant to Buss, poked his head in the door to ask if his boss needed any last thing.

"Yeah," Buss told him. "Go upstairs and bring us some rum-and-cokes."

"How many?"

"Bring us a dozen."

I suddenly realized that I was going to stay in The Little Kahuna's room for a long time.

Buss could probably sense that I was in tremendous pain. The tone of our discussion was matter-of-fact, but kind. He told me how proud he was of the team, and of the job the coaching staff had done all season long. He told me something that I remembered and later relayed to the team at our final meeting of the season two days later. He said, "It could have been our greatest moment. If we have to lose our championship sometime, I can't think of a better way. Against a young, hungry, and talented team. Going down fighting. Showing tremendous pride. It took a miracle shot to beat us. Even though we lost, I have no disappointment at all in the team. You did as well as you could."

We talked on and on. Gradually the empty glasses on that tray became a majority. Buss surprised me with an offer. He wanted to extend my contract. Now, this might have been strictly a smart business move, offered because I was in a vulnerable position. Or it may have come out of tremendous compassion, wanting to alleviate any feeling I might have that my job was in jeopardy. Either way, I thought it was a wonderful gesture. He said to have my business representative get in touch with him right away. We drank to it.

We rambled through more topics. An hour or so later, he fixed me with a look and said, "Do you realize you just cost me three million dollars?"

"This is great," I thought. "He gives me the new contract and now he's going to lay this on me."

"No," I said. "How do you figure that?"

"We aren't going to the Finals," he said. "Which we're used to around here. We aren't playing a seventh game at the Forum. That's about three hundred and fifty thousand dollars in gate. And then there's concessions and licensing, television and radio revenues, and so on. I would probably generate another three million dollars if you made the Finals."

I did some figuring of my own. "That's great, Jerry," I said. "I cost you three million this year. If three million is how you value getting to the Finals, then I've been there four straight times before this." I broke out in a smile. "That makes twelve million. So I'm still nine million dollars ahead! I've got another three years to go before I get down to a zero base. There's still a big cushion, right?"

He gave me a raised eyebrow. I think he either wanted to pull back the contract or break out laughing and he couldn't decide which.

We continued to get quietly blitzed. Challenges were set up for pool games. Dinner plans were arranged for summer get-togethers at Pickfair, the old Douglas Fairbanks/Mary Pickford estate where Buss lived then.

It was close to two-thirty in the morning when Chris knocked on the door. Buss said, "Are you still here? My limousine driver would've taken you home. I meant to keep Pat up until seven in the morning. That's what this is all about, to sit here in the training room and wallow in your misery and be with your friends and forget about it and go home." We were really flying by that time.

I pulled myself up and said, "It's time to go." He offered me his hand. I brushed it aside and gave him a big hug. I said, "Thanks, boss. Thanks for everything."

The Forum was eerily empty upstairs. I passed through the Press Lounge. The usual postgame scene there is noisy, crowded, electrified. Buss and his friends at their table. Some ex-players. Movie stars. Wives and families and Forum staff. Talking, laughing, shouting to whoever comes through the door. I can't cross the room in less than five minutes. Now there was just Lynn, the bartender, picking up the last napkins and popcorn bowls, trying to go home.

Chris and I walked back to my office. I had to collect my coaching stuff for the last time this season. There was Randy Pfund sitting alone in his chair. I said, "What the hell are you doing here?" We embraced. I was pretty sure I could see tears starting to form in his eyes. All he said was, "I thought somebody should be here for you when you came up." I think this was about the worst disappointment he had ever been through. Randy is the kind of person who is always concerned about doing the right thing. He almost seemed to be placing the blame on his own shoulders.

Chris told me that she had urged him for hours to go on home. He wouldn't budge. He just kept saying, "No. He's going to need somebody." That's something I'll never forget. "Hey," I told him, "just don't worry about it. You did a great job. I couldn't have asked for anything more."

Chris and I quietly gathered our stuff, said good-night to Randy, and walked out to the parking lot. The season was over. We hit the 405 Freeway northbound for the 9,786th time. And we went home a loser that night.

Decisions

The summer of 1986 was a summer full of difficult questions. The morning sports pages of Thursday, May 22nd, one day after our playoff loss, kicked off a string of articles dissecting our failure and probing our corpse for signs of life.

We lost because we didn't pick up Bob McAdoo's option one year ago. We lost because Kareem is too old. We lost because the Twin Towers era has arrived and the Lakers can't ignore the fact any longer: they need two seven-foot guys on the floor at all times.

On the Tuesday after our loss, at the final team meeting, I had my own answer worked out. There were several things to point to. James Worthy's neck injury. Some difficult matchups. My failure to make the right coaching adjustments.

But one thing stood out in my mind.

I said to the team, "We lost because of our attitude. Throughout the season, and particularly during the Houston series, we had the wrong attitude."

Our attitude wasn't negative. But it wasn't the proper one. There's always the motivation of wanting to win. Everybody has that. But a champion needs, in their attitude, a motivation above and beyond winning.

We didn't have the emotional fiber, the mental toughness, that the team had a year before. It wasn't individual letdowns. It was the idea that somebody else would get the job done. It was forgetting that it takes continued hard work to stay on top. It was the belief that we were a miracle team, that all our talent meant we had it made. Nobody in the NBA has it made—ever.

Any team can be a miracle team. The catch is that you have to go out and work for your miracles. Effort is what ultimately separates journeymen players from impact players and the one-year champs from the teams of lasting greatness. It might be the effort spent since schoolboy days, taking a few dozen extra shots after practice, building habits that will pay off throughout a career. It might be the effort at one very crucial moment in a tight game. Great effort springs naturally from a great attitude. It was obvious that all of us—team, coaches and management—hadn't developed the right one.

We had not deserved to win. We weren't the better team during that crucial four-losses-in-eight-days stretch. Because of our attitude, our effort was below par. We had nobody to blame but ourselves.

Finger-pointing and blaming are enemies of teamwork. We've learned that the hard way on the Lakers. One reason we stay solid, in spite of all the potential jealousies and ego problems that can explode in any team's face, is the method we use to handle family disputes. Any dispute is an opportunity to solve the underlying problem, not to inflict wounds on each other. It's part of our team culture now to keep those family matters within the family.

We keep a very detailed set of numbers on each player. They cover their every game as a Laker and, as much as possible, every game of their career—even extending back to college.

Every team in organized basketball charts the major statistics: rebounds, points scored, shooting percentage, minutes played. We get all those numbers, then we go beyond the basics to chart the effort areas. Jumping in pursuit of every rebound even if you don't get it. Swatting at every pass and shot whether or not you have a prayer of blocking it. Standing your ground when an offensive player comes smashing into you in order to get yourself, fresh bruises and all, up to the free throw line for a chance to make a difference in the score. Diving for loose balls. All the things that take tremendous energy but don't look pretty while you're doing them. These are the Effort Areas.

It only takes a few minutes after each game to have our statistical analysis punched into the computer. We come out with a factored number that reveals how much effort each person put into the game. It's like a report card. Each player has a number, called their plus/ minus number. It reflects the standards they've set over their career. In other words, they aren't judged against Joe Superstar. They're judged against themselves individually, against their own past efforts.

The numbers from our Houston series showed that only two players had consistent effort levels. Earvin and Kareem earned their money. The rest of the team had not played up to its potential. We showed indecisiveness at key moments. There might be a strong individual effort, but it wouldn't be built upon or added to by someone else's performance. It would just vanish into the fabric of the game. We couldn't piece together a surge of teamwork, where the whole would be greater than the sum of the parts.

In the meantime, Houston forged ahead. They blocked a dozen shots in one game. They swarmed over every loose ball, every opportunity. They probed every little crack in our performance where a wedge could be driven in and the game split wide open.

We wrapped up the meeting and the players went off to their wives and families, to their bachelor apartments, to their hometowns in Oregon and Michigan and all around the country. Bill Bertka spent the rest of the afternoon at Hollywood Park. He watched Willie Shoemaker aboard a horse called River Drummer. If Shoe could keep himself near the top of his profession for years and years, maybe there was hope for the Lakers.

Demise-of-the-Lakers stories kept on turning up. One sympathetic reporter asked me if I was upset or disappointed by the press coverage. I said, "No. I don't think we're getting it hard enough. I want to take my hat off to the media for treating us with some dignity and respect."

Of course, they have to offer their perspectives. That's what they're paid to do. So all the writers were prognosticators. They all knew how to change the team; everybody was brilliant now. But at least they weren't nasty. No one rubbed salt in our wounds. They just puzzled over and over about how a brilliant team had faded, suddenly and unexpectedly.

The only commentary that made sense to me that summer came

out of the coaching staff. We had a team attitude problem to correct. We didn't need a Twin Towers starting lineup.

In fact, we had already hurt the team by overreacting to the height-and-strength trend in the league. We had slotted Maurice Lucas into the lineup to give us size and bulk and savvy in the low post. He did all that. He also became our team's leading rebounder. But as a 238-pounder in his eleventh pro season, Luke did not possess a fast set of wheels. Getting a big man who made us slower was the wrong strategy. We had to get back to the core Laker concept: speed and quickness.

As coaches, we realized that the Houston series could have been won if we had reverted to a fleet-footed lineup. We had tried to pound big for big. But their big was bigger and better than our big. Instead we should have exploited them with trapping and fast breaks. We had snookered ourselves into playing their game, the Twin Towers game. We didn't play Laker basketball.

The first thing we developed in the summer was a resolve to throw our quickness at people, to gamble that our style could prevail. Let small and quick go after slow and big. See who could beat who first.

We still needed a legitimate backup center, but no way would we bring in someone who was slow, average, or over the hill. We were out to make other teams worry about matching up to us, instead of the other way around.

The only full-scale remodeling job taking place was the one at my home.

The arrival of our son, James Patrick, meant that our old two-bedroom house just didn't fill the bill. It was the same one we had bought back in 1973. I had torn down the old shed in back and built a cabana that served as an exercise room and office. I had built a fence and refaced the whole stucco house with rough-sawn cedar. We were definitely well dug in, but everything changes when there's a newborn in your life.

Our new place, which we bought in midseason, was only about one mile away. We'd still have the same stores, the same church, the same atmosphere.

Home number two needed fresh paint, inside and out. It needed a complete relandscaping. The woodwork had to be stripped. An enclosed back porch had to be turned into a den and the front-porch roofline reshaped.

While Houston and Boston thumped on each other in the Finals, providing a constant reminder to me that our team had failed to advance, we lived around boxes and crates and papers. Every bit of it got shuffled again and again into safe places as the painting and carpentry and plastering crews progressed from one room to the next.

The backyard was what really charmed us into buying the property. It fades back a long way and ends with a small rise where there's a family of old eucalyptus trees. There's even a tiny creekbed and a short wooden bridge.

Throughout the remodeling, the backyard was a parking lot for tractors and backhoes. There wasn't a single living blade of grass. One weekend afternoon I wanted some rays and some solitude, so I dragged an old chaise lounge out into the dirt. I put it in a clear spot and draped a towel over the top, then I spread myself with suntan lotion and settled back. James sat down by me and maneuvered one of his toy tractors. Somehow, watching all the men at work had given him a love of tractors that lasts to this day. If you want to make an impression on my son, come around on a John Deere.

Every little breeze stirred up loose dirt. Every speck of dirt stuck to my suntan oil. Chris had to come out and photograph the moment. Father and son dirtballs. I looked as if I had escaped from a chain gang wearing a swimsuit.

On May 27th we called a strategy meeting. The coaching staff convened with General Manager Jerry West and President Bill Sharman. As longtime basketball fans know, West and Sharman are not only two ex-coaches. They're also two of the toughest players in NBA history. We all compared our notes and our gut feelings about what had gone out of sync. We talked about how we should proceed, in an administrative way, to set a course for the future of the Lakers. We talked about trades and the players we liked in the upcoming collegiate draft.

Naturally, because we finished second only to Boston in league win-loss standings, we had the next-to-lowest first-round pick.

West was sold on Billy Thompson. At 6'7" and 195 pounds, he had shown tremendous quickness and leaping ability on the Louisville team that had just won the NCAA championship. But we were convinced some other team was bound to snag Thompson before our 22nd pick materialized. There were also some impressive big men coming out. We had great interest in Roy Tarpley, a 6'11", 230-pounder out of Michigan. West had already been dickering with other teams. Somebody out there had to want one of our players bad enough that they'd swap an early draft choice. We might have to exchange a proven veteran for a promising rookie. The question was, which veteran?

West and Bertka left after the meeting and caught a flight to Chicago. They were headed for the annual tryout camp, a predraft ritual where promising seniors showcase their abilities. The idea is that coaches and scouts might see more mature potential than was revealed in their college play. Some colleges play systems that develop great fundamental skills, but don't showcase players' one-on-one capabilities. Oregon State is one example. That's why we had been able to get A.C. Green, a player of incredible potential, in the previous year with only a 23rd pick.

This was the first time that a Laker coach had appeared at the tryout camp in at least five years. We had always been busy playing in the Finals instead.

On Tuesday, June 3rd, Dr. Buss called Jerry West to a meeting at Pickfair. He had been looking at tapes of the playoffs over and over, searching for his own answers. Some of his optimism was beginning to wear thin. His mind was open to making trades.

"I'm having a hard time believing what I see," he told his general manager. "I can't believe some of the defensive play. I don't like the way they're responding to pressure. What can we do to strengthen our position?"

Buss's philosophy as a businessman is to hire people he trusts and give them almost full rein. Most of the key people in the Lakers organization have been with the team in one capacity or another for many years. That breeds continuity, which also breeds stability. But, like B.B. King says, you've got to pay the cost to be the boss. The organization rolls forward on Jerry Buss's money. He traded away a major hunk of his real estate empire for ownership of the Lakers. When he has a profound opinion about the needs of the team, he wants that opinion acted on. Nevertheless, West wanted to hold all of our starters out of trade consideration. I agreed.

Meanwhile, on the eighth of June, Boston crushed Houston 143 to 97 in Game Six of the Finals. Larry Bird averaged almost a triple-double for the series—24 points, 9.7 rebounds, and 9.5 assists. I happened to be there in Boston for the game, as a halftime guest on CBS. At least now that Boston had won it I could stop paying attention to basketball news and concentrate completely on addressing the needs of our team. I felt like someone in a collapsed mineshaft who just got a timber lifted off his body. I could start moving toward daylight.

Back in L.A., we reviewed our draft and trade options. The Atlanta Hawks needed an experienced reserve guard. They were willing to trade their number 18 pick for our number 22 if we would give up Mike McGee. McGee stands 6'5" and weighs 190 pounds. He was an important part of our rotation at the guard spot. Every so often, after a great relief performance, he would be cited by a sportswriter as someone who "could probably start for any other team in the league." But he had had enough of playing off the bench. He could hit the long shot. He was explosive enough to earn the nickname PPM, "Point Per Minute." He wanted to join a team where he had more of a chance to play significant minutes. But the deal hinged on whether Billy Thompson was still available on the 18th pick.

On June 11th, six days before the draft, came a summit meeting. We all agreed on the need for a quality big man. A fleet-footed reserve to back up Kareem. The quality big men were sure to be the first players taken. So far, we hadn't scored a potential trade that would yield one of the top draft-choice positions.

Buss had dug back deeper in the tapes, looking at our series with Dallas. He was very impressed by the hot play of Mark Aguirre and his furious outside and inside scoring. It had played hell with our defense, forcing us to edge out from their low post players. Buss wanted Aguirre. He saw in Mark a tool to pry defenses off Kareem and to create lane-driving opportunities for Earvin.

Mavericks management was receptive. There was a long history of trouble between Aguirre and his coach, Dick Motta. A potential trade was discussed. James Worthy for Mark Aguirre and Dallas's first draft choice. That would probably translate into Roy Tarpley, since Dallas held the seventh pick. All kinds of names and deals were discussed as the offers and counteroffers were relayed between Dallas and L.A. But nothing concrete happened.

It was an uncertain bargain. Worthy, on the one hand, is an All-Star and the first player chosen in the 1982 draft. 6'9", with great hands, a lean upper body, a powerful torso, explosive speed, devastating one-on-one moves and outstanding leaping ability. If you used a computer to design a prototype NBA small forward, it would create a picture of James Worthy.

Aguirre was the first draft pick of 1981. A two-time All-American from DePaul. Averaged over 24 points a game. An All-Star. But would his feuding-with-coach days be over once he got away from Motta? Nobody could tell. Besides, we didn't want to disrupt the core of the team. It was still the same group that had nailed Boston on their home floor. We still had a world championship unit. We just had to unlock another championship performance. You don't back the Bekins truck up to your doorstep and move out of town because of one downturn. You dig down to your fundamental strengths and reassert them.

Just before draft day, Buss called Don Carter, the owner of the Mavericks. Both men also hold soccer franchises. Buss wanted to talk about a certain player, Tatu, that he desperately wanted. During the conversation, Carter asked, "Why did you call off the Worthy and Aguirre trade?"

Buss said, "I didn't call it off. I understood that you called it off."

Carter replied, "No. I think you called it off."

"That's strange. I thought you called it off. I'll get back to you."

Buss called Jerry West and asked, "What do you think about this trade?"

"No way," West said. "I don't want to do it."

So Buss called Carter back and said, "You're right. We can't do that deal. We were the ones that called it off."

Meanwhile, the newspapers reported that Buss had been pushing the deal. No reporter ever asked him to comment.

We cinched our bargain with Atlanta. It went down just as we had hoped. They got Billy and asked us to select Ken Barlow, a 6'10" player out of Notre Dame. McGee became an Atlanta Hawk and we additionally got the rights to a later draft pick, Ron Kellogg, a small forward from Kansas.

Shortly after the draft we rounded up our rookies and staged a four-day mini-camp. Thompson looked like a jewel. He looked like a full-grown man playing against schoolkids. We started to feel like there was a path out of the woods. The core was intact. The newcomers had substantial promise. The two-week Summer Pro League, where rookies and other young players from around the league come to hone their skills, was just around the corner. We had some exciting people to invite.

Jerry West made a special trip to Pauley Pavilion, on the UCLA campus, to watch Adrian Branch, a 6′8″ former Maryland player who had averaged 25 points a game in one year of Continental Basketball Association experience. Jerry was out to find a tall reserve for the off-guard spot, which calls for accurate outside shooting. He liked what he saw. "Sign Branch up," he said. "Bring him into camp." I had only seen Adrian play on television, during his college career. But I don't know of a better judge of basketball talent than Jerry West. I took his word for it. Adrian was brought in before any other team could get a good look at him.

Vada Martin had played in European pro leagues and looked like a promising small forward. Ron Kellogg was an excellent defender. Andre Turner, a third-round choice out of Memphis State, was an exciting little point guard. Only 5′11″, but he could push the ball up very fast on offense. Roger Harden came out of my old school, Kentucky, and he was hard as nails. Dale Blaney, out of West's home state, West Virginia, was a deadly shot from outside. Altogether they presented some very fresh young faces. We knew we could create a good situation.

A.C. Green missed the first couple of Summer League games. He was up with his family in Portland, Oregon. But as soon as he checked in, he was a major presence. In one of the first team victories he matched up strong against Cliff Levingston, a four-year pro of similar size from the Atlanta Hawks. A.C. scored 28 points and 14 rebounds.

As the only rookie on our '85–'86 squad, A.C. had had limited playing time. His primary role was to be a rebounder, not a scorer. But we liked his determined character, his willingness to work and his speed. We believed he could eventually be a dominant player in the league. He was starting to look like one.

Bertka and Pfund and I went to Playa Del Ray for Mexican food after the games. We were like prospectors, discussing every fleck of gold we saw in the stream.

Our commitment to speed called for special work. Most people assume that any professional basketball player is a good runner. Especially any player on the Lakers. But all players have strong and weak facets to their games. At least half of our guys needed some measure of help with their running.

Henry Hines is a former USC long jumper who now specializes in coaching speed. John McEnroe and Martina Navratilova and Chris Evert had all hired him for guidance on their quickness and footwork and explosive movements.

Hines came in and put on a demonstration. We were impressed. He started in with the fellows in Summer League. First off, he watched each man play. Then he wrote his observations in a notebook. Then he zeroed in on specific needs for each player.

Some of them didn't know how to use their arms or how to use their body weight to help them get downcourt. Some of them had the habit of drawing one foot back when they wanted to generate an explosive takeoff. It's an instinctive way to establish a base for a strong push, but it also tips off defenders that something is about to happen. Watch James Worthy to see the difference. He taught himself a long time ago to eliminate the step back. When he catches the ball on the wing and faces the hoop, there's never a clue whether he'll spin around his defender on the right or blow past him on the left.

Hines noticed right away that A.C. Green had a habit of pushing off from his heels as he ran, instead of from his big toes. Eliminating that trait made A.C. a little faster downcourt and a little more explosive in pursuit of a rebound. It's a tiny advantage, but accumulate enough tiny things and you can change a player's career—or a team's fortunes.

If we could generate enough added increments of competitive advantage, maybe we could answer some of the summer's difficult questions. Maybe we could start seeing a different kind of story in the papers.

Career Bests and Career Changes

Three key moves got the Lakers back on top.

The first was when we avoided any trades of core players.

The second was when we set ourselves on a program to revitalize the team's attitude.

The third move was to make some simple and profound changes in our offense and our defense.

The Worthy situation, unfortunately, didn't come to an end when the proposed trade fell through. There were complications.

James is a preacher's son from Gastonia, North Carolina. The Worthys are a tight-knit family. They get strength from the bloodlines and religious values and gospel traditions they all share.

James Worthy came to Los Angeles with a tremendous sense of purpose, but also with tremendous reservations about some of the people he was likely to meet in Tinseltown. Los Angeles isn't really the festering palace of sin that some people believe it to be. It's just a big, sprawling city, full of good people and bad, pushed along by a healthy economy that includes an exceptional amount of get-rich-quick opportunities. For James, though, Los Angeles is a far cry from his roots. It inspires him to remain guarded.

The trade rumors made James mistrustful. As it turns out, the same business agent represents both Mark Aguirre and Earvin Johnson. That gave James, and a few sportswriters, the erroneous idea that Earvin was pushing for the trade.

Earvin and James have very different personalities. They've always had high respect for each other as players and they've always liked each other. But where one is gregarious and always ready to joke and create a loose atmosphere, the other values his dignity and is more of a solitary presence. It wasn't hard for James to think out a connection like this: "Earvin is in tight with the owner. I was never a rah-rah guy, but I always did my job. Now they think they'll be better off without me."

The fact was, Buss had conferred privately with Earvin about the trade idea. Earvin's take was, "Do whatever you think is best. Mark's a great player, but I think James is the best player for this team." You see, a great team isn't simply built by hiring the top talent. Just as in any other form of business, it also matters how those top talents combine with each other. The Lakers are a fast-breaking team. Earvin can push the ball upcourt at an incredible tempo, but he needs someone even faster than himself to break for the wing and fly upcourt. James is the fastest man of his size in the NBA. In terms of finishing the fast break creatively and swiftly and deceptively, no one else compares. His attributes synchronize with those of our other stars. It's no accident that we selected James first in a draft year that also offered a choice of Dominique Wilkins, who led the league in scoring through '85–'86, and Terry Cummings, who was subsequently named Rookie of the Year. Those two are undeniably great players, but James fits better than either of them into the Laker style of basketball. That's what is called chemistry. Attitude and chemistry are the factors that can kick people up to higher levels of winning, no matter what talent they have.

A great collection of talent with unbalanced chemistry and inappropriate attitudes can get knocked over by teams of lesser talent. Because of that, and because he didn't want a teammate feeling bad, Earvin got together with James during the summer. They worked on building their understanding of each other. They had a breakthrough. The trade rumor stuff got put away and now I think the two are far more accepting of each other's differences. You won't likely see James at a disco or at a tailor shop ordering a custom leather suit, and you won't see Earvin headed to a relatively modest home in a used Toyota either. But they don't pass judgment on each other's lifestyle.

For his part, James had to absorb a lesson. Life in the NBA, as in any competitive business arena, is full of contradictions. One of the ultimate contradictions is this: Even though loyalty between the players and the organization is part of the lifeblood of the team, no one in the sport is above being traded or fired. Jamaal Wilkes was demoted to the bench, and eventually traded, to make room for James's emerging talents. Kareem Abdul-Jabbar was traded, as were Wilt Chamberlain and Dave Bing and Walt Bellamy and dozens of other great names.

Very few number one draft choices remain over the years on the same team that selected them. Earvin Johnson and James Worthy are two of the exceptions.

I once had a conversation with Jerry West about this ultimate contradiction of loyalty versus the team's need to stay competitive. He said, "You know, there might come a day when I have to fire you." Jerry was perfectly serious. He was my closest friend when we were Laker teammates in the seventies and is still among my best friends today. I told him, "That's right. I understand that. And there might come a day when I decide to walk away from the team." He cracked a smile and said, "I never thought about it like that."

Just as the '86–'87 season was about to get underway, a James Worthy article appeared in *Los Angeles Magazine*. They called him The Invisible Man. The interview capsulized James's dilemma. He's a two-time All-Star, emerging and improving with every season, but he's teamed with Kareem and Earvin, two men already recognized as among the greatest to ever play the game of basketball.

James has the potential to be the greatest forward in the game today, but sometimes, no matter how incredibly he slashes to the hoop or how creatively he executes the finish of a fast break, he doesn't get all the acknowledgment he deserves. He continues to play brilliantly regardless. Maybe that's another measure of his strength and his greatness.

The potential trade and its aftermath aside, another danger threatened our core player group.

Michael Cooper's contract had expired. He knew that he was worth plenty to the team. Management had to decide just how much. And they had already decided not to write any more long-term contracts, unless those contracts contained clauses saying the player involved must remain healthy enough to play. The Lakers are still paying hundreds of thousands of dollars annually to people who are no longer able to compete.

"I've come in and I've played with a broken nose, I've played with a broken hand, hamstring pulls—every injury," Cooper told reporters. "So how can they give me a contract contingent on my health?"

The negotiations had been going on since January. They weren't going fast and they weren't going smoothly. Coop, just like he plays, was going all out. He expected a deal that would make up for his low-paid early years. If there was anyone who really could go be a starter for another NBA club, who had sacrificed a lot of potential glory and income, Coop was the guy.

In one game Coop physically challenged James Donaldson, the Dallas Mavericks' center, because he thought Donaldson was abusive. All Mike gave up in the exchange was seven inches of height and 108 pounds! He was just as reckless about going head-to-head with a master deal-maker like Jerry Buss, a man who had once acquired the Chrysler Building so he could use it as a bargaining chip to buy the Lakers.

It was a tough negotiation. Offers were made and rejected. Neither side would really sit down and hammer out a deal. Management finally just said, "The hell with it. Wait and see what you're worth on the free agent market. If we think it's realistic, we'll match it."

Besides being intensely competitive, Michael gives away lots of time every year to community causes, things to provide for people and keep them away from drugs. His father was absent in his childhood. Lots of other adults, especially aunts and uncles, filled in with nurturing and coaching and support. Loyalty and demonstrated affection are two of Michael's highest values. The more the negotiations began to resemble a high-stakes poker game, the less he perceived those qualities in his employers.

Some people, if you give them a wonderful contract, will suddenly go soft. Michael is the opposite. Let him know how much you care and he'll get stronger and stronger. That's the way his heart works. When negotiations stalled, he started thinking, "Forget them!

I'll play so hard that other teams will outbid the Lakers." Trying to play tough at the same time he was hurting emotionally made him tighten up. He started to worry too much about making mistakes. He constricted himself.

By the time of the playoffs he was under extreme pressure. He had to do well. He had to win a contract. And he played exactly like someone under that kind of pressure: a little bit afraid, tentative. I'm convinced the Houston series would have gone down differently if Cooper's contract had already been settled. Ironically, when Cooper's agent started calling around the league for a better deal, Houston was very interested.

I usually stand apart from contractual dealings between players and management. I say to the players, "Get as much as you can for yourself, then come in ready to work." This time I pushed a little on both parties.

I also had a number of conversations with Mike. I had gone through the same contractual thing as a player. In fact, I was negotiating my own new contract with Jerry Buss at the same time. I wanted him to keep it in perspective. I told him, "In these kinds of situations, just because you feel you want something and you think you deserve something, that doesn't mean you're going to get it. You can't ask for A, B, C, D, E, and F and expect that they'll give you everything you want. Look at the whole picture. For the one hundred thousand dollars more you might want, or whatever, don't throw away seven years of what you have built up. You're a highly respected player here, well known in your community. Your family's from this area. You're in Los Angeles, you're on a championship team, you play with players you love.

"Some other team might give you everything on your list and you'd walk into a situation that you're going to hate. You've seen veterans come to this club. The only thing they can think about is that now, finally, they're on a team that has a chance of winning a championship. Isn't that where you want to be? Isn't that worth something?"

The coaches worked all summer long on how to address our team attitude problem. It boiled down to this: How do you keep motivation high, how do you keep goals in focus, when they already believe they're on top of the world? How do you keep the hunted moving always a few steps ahead of the hunters?

Career Best awareness was our strategy. The root concept was, every player should aim for the best statistics of their career, in at least one—but ideally several—areas. Each player would have a different emphasis, depending on his role within the team. They could try to score more or they could strive to give out more assists. Or they could push for an increase in rebounding or drawing fouls.

Whatever their position or their place in the rotation, everybody should be able to improve one facet of their game. Some might have Career Best years in more areas than one. A few might have overall the best season of their whole NBA career.

We already had a thorough system in place for keeping track of performance. For Career Best, we extended the system. We programmed the computer to compare their play in every area, in every facet, to the best they'd ever done—current production versus lifetime best.

First, we wanted everybody to think about their output in a new way. Career Best gave everyone something sharper and more defined to aim for. The better you can see a target, the more likely you are to hit it.

Second, we wanted to bring the less focused players up to an even higher level of pride. The greatest ones, like Kareem Abdul-Jabbar, persevere because of pride. On top of all their physical equipment, the greatest ones have an attitude that says, "I want to come out on top. If somebody has to win and somebody lose, my choice is to win. I don't want anyone to take that away."

John Robinson, the coach of the Rams, saw it in the 1987 championship series. He expressed it to Scott Ostler of the Los Angeles *Times*. "I'll never forget that first Lakers-Celtics game," he said. "Watching Magic! Not the skill, but the determination. And Kareem. You look at those people and you say, 'There's that look.' Boy, did those two have it. Wow! That's one of the hardest things to do, come up with the ultimate performance."

Robinson is right. It's easier to back away from excellence than it is to give everything you've got. It's easier to let the frustrations and distractions and fatigue of the long season erode your performance. But it's not satisfying in the long run. I want the Lakers to be always conscious of the long run. I want them to think about securing a place in history, to separate themselves from those who are considered today's best and to become ranked among the greatest teams that ever played. I believe that the Lakers can ultimately leave those kinds of footprints. That's why I hung my ass out on the line and told the world I could guarantee a repeat championship in '87–'88.

I have never questioned the fact that our players all want to excel. Our Career Best plan was just a mechanism to keep that desire up at the top of their minds. We wanted any voice saying "It's okay to slack off now" to be blocked out by concentration on Career Best goals.

Third, we believed that a Career Best awareness was our best tool for weeding out complacency. Before we got upset by Houston, we had won 62 regular season games. We were like a track star who is ahead of the pack and who begins to run just hard enough to stay in front. If that runner was after his Career Best time, he'd try to widen the gap. What he's doing is allowing someone in the pack to keep his courage up and be inspired to give it a hard kick in the last turn.

There's a lot of motive power in being an underdog. "I'll show you" is powerful fuel for a short burst. It carried us past the Celtics after the Memorial Day Massacre, and it carried the Rockets past us after we had pinned their ears back throughout the season and in the first playoff match.

What happens to the underdog when he bites and scratches his way to the top? The old leader of the pack is bloodied. Who does the underdog measure himself against? Obviously it takes a higher kind of motivation to make people sustain their winning ways. As the '85–'86 season was in its last few dozen games, I think people around the NBA sensed that we were losing some of our competitive spirit.

Once you've been around sports long enough, you see how success softens some performers. To stay on top you have to develop an attitude that excellence is always defined as wanting to do better. When you understand what it takes to sustain greatness and championship form, then complacency is something that isn't part of your life. You don't allow it.

Lod Cook, the chairman of Arco, has remained a good friend ever since I met him at a speaking engagement a couple of years ago. Arco keeps a big house near the beach in Montecito, near Santa Barbara, about ninety miles up the coast from Los Angeles. It's a two-bedroom place that has extra conference rooms and audiovisual facilities. They use it for executive meeting sessions when they feel the need to have a relaxing, distraction-free setting. Lod called up and offered use of the Arco house to the Laker coaching staff. I didn't have to think twice about saying yes.

The coaches settled in there for a long weekend of talking basketball. We wanted to make the Lakers less predictable on offense. We also needed to take our defensive philosophy to a higher level. Actually, we hadn't ever really had a defensive philosophy, just a set of tactics. There's a difference. I'm basically offense-minded, so polishing the defense drew heavily on Bertka's and Pfund's input.

Randy Pfund comes from a basketball family, as some people come from farm families or show business families. His dad coached at Wheaton College in Illinois. Father and son are both the kind of coach I call a lifer. One of the reasons I hired Randy, besides his great attitude and tremendous eagerness to learn, is his defensive expertise. Bill Bertka was the only man I wanted for the job back when I had my first opportunity to hire an assistant coach. He worked for the Lakers when I was a player. He was once a college coach, at Kent State, and he's also been a general manager and a director of player personnel. And he knows the game cold. One time when Randy and I were getting elated about a new idea we had for defense, Bertka looked at us both and said, "Wait a minute." He left the room briefly and returned with some dusty, dog-eared basketball book published in 1942. He opened it to a page somewhere near the middle and dropped it in front of us. "There," he said. "There's your brand-new defense. Hank Iba was using it thirty-five years ago." Bertka keeps everything in perspective.

We went out and had dinner every night and discussed the game. In the late afternoons Randy and I played some real competitive tennis. Randy used to live in Santa Barbara and he still knows everybody. He called up a woman friend to make up a doubles match against Chris and me. They blew us off the court. "Where did you find her?" I asked. "She's an A-list player," he explained. "I'll go easy on you tomorrow. I'll bring someone from the C-list."

Montecito is one of my favorite places in California. It reminds me of how things probably looked in the fifties. It's uncrowded and unhurried, a villagelike place that's perfect for relaxation and reflection. You just go down Olive Mill Road a little ways from Montecito's shops and you're at the shoreline. Over on the right is the Santa Barbara Biltmore, which is one of the great examples of Old California grandeur. Red tile roofs and thick, white adobe walls and sprawling Mission-style bungalows on a big green lawn. The Pacific Ocean pounding beneath the bluff just across the road.

The Arco house sits between the Biltmore and the center of Montecito. We sat out on a big porch that faced the ocean, overlooking the top of the Biltmore. We had flip charts and we brought sandwiches in and we sat there running through our notebooks. We talked and improvised plans and filled up three or four flip-chart tablets with our X's and O's and schemes. Actually, some of them looked pretty good; they could have been pieces of art. Red, blue, and green, X's and O's and lines slashing in every direction. We thought about selling them to a gallery for hundreds of thousands of dollars. Let somebody else worry about the Pistons and the Hawks and the Rockets and the Mavericks.

We took our dinners at The Grill, a classy little informal place in Montecito. Inevitably, after spaghetti and meatballs and long-necked bottles of beer, we'd be back onto basketball. The Grill puts out oversize paper place mats. Randy would pull a pen from one of his pockets. We'd stay another hour, messing up our place mats with more play sets and terminology and scribbles.

It took a large part of the following season to actually get the team in tune with the new offensive and defensive patterns. All we could do initially was to sketch out some approaches. Later on we introduced these things and elaborated on them gradually.

Basketball is a game of flow and spontaneity, but it's based on well-drilled patterns. Because the players know so well how to be in the right place at the right time, they can branch off and do unexpected things that surprise and upset opponents. Then they can slip back into the pattern again. But if you try to impose too many pattern changes at once on a team, you risk chaos.

Our defensive concept was three words: *Contain, Protect, Contest.*

Every team, when it goes on offense, already has in mind exactly what it will try first to score. When that first option is unavailable or is not working, there's a second and a third. The first option is their bread-and-butter play, their hottest offensive weapon.

Contain means we will make it our top priority to stop that first strike. The ball would come down against us, and it would be passed to the first-option player. For the Bulls it would be Michael Jordan. For the Portland Trailblazers it might be Clyde Drexler or Kiki Vandeweghe. We wanted all five players to move with that first pass. When that first-option player catches the ball, he sees nothing but a wall. He has to give up the ball in favor of their second option. By now they've eaten up about ten seconds from the 24-second clock.

The first threat is contained, but now that player will try to zip a pass out to an open man and let him pop the shot, the way Bird loves to feed Dennis Johnson or Danny Ainge. *Protect* means we have to shift back in a very coordinated way. This is a tremendously vulnerable moment for the defense. This is where teamwork has to be at a peak. Somebody slides out to pressure the new man with the ball. Somebody else slides into the open position, becoming a helper for the man defensing the ball. Other players shift position to help the helper. This is alertness time. Doing it well puts a lot of pressure on an offense. They've got to make great passes to exploit how we're shifting and stunting. And they might make one or two, but over the course of the game they're not always going to be able to thread the needle.

Now their offensive plan is gummed up and they're improvising, passing away from the pressure and hoping for some surprise opening. *Contest* means that we keep the pressure on, all five defenders concentrating on the movement of the ball, until they force up a low-percentage shot or turn over the ball with a 24-second-clock violation.

The soul of our Contain/Protect/Contest philosophy is to control their clock. Of all plays run in this league, the shot is taken on the first pass seventy-five percent of the time.

That's a very basic sketch of the system. To make it work we had to get five guys working in unison as they adapt to quick, aggressive changes. Anyone daydreaming for a tenth of a second would create an opportunity that another team would spot and exploit. And there could never be an attitude of "I had my man covered, it was so-and-so's fault." Our people had to have an awareness of every shift being made on the floor, not just by their designated man, but by all five of the opponents.

Kareem Abdul-Jabbar's skyhook is the most deadly and unstoppable offensive weapon in any sport. For years and years, the Lakers picked up their paychecks regularly because Kareem dropped that shot in, right hand or left hand, whenever the game was on the line. That's why everyone calls those crucial seconds "money time." We had plenty of other offensive weapons, but that was the one that came out of the holster when we got into a make-or-break situation. You can hear Chick Hearn announcing it: "Magic dribbles out to the wing. Kareem is fronted in the low post, but Magic feeds him with a lob pass, right between two defenders. He swings left and hooks right. They're on his arm. He gets the shot off and there's a foul called. It'll count if it goes. It's . . . good!"

In our half-court offense we went into Kareem in the low post so much it was an act of arrogance. We didn't even try to disguise it. It was like saying, "Here's what we're going to do. It's what we always do. We just don't think you can stop it." Over the years Kareem has become excellent at reacting to double- and triple-team pressure. But especially with taller and faster lineups, the intensity of that pressure has increased. They clog the middle and Kareem has to kick the ball to the perimeter for an outside shot.

The big trouble with that is, outside shooting is a hot-and-cold proposition. Outside shooters are like quarterbacks who have to throw a long bomb for a touchdown. One slightly wrong twitch and you get a shot that caroms off the rim. Maybe their brain computes and corrects that tiny miscalculation next time, or maybe the brain has to try out a few theories. Each wrong theory is a missed shot. Too many missed shots and that player may need an hour of practice to regroove his shooting motion. So we needed more diversity in our half-court attack.

We had personnel changes, too. McGee was bound for Atlanta. Ronnie Lester, a reserve point guard, and Larry Spriggs, a forward, were also gone.

Larry Spriggs was a well-traveled veteran. He played for the Rockets and the Bulls and for CBA teams in Las Vegas and Rochester and Albany before he joined the Lakers. Ronnie Lester was our longtime insurance policy at point guard. He was my first choice if Magic couldn't play. But Earvin is such an impact player that he'll always play a lion's share of any game's minutes.

Like McGee, Spriggs and Lester were eager for more playing time. Each had reached a stage in his career where he felt it was time to go for it, to see if the grass was greener. Ronnie became a factor in a trade we made with the Seattle Supersonics. Larry packed off to Real Madrid, a Spanish pro team.

Basketball is becoming huge in Europe. Bob McAdoo, who helped us win a couple of championships and who was the NBA's leading scorer in '74, '75, and '76, is now a big star in Milan. After the New York Knicks cut Kurt Rambis in his rookie tryout, he used a Grecian team as a place to refine his skills. Then he came back to the States and won a place on the Laker roster. I went to Milan one year to participate in a camp. More people recognized me on sight there than they do in Los Angeles. The Europeans are truly in awe of our basketball players, just as they are of our jazz musicians. So that's where Larry Spriggs went to ply his trade. Michael Cooper, in the depths of his contract negotiations, gave a lot of thought to jumping over to Italy himself.

Another personnel change was the retirement of Mitch Kupchak. The first game I ever coached, a win over the San Antonio Spurs, Mitch was 11 of 11 from the floor. Later he suffered a knee injury so severe that it was believed he would never play again. He could have easily sat back and collected the guaranteed money in his contract, but he returned and played through the pain and gave us three more seasons. He also started a graduate school business program at UCLA. Jerry West brought him into management, as an assistant general manager, after he retired.

The last departure was Maurice Lucas. We brought him in for the '85–'86 season to make us better matched against Twin Tower lineups. He came to us as an eleven-year veteran with experience spread across seven ABA and NBA teams. In 1977, the year Portland upset Philadelphia to win an NBA championship, Luke averaged over 20 points for the Blazers and established himself as the best power forward in the league.

He came to us as a veteran ready to accept a reserve player's role. His speed was diminished from the glory days at Portland, but he compensated with a lot of savvy and with his tough guy "enforcer" image. The truth is that Luke is a good man with a gentle side that you will only see off the court. When strangers would want to talk to him in our locker room they'd expect to get growled at, but Luke would greet them with, "Hey, big guy! How's it going?" He sold that evil enforcer image to the hilt, though. It's part of the Maurice Lucas Professional Package.

We realized that we needed more speed than Luke could provide. Also, we couldn't continue to play a lot of veterans at the expense of building up our younger players, such as A.C. Green and Adrian Branch and Billy Thompson.

The week prior to training camp I called Lucas because I wanted him to know that we were about to put him on waivers. There were already rumors on the grapevine, and I wanted to tell him directly. I called the house in Portland, where he still lives in the off-season. Rita, his wife, answered the phone and told me he was working out at a gym. "Have Luke call me," was all I said. Rita knew what that meant. She's been the wife of a warrior a long time.

"Is it over?" she asked.

"Yes, it is, with us," I told her. "It's not over for Luke, but it is with us."

"I understand," she said. "I just want to collect my thoughts before I call him. I just want to say the right words to him."

Luke called me back about ten minutes later. I wanted to make sure that I didn't stumble at the beginning. "Luke," I said, "we made a decision that we're going to put you on waivers and we're going to go with A.C. Green." I knew a direct message would be better than any attempt to soften the blow.

I remembered a story I once read about a pro football coach. He always came up to the players he meant to cut and tapped them on the shoulder as they were walking off the practice field. It became legendary. The men would talk about their dread of "the tap on the shoulder." It was like the angel of death to them. One guy noticed the coach coming up to him. It was late in preseason and he wasn't a standout player. He knew that his tap was coming. Before the coach's hand could touch his shoulder, he dropped to the ground. He said, "Look how strong I am, Coach." He started doing push-ups like there was no tomorrow.

The coach didn't have the heart to cut him right then. But he did twenty-four hours later. All the guy achieved was one more day of anguish.

Luke showed class. "Thanks," he said. "I appreciated the opportunity. I was happy there. You treated me well." It turned out that Seattle wanted him, but they couldn't see springing for the salary he would have had as a Laker. So our team paid the first $300,000 of his salary, the Sonics paid the rest, and they got a veteran to balance their youthful lineup.

The announcement of Mitch Kupchak's retirement hit the papers right after the news of Lucas's trade. Training camp was a couple of days away. Michael Cooper was still unsigned. Everybody wondered what we were going to do. This much was for sure: Lucas was cut, A.C. Green was starting, Mike McGee was gone, Larry Spriggs gone, Kup retired, Ronnie Lester due to join Luke in Seattle. The closet was cleaned out. For the first time in five years, there was a legitimate chance for several newcomers to win a place on the Lakers. There was one major criterion: These newcomers had to be fleet-footed.

We were close to a trade for Jawaan Oldham, a good-running 7-footer playing for the Bulls. But one day before we hit the road to Palm Springs and training camp, West had bad news. "The deal is dead. Three days ago I thought we had a deal, but now we don't."

Oldham's agent, Fred Slaughter, told reporters, "I get the impression Chicago can't let him go. Rumor has it that one of their backup centers, Mike Smrek, hasn't fully recovered from a foot injury. So if Jawaan left, it would leave Chicago thin at the center spot."

Being thin at the center spot was something we knew about. Kareem Abdul-Jabbar is the greatest player in the history of the game. He has gone to more playoffs and has scored more playoff points than anyone else in NBA history. In various years he has led the league in scoring, in shooting percentage, and in rebounding. He has been league MVP six times and a member of the all-league team ten times. In the '85–'86 season, at age thirty-nine, he was voted the greatest center currently in the game.

But he was still just one man. And Coop was still talking about going to Italy—or the Rockets. On the road back to the top, we needed Michael Cooper alongside. And if we could just find another companion for the trip, someone with long legs and fast feet and a master basketball mind . . .

Start Me Up

Here comes October first. I had been ready to go since the middle of August. I was driving the people around me crazy. I wanted to do more, prepare more, change things. Everyone was relieved when the time came to open training camp. We were going to start the machine now.

The Summer League showed us that we were going to start A.C. Green at power forward. We didn't tell him, and we didn't tell Kurt Rambis, our veteran power forward, during the summer. Now was the time to reveal that plan. We had to boost the quickness and versatility of our lineup.

This was the start of Kurt's sixth season with the Lakers. I knew what he could do, and I believed he could be just as effective off the bench as he was in a starting role. A.C., on the other hand, was just beginning to blossom as a player. If we got him into the flow of the games right away, he would mature sooner and give the team more offensive punch.

When I saw A.C. come as a rookie the year before, I said to myself, "That's it. He's gonna play!" He came from Oregon State, under Coach Ralph Miller, where they profoundly emphasize teamwork and fundamentals. Like Earvin Johnson, A.C. arrived already understanding how to play unselfish basketball. The footwork and the fundamentals were all perfect. And he was blessed with a young, 6'9", 230-pound body that could just propel itself up and down court all night long. His build is much like James Worthy's: slender from the waist up, exceptionally powerful from the waist down. A prototype leaper's body, one that can explode into a quick sprint and also run continuously at speed.

A.C. doesn't have the offensive skills of James, but he was showing a capability to grow as an offensive player. A.C. has tremendous respect for coaches. He works hard and he learns very quickly. He has had to overcome some tentativeness and to develop more confidence as an offensive player.

Ultimately, every offensive player has to master a certain shot. It becomes his stock-in-trade. Everybody in the league learns to respect it. Then, out of that shot and out of that certain place on the floor, he can develop enough variations to keep the defense guessing. Kevin McHale has his ability to turn in the low post and suddenly, with those skinny shoulders, slide laterally past his defenders and lift the ball to the hoop. Kareem has his skyhook. He faces away from the basket and rolls either left or right for his launch, depending on where the opponents are the most vulnerable. Earvin has a variety of shots. A.C. needs to develop a special one of his own that he can put up from somewhere in and around the lane. That will be his next breakthrough.

But we had seen enough of his 30-point, 15-rebound games in the Summer League to believe that he could flat-out score when he was the first line of offense against lesser players.

Kurt Rambis always reminds me of a great statement Bill Russell made when he was a player/coach. Russell said that the talent he looks for is hustle, and hustle really is a talent.

Hustle isn't a God-given talent, like quick feet. It's something that a person develops through sheer will. It's a state of mind. Every coach in the world, from the pros to the youth leagues, prays for his players to develop more hustle. Every coach needs a Kurt Rambis.

Kurt Rambis doesn't have the quickest feet. He doesn't have the end-line-to-end-line explosion. He doesn't have the lift. He doesn't have the flair or the flow. His whole game is based on hustle.

He does have talent. He's a coordinated, 6'9", 235-pound blue-collar forward. But his greatness is in his heart. In my playing years I tried to be what Kurt Rambis is, because I had to rely on hustle. You have to have that element on a team. You have to have a player who is smart, who might be limited in certain skills, but who has that spark that can incite and inspire teammates. We always told Kurt, when he became a starter, "Your first six minutes of the game have to be played like they're the last six minutes you're going to play in your career." He can never say, "I'm gonna pace myself." His role is to be an inspirational player.

I've talked to some guys who play in city leagues and YMCA gyms. They look to Kurt as a role model. They look at an Earvin or a Michael Jordan and think, "That's fabulous, but I could never do those things." They look at Kurt and they think, "He's busting his ass out there. Look at the results he gets. If I bust my ass, maybe I can be a factor in this game." There are people who come to Laker games and sit together, all dressed like Kurt—the same plaid shirts and casual pants and the same heavy-duty plastic-frame glasses with the hold-down strap across the back. That's the kind of admiration he has inspired.

The problem was, Kurt embodies all these things because he is full of competitive desire, as anybody who climbs the ladder must be, no matter what they do in life. Kurt is the leading scorer in University of Santa Clara history. As a third-round pick by the New York Knicks in 1980, he was waived, then signed to a ten-day deal, then let go again. He went off to work in Greece, which is definitely the outer margins of the pro game.

By the time he came to the Lakers' camp in '81 he was strong enough to win a spot on the roster. He built that break into a starting role. In time, other teams around the league noticed his impact and started looking for "Kurt Rambis types."

Now, just as he had sublimated his competitive desire and assumed the identity of a role player, Kurt had to adjust once more. A great role player is really just as valuable as a star, and almost as hard to find or develop. A great role player has to go through difficult phases. You have to say and do the right things, the limited and the supportive things, while inside you there's the hunger to be a star. Eventually you have to really believe in those things. That is who you are, that is your being.

The team needed more quickness and versatility, but it came at the expense of Kurt's starting role. He gave up a little bit of his identity. He was at a crossroads. Another role was being defined for him.

Kurt told reporters, "Pat says that there's a possibility I might not start this year and to me that's fine. I've always said that all I want to do is play—whether I get that time coming off the bench or starting is perfectly all right with me." He was saying the right things, but I could tell that he was not really feeling them. His breakthrough is going to come when those words flow naturally.

Mitch Kupchak announced his retirement formally on October 1st. He played on our Olympic team in '76. He made the NBA All-Rookie team the next year and went on to ten pro seasons, in spite of a knee that blew out on him like—as one sportswriter said—a cheap inner tube. Mitch carried through, regardless of pain. He went out with class.

On the same day Mitch retired, the newspapers reported that Kareem said he intended to play at least two more seasons for the Lakers. This was news that lifted everyone's spirits. One more thing to make the team environment positive.

A friend of mine was across the country on business last year. The only place he could see one of our games was in a barroom right in the opponent's hometown. A local guy kept pressing him about the matchups. "What about Kareem?" he said. "He's gonna be forty!"

"Yeah," the Laker fan answered. "And in forty more years he'll be eighty. And he'll still be kicking your guy's ass!"

Other people talk about Kareem's age. They say he's obsolete. I say we don't win a championship without him. Certain things have slipped, like the ability to go after a rebound two or three times in a row, or the lateral movement. Don't let those things distract you. He can still put the ball in the hole better than anybody. He is still the most vital force at the end of a game, to get us the best possible shot and put it down.

If I ever had to choose up sides and play a game for life or death, I would choose Kareem first.

We were still trying to acquire Jawaan Oldham as his backup. We weren't looking to build a Twin Towers lineup. We just needed a quick, quality big man to relieve our starting center. Having Kareem Abdul-Jabbar on the team is like owning a mint condition Mercedes 300SL Gullwing Coupe. You don't want to drive your classic every single day in rush hour traffic. You set up a good maintenance schedule. You perpetuate its useful life.

We liked Oldham because he could run. We liked it that he could

play facing the basket. Most big men play the game with their backs
to the basket. With less speed, they have to make slow, deliberate
offensive strikes. A big man who faces the basket adds a new element
of terror for defenders, a fifth quick-strike option. I was eager to see
what Oldham could do on a team with four greyhounds.

On the same day as Mitch's retirement and Kareem's announcement, Jerry West reported confusing news about Oldham. The Chicago Bulls were apparently ready to accept our first 1987 draft choice
in exchange for his contract. Oldham's agent said, "Jawaan would
love to come to L.A. He and I are working feverishly to get it done
tonight or tomorrow." But West said, "The surprising thing to me
is that he apparently hasn't decided yet whether he wants to play
here. Until we find out and go from there, we're just spinning our
wheels."

October 2nd, the following morning, was our annual Media
Day event in the gym at Loyola Marymount College. This is where
the team officially tells the world, "We're back. We aim to make
our city proud of us. Please take our picture and run it in the
sports pages. If they don't sell some tickets, we might have to get
regular jobs."

The same reporters showed up as last year. They asked the same
questions. It was probably the same doughnuts and the same coffee.
But something fantastic happened to upset the routine. As a complete
surprise, Michael Cooper came in the door with his Laker uniform.
He was still unsigned, a free agent, but he wanted to declare his
loyalty to the guys. The cameras started flashing, the players were
in heaven.

"It's close," Coop told everyone. "We just need a dot over a
couple of *i*'s and a period at the end of a sentence. In a day or two
it will be over. Maybe sooner."

All of us left the Media Day event and drove to the Ocotillo
Lodge in Palm Springs. That's where we stayed for training camp.
Far from big-city distractions. It's a resort, but it's also an isola-
tion post.

When you drive to Palm Springs, you climb slowly for the first
hour or so, heading eastward from L.A. You run through a chain of
suburbs built over old citrus orchards. West Covina, Montclair, Guasti,
Bloomington. Then you go by San Bernardino and make a final, steep
climb through the pass to enter a big desert bowl. The air is hot and
dry. You're almost coasting on the way down. It's like flying a light
plane into a dry sauna.

We mark the start of camp with a dinner. With all our longevity, the core players on the Lakers have invented lots of rituals. The rookies have to stand and sing their alma mater. Then Earvin assigns each one to a veteran player. As long as they remain in camp, they'll have to fetch water and carry the gym bag for their man. Plus provide a wake-up call service and food delivery.

Knowing that Roger Harden played at Kentucky, where I had played in the 60s, James Worthy challenged him to name the greatest guard in Kentucky history. He said, "Pat Riley." When everyone stopped laughing, I looked at Dale Blaney. He played at West Virginia, where Jerry West averaged nearly 25 points a game in the late 50s. I asked him, "Who is the greatest guard in West Virginia history?" Blaney answered, "Rod Hundley." The whole room roared.

Opening night dinner is like the overture to all the emotions of our upcoming season. It seems like there's no mercy in the joking and verbal hazing, but there's always an undercurrent of love and respect. When Cooper arrived, Kareem shouted, "Get that guy out of here. He's unsigned."

We show videos from past years. We make about five new videos every year, setting the season's highlight moments to music about joy and victory and love. I want the team to remember, always, the feelings that go with winning. I want them to remember the striving it took to get themselves in a position to be winners.

Of course, I have a few critics as a video artist. I love to use soul music, rhythm and blues, and jazz. Rambis and Kupchak got on me to provide equal opportunity to Bruce Springsteen, which is their kind of inspirational music.

After the videos, each rookie has to get up and sing his college song. It goes hard on anybody who doesn't know the words to his own alma mater.

After dinner each veteran will come up and give an unsolicited testimony. Each one talks about what they feel they have to do this year, as individuals and as players. They make solemn commitments to their teammates.

Finally, I give my State of the Union message. This year, I talked about attitude. I emphasized our transition into our break, which was going to be a key to running-game dominance. We feel that any time we can make the game a fast one, our opponents are going to be disadvantaged. We need a quick, opportunistic transition to get the running game into gear. I finished by saying, "Obviously, you can all see that there are five faces gone from last year. The opportunity exists for you to win more playing time. The opportunity exists for our rookies, for the first time in five years, to have a legitimate chance of making this team. You rookies, I don't want to see you deferring to our veterans at all. You're here to win a job, not to pay homage. Tomorrow, when practice starts, those veterans are going to be the guys who stand in the way of your getting a job. And if you defer to them, you might not make it. You've got to compete with them."

At 10:05 A.M. on October 3rd, Earvin Johnson drove the lane for a breakaway layup. Roger Harden planted himself in front to take a charge and Earvin ran right over him. Turning to sprint back downcourt, Earvin flashed a smile down to the rookie and said, "Welcome to the NBA."

Palm Springs

This was a teaching camp. In the past we might have had only one or two newcomers and twelve veterans. The regulars would be familiar with all our patterns and the rookies would scramble to learn them fast. We just played. We ran them and got them in shape. We put in our play sets and they clicked right away. This time only six men in camp had been Lakers the year before. The rooks were a majority. The offense and defense had been redesigned. We had one week to make it from kindergarten to Ph.D.

There was one newcomer we didn't have to be concerned about teaching. As camp opened, West announced that the Jawaan Oldham deal was dead. "Three days ago I thought we had a deal," he said, "but now we don't." The quest for a backup center would go on for a long time.

Meanwhile, our captain arrived in terrific shape. Kareem pumped iron all summer. A special training consultant kept him on a demanding program, emphasizing squats and abdominal work. He wanted to muscle up his lower body and become harder to push around in the low post. His body weight was only up three pounds, but the percentage of fat in his weight dropped incredibly, from thirteen to just eight percent. Some of our other players didn't report to camp in such great shape. We had an epidemic of blistered feet, sore calves, and little muscle pulls, all the signs of underconditioned athletes. By the middle of the week those fatigue injuries brought us down to only ten able-bodied players.

I hate to do a lot of talking in camp. I hate to hold up practices. For the first half hour every day, before the players were stretched and ready, we walked through our new situations, step by step. Then we would stretch, run, and begin practicing in earnest, two sessions a day. "We're going to emphasize flying," I told them. "We have always run. This year we're going to fly."

Petur Gudmundsson, our 7'2", 260-pound reserve center from Greenland, didn't make it off the runway.

Gudmundsson had a brief NBA apprenticeship in Portland and Detroit after graduating from the University of Washington in 1981. When Mitch Kupchak was on the injured reserve list near the end of the '85–'86 season, we first tried out Jerome Henderson on a ten-day contract. Then we picked Petur from the Kansas City Sizzlers of the CBA. The results were promising. He wasn't ready to be a pillar of the team, but he had the makings of a good stand-in.

Two hours into our first practice, Petur pulled out of a wind sprint and said, "That's it. That's all I can do." He just broke down. It took weeks of waiting, watching, and testing before we knew why. A vertebra had torn one of the discs in his spine. The damage was microscopically small and extremely hard to detect. But in the eventual surgery, doctors had to cut through muscle fibers. On the first day of practice our only reserve center went down for the season. The conditioning and maintenance of Kareem Abdul-Jabbar suddenly became even more crucial.

In order to drill the team, there have to be two players for every position. You need to assemble two squads and have them vie against each other. We have a gold squad, which is usually the top six players, and a blue squad, comprised of the next six. I had to use Kurt and A.C., both power forwards, in the pivot for the blues, even though it was essential for A.C. to work on mastering his position in order to be a starter. Then Kurt sprained a hip muscle and was confined to exercise-bike workouts.

Cooper sat on the sidelines in sweats and sneakers. All he could do was perch on the bleachers, wrap his arms around his knees, sit back, and watch. It was killing him, but to practice before the contract was signed would be against league rules. On day three of camp a courier arrived with his completed contract. Cooper signed on and took the court before the ink had time to dry. He lifted that tired team. Our fifth practice, the afternoon session on our third day, was the best practice we had.

Fortunately, it was also a practice that Jerry Buss came to see. The energy level was way up. Our break was clicking. The outlet passes, both after misses and made baskets, were crisp. Transitions were quickly made. James and A.C. were in great form. Buss had a happy look in his eyes.

Kareem walked up beside me after practice. I had wondered how he would feel about our diversifying the offense. After all, he had been the number one option on every team since his grade school days. He said, "The changes are working great. The guys seem to love it."

The coaches went out to dinner together. We felt great. In terms of effort, this was the best camp we'd ever seen the Lakers have. "We're on the right track," Bertka said.

Jerry Buss always puts on a big dinner in midweek of camp. Up to now he had been watching from the sidelines. This was his first time to mix with the team, and we went to Kobe's Steak House. There weren't any speeches, just casual conversation and good food.

Late in the meal, Buss told Jerry West and me that we would "wait and see" about the decision not to trade James. I think he was still upset that we had swayed him. Not upset about the decision itself, but about feeling he had let go of some power. There was a hint of finality to Buss's message, as if our tenures were directly connected to James's growth and contributions in the year. Buss wanted us to remember who runs the ship.

Frank Brickowski, a reserve power forward/center, arrived on the next day, October 7th. He was the final installment from our trade of Lucas and Lester to Seattle. Frank had been impressively physical whenever he guarded Kareem. At 6'10" and 240 pounds, he wasn't the complete solution to our size problem, but he certainly took off some of the pressure.

Another kind of pressure was being applied to Billy Thompson, our number one draft choice. Without the slightest trace of malice, Billy was driving the coaches crazy. Five minutes late for prepractice taping on the first day, fifteen minutes on another. Twenty-five minutes late to the evening practice session. We levied fines, which all go into a general fund for team parties and charity donations. Kellogg and some of the other rookies were also late a few times, so it wasn't a federal case. But Billy wasn't picking up on his assignments as quickly as we had hoped. The great skills were still evident. Every so often we'd get another glimpse. A quicksilver offensive rebound brought back up and dunked cleanly before the other players had time to react. An extended leap to control an alley-oop pass and jam it through in one unbroken motion at the top of the jump. But when it came to meshing with the team, his concentration seemed to drift. We wondered what had happened to the guy we had watched in the Summer League.

On the day Brickowski arrived, the San Antonio Spurs upset the Dallas Mavericks in the first NBA exhibition game of the year. Mychal Thompson, the number one pick in the 1978 draft, scored 12 at center. It was his first game for San Antonio after seven seasons at Portland, where he had replaced Bill Walton. Reading that news, I remembered how Earvin and Cooper used to talk about wanting to play with Mychal: for his size, his speed, and most of all, his intelligence.

We always break training camp with an intrasquad game at College of the Desert. All the proceeds go to their athletic fund. It's always a packed house. Early in that final day, Dale Blaney approached the coaches with a revelation. He wanted to go back home and become a race car driver like his older brother. "You've done yourself a lot of good here," we told him. "You have a reasonable chance. If you leave, you're going to throw that all away." But his heart was set on going back to West Virginia. After he went off to pack, Bertka shook his head and said, "In all my years in basketball, I've heard every possible reason for giving up. But I never heard of someone quitting to race stock cars. This is the first in NBA history."

Our exhibition game was sharp. All the things we had been talking about and working on all week long clicked. The open break was executed extremely well. Our veterans were completely on top of the new offensive system and the rookies were getting the hang of it, too. It got hot in that gym, in both senses of the word. A.C.

scored 23 and pulled down 13 rebounds. Adrian led all scorers with 30. Cooper showed the rookies what it's like to play against the best defenseman in the NBA. Byron had 28 points.

When we walked out after the game, the sky had become deep black. In the clear air you could see enough bright individual stars and white, dusty patches of galaxy to get a brief hint of what "infinity" means. Camp was officially over. Everyone got into his car and headed home.

I made the slow ascent out of the Coachella Valley, through the pass and into the Los Angeles Basin. We were headed back to the realities of a barnstorming exhibition season, an 82-game regular season, a heavy load of expectations, both positive and negative, competition from twenty-two other determined teams, attitude adjustments, and hard choices about who should be on our final, twelve-man roster.

In two days we would play Chicago in the Forum. There was no scouting report, no special preparation. Gudmundsson, Rambis, Kellogg, and Harden were all injured. Blaney was back home trying on a crash helmet.

I stuck a cassette into the car's player. I constantly review motivational literature, looking for pearls. The team needs them and I need them. This time I selected Wayne Dyer reading from his book *Choosing Your Own Greatness*. While my mind worked on fine-tuning an approach to the challenges laid out against our best-in-history/over-the-hill team, Dyer said, "Attitude is an inner concept. It is the most important thing you can develop in your life."

For the Lakers this year, I'd never heard truer words said.

Exhibition

Idon't like the exhibition season, never have. We start a month before the first official game, and take a week to get in shape and learn systems. For another week we rip around the country playing noncounting games. Then we play exhibitions locally for a week, practice a little more, and rip around the country again to play *more* noncounting games before coming home for final preseason adjustments.

Everybody should be limited to two weeks of practice: one week to drill, one week to play three exhibition games. Cut two weeks off the season. They never really address the issue of the length of the season. It just gets extended every year.

What happens now is that you lose the conditioning you worked so hard for in camp. The starters can only play limited exhibition minutes because you need to evaluate the rookies. That's something you could do better in team scrimmages. Everybody gets out of game shape. You generate enough money to pay training camp expenses, but at the expense of developing the team.

We hadn't played against Michael Jordan in a year. Foot injuries kept him out of both L.A.-Chicago games of '85–'86. Subsequently, in a single playoff game with the Boston Celtics, he threw down 63 points. That got our attention. This was the first game for Doug Collins as the Bulls' new coach. We knew him as a four-time All-Star at guard for the Philadelphia 76ers, and we figured his team would be scrappy and competitive.

On the day we broke camp, the San Antonio Spurs waived two guards: Alfrederick Hughes and Wes Matthews. Hughes had entered the league last year with the nickname "Alfrederick the Great." College glory fades fast in the NBA.

Matthews was a first-round pick by the Washington Bullets in 1980. From that start, he bounced between six different NBA clubs and three CBA outfits. His past record included insubordination and drug problems. But he also had brilliance. He could be fearless against anybody. In the first round of the '85–'86 playoffs Wes tagged us for 90 points over three games.

We've had good luck in the past with accepting players of checkered reputation. They come in and see the attitudes and behavior patterns of our stars and they get a new outlook. All of a sudden they see that no one with destructive habits has a prayer of lasting.

Wes was the kind of whippet guard a fast-breaking team needs. At twenty-eight, he had experience to go with his speed. Bertka and I talked about him with Johnny Bach, the former Golden State coach. We were concerned, as any coach would be, about the character of a potential new player. Bach looked at us and said, "You don't want all milk drinkers on your team!"

He was right. A team has to be a melting pot. It's going to face a lot of different challenges and it has to have a lot of potential responses. A few sinners mixed in with the saints can create a powerful brew. We called Matthews's agent. In five days he was competing for the reserve point guard spot against Andre Turner.

Wes had his work cut out. The headlines following our first exhibition said, "5-10 Andre Is a Giant for Lakers," "Turner Hot as Lakers Win Debut," "Rookie Point Guard Impressive."

Turner went on to win a lot of positive ink throughout our exhibitions. In this game against the Bulls he scored 11 and had 6 assists in twenty-five minutes. We were giving him a thorough look.

Magic Johnson is of paramount importance to the team, and the guy who replaces him when he needs a blow has to be able to keep the momentum alive. Turner showed he could push the ball upcourt. He came in when we were down by seven in the first quarter and he helped light up a 17–9 scoring burst. The Forum fans picked him as a favorite. The reporters said he gave us a "Spud Webb–like" dimension.

We also needed to prove we were viable against a Twin Towers lineup. New York came in on the 12th of October. They brought in 7', 240-pound Patrick Ewing at center, the first pick of the 1985 draft and the 1986 Rookie of the Year. They also brought 7'1", 245-pound Bill Cartwright, the third pick in 1979's draft and a former All-Rookie choice, to join him at power forward.

Cartwright stretched his arms in the dressing room before the game. His left hand shattered a fluorescent light fixture. The glass lacerated a tendon in his middle finger. The doctors splinted him up and New York was suddenly a Single Tower team.

Coop got five quick points, a steal, and an assist to start a scoring surge late in the first quarter. We won the game. But it wasn't the vindication we needed.

We waived Vada Martin and Roger Harden just before an eastern road trip. Chicago fell to us 109–99 at their arena and then 123–101 in a game staged at Chapel Hill, North Carolina. Over 21,000 local fans came to see James Worthy and Michael Jordan, who were teammates on North Carolina's 1982 NCAA championship team. We had an incredible performance—up 30 points for a while. Chick Hearn, the veteran Lakers announcer, almost missed it. Bertka accidentally left him at the hotel.

While the crowd looked at the Worthy vs. Jordan matchup, the coaches focused on A.C. making 19 on 8-for-10 shooting to lead team scoring. Adrian had 14 and Wes Matthews, playing his first minutes as a Laker, got 10.

Two days later I was walking through Times Square, grabbing a hot dog at Nathan's. We were in New York to face the Knicks again. This time Cartwright would play. Hubie Brown, the Knicks coach, had been playing up the game to the fans and his team. It was an exhibition, it meant nothing, but there was big-game electricity in the air.

When I got back to the Grand Hyatt Hotel there were messages from Jerry West. Dale Blaney wanted to come back. "Let's give the kid another chance," Jerry said. I hated the idea. I knew it would lose me respect from the team. The guys who hadn't quit, who had hung in tough, would see us bring back Blaney and think, "Uh-huh. They want to keep a white guy on the end of the bench."

West had heard that Gerald Henderson, a guard, and Alton Lister, a center, might be available from the Sonics. Lister had just arrived in Seattle. He was traded there by Milwaukee for Jack Sikma, but he balked at the Sonics' contract offer. Rumors such as that are a general manager's daily bread. The NBA's gossip pipeline has an open valve. Most of the time you can ignore the personnel movement talk. Ninety percent of it will never materialize. But when your team needs players, you suddenly start paying close attention.

Bill Bertka thought we should discuss Rick Robey. Robey was a first-round pick out of Kentucky in 1978, a 6'11", 230-pound power forward who could play center. He was with Boston and then Phoenix, but he had just been waived. He had gotten woefully out of shape, ballooned up to 275 pounds, and developed chronic injury problems.

Bertka called Robey at home with a chance for a fresh start. "Before we bring you in for a look," Bill said, "we want you to get some basic tests run. Cardiovascular, fat, and stress." Robey replied, "Well, I'll have to check with the Players' Association whether or not you can make me do that." That was the last time we talked to him. We found out he didn't have what we wanted.

While we waited for New York's Twin Towers on October 21st, Houston's were going up against the Washington Bullets on the same night. We sent a scout. Our first scheduled game of the season was a Houston rematch. Rockets against Lakers on CBS-TV. People couldn't wait to see if L.A. would stay down like they wanted us to.

Kareem drew three early fouls guarding Cartwright. Ewing scored 21 points and 10 rebounds matched against A.C. Green and Kurt Rambis. Brickowski, our only backup center, was out with a hyperextended elbow. Cooper, Scott, and Matthews went cold offensively and we shot under 45%. The headlines of October 22nd said it bluntly: "Knicks Dwarf Lakers 110–101."

There was one last stop for the barnstormers. We arrived on October 24th in Albuquerque, New Mexico, to play the Phoenix Suns. As with James in Chapel Hill, this was a homecoming performance for Michael Cooper. He played at New Mexico State and they remember him as one of the greats in their university's history. The

Cooper family plans on retiring in Albuquerque when he leaves pro sports.

We lost by one. A.C. Green scored 24 points and pulled down 13 rebounds before noticing his left thumb hurt like hell.

He asked Gary Vitti to take a look. Gary called in the Suns' team doctor. He said, "Doc, I have a hard time believing this. Would you check it out?" Later Gary got on the phone to Dr. Kerlan, our team doctor in Los Angeles. When he heard the diagnosis, Kerlan said, "Are you sure?"

A.C. had torn the radial collateral ligament. That's a rare injury. I had the same thing when I played for the Lakers. They had to put steel pins in to stabilize it. I wore a splint for six weeks.

Thumbs are usually injured by being pulled backward and hyper-extended. Like when a skier has his thumb in a pole strap and the pole sticks in one place while momentum carries the skier forward. Somewhere in the heat of battle, A.C.'s thumb had gotten hyper-extended up and over the back of his knuckles. He hadn't even noticed when it happened.

At the tail end of these meaningless exhibition contests, just before we were to march off into an 82-game war, the young player on whom we had built big hopes was headed for the hospital—with the kind of damage that stumps the experts. "This can't happen to us now," I thought.

They had A.C. in surgery a couple of days later. They fixed him up with a monster splint. It looked like he was trying to shoplift a Ping-Pong paddle. That splint stayed on for months. By midseason The Little Kahuna was able to give him something smaller. But the second splint had to stay on until the end of the season.

There was another personnel problem. Byron Scott was having a horrendous exhibition season—0 for 6 in Chapel Hill, 1 for 7 in Albuquerque, and struggling in the other games. He's an off-guard, a shooter, and shooters are going to be erratic. That's the nature of the beast. The outside jumper is a low-percentage shot. The off-guard has to beat those percentages. He has to have unflinching nerve. The off-guard's motto is, "Shoot it up and sleep in the streets."

I told Byron, "This is your fourth season. We're not developing you anymore. You have all the talent in the world. We've seen flashes of it. But it's always been up and down. You'll have a great series of games and then a bad one. That has to change."

Byron is a player who is really just beginning to grow into his profession. He has a great body. He has a lot of talent. His weaknesses have been more emotional and attitudinal than anything else. He arrived as a rookie in a pressure situation. Management dumped Norm Nixon, a veteran, to bring in Byron. The general public didn't know that trouble had been festering on the team because Nixon couldn't come to terms with being less of a star than Earvin. It was an ugly situation, and Earvin did all he could to defer, but it was creating factionalism. Nixon was popular because he's a tough, don't-back-down player. Byron would have had to have been godlike to please the people who didn't understand why we traded Nixon.

Only a few players come in as rookies and have the confidence and skill to be major forces on the court. Byron is one of the many who need time. The media and the fans didn't want to grant it.

Byron's challenge has been to learn a way to deal with the pressure. In the past, if he didn't get good offensive numbers, he assumed everyone was down on him. He would lose concentration on defense. From three consecutive misses on 18-to-20-foot jump shots, his whole game would begin to drift. When I would bring in a reserve for him, it would be almost like a penance. I don't want him thinking like that. I have confidence in him. I know he's going to get nothing but better.

This had to be a year where he played great and then continued to play great. He needed to break through barriers of concentration and confidence. Every time he missed, he had to think, "That's okay. I'm gonna nail 'em. I'm gonna get 'em somewhere along the way." This year, Byron had to understand that more than ever. It was time.

Two days after the Albuquerque exhibition there was a charity intrasquad game at Loyola—the Save the Books Fund. People were trying to rebuild the main L.A. Public Library after an arson fire. It was a good cause, but not a good game. The team was flat. The veterans had their minds on Houston. The rookies had their minds on surviving the upcoming cuts. Byron and Wes provided the only bright spot: 25 points each.

Chris was carrying James in her arms after the game. He was 20 months old. This was his first time to actually be among the men he had seen on television and from a seat in the stands. He caught sight of Earvin. As if he was talking to someone who was part of his everyday life, James called out, "Hi, Magic."

Ron Kellogg was let go on the 27th of October. In practice that same day, Kurt Rambis came running over to Gary Vitti on the sidelines. Ligaments were torn in his left ring finger. Another power forward was going to go around wearing a splint. It was a fashion trend I didn't like.

Andre Turner was cut the next day. He felt terrible. His hopes had gotten up extremely high. But a coach can't let the media pick the team. Turner, at his size, needs a consistent outside shot. Because he couldn't hit the outside jumper, teams in exhibition started to back off him on the outside and pack their defense in the middle. He was a very likable player, cooperative, able to give the team a spark. It was hard to cut him, but Wes Matthews gave us a more complete package of skills.

Blaney returned on the same day. So did a controversy we had hoped was extinct. "Lakers should trade Worthy for big man" was the printed opinion of one of our local media experts. "It's the only option left."

The doctors were still not sure what was wrong with Gudmundsson. He hadn't gone into surgery yet.

I call the end of October "Coach's Delight." All the clubs have to trim their rosters to twelve. There's always hope that someone will release a player who can help your team. This year the waiver wire was heavy on guards, thin on big men. We made a list of eighteen players to think over. I guarantee you, you wouldn't recognize any more than two names on that list.

On the evening of the 29th, I was inducted into the L.A. Athletic Club Hall of Fame. A nice honor that included a year's free membership in the Riviera Country Club, which is close to our home. Chris and I were ecstatic. We both enjoy tennis, and pictured ourselves having some wonderful afternoons there. As the year unfolded, we never had time to take advantage of the membership. But the idea was exciting.

After the banquet we took Chris's parents, Frank and Dorothy, upstairs for a drink at Rex Il Ristorante, which is a wonderful place in the old downtown of Los Angeles. It was a swanky clothing store in the twenties. All the walls are beautiful wood paneling, all the light fixtures are Lalique crystal.

We drove home thinking about the tennis we wanted to play and about a new season that might become one of the most exciting we had ever known.

When we walked through our front door, we found Cia, our housekeeper, sitting on the staircase crying hysterically. She kept saying, "James almost died." I ran up the stairs and found him safe asleep. Cia explained that he hit his head when she was giving him his evening bath. He cried so hard that he stopped breathing and turned blue. He went into convulsions and his eyes rolled back. She splashed water on him and he came around. Then she tried to reach us at the banquet, but somehow she couldn't get through.

We called our pediatrician, Jay Gordon, who lives close by. He came over and reassured us that James was all right now.

Chris is home almost every night. It made the emergency much more frightening that it happened on one of our rare nights out. We stayed up with him through the whole night, waking him every so often to be sure he was breathing right. He was fine and there was never a recurrence. But we watched him extra closely for a long time.

The next day, the 30th of October, was the final day for making changes in the roster. Billy Thompson came late to our morning shootaround. Houston's Twin Towers were coming in sight.

The Good, the Bad, and the Ugly

When I leave for a game, I gather Chris and James in the hallway by our front door. Chris lifts James up in her arms. I stick my face in between theirs and nuzzle in for a triple kiss. Sometimes James can't handle the action and he has to rub the spot I kissed on his cheek with the back of his hand. He forgives it, though. If he's awake when I come back, he asks me, "Lakers win, Daddy?"

On Halloween morning I collected my triple kiss, threw a bag in the car, and headed down the San Diego Freeway. If we lived through trick-or-treat night, we still had to face the monsters in Houston's lineup. Our mission for Saturday, November 1st, was to prove that quicker players can beat bigger players. If we won, people would say, "They're supposed to." If we lost, they'd say, "The Lakers are on a slide." You could write the stories before the game even started.

We practiced at ten and caught a 1:35 flight. Gudmundsson came along in case we needed him. And we did. But he was still having back spasms. A.C. had the cast removed from his thumb, and the splint was taped on. He wanted to play, but the thumb was still tender from surgery. A.C. hadn't missed a game since grade school in Northeast Portland. Sampson was out for the Rockets with an ankle sprain, but the Rockets had big backups in 6'10" Jim Petersen and 7' Dave Feitl.

Sports Illustrated signaled the start of the new season with a feature that revealed there were thirty-two 7-footers in the league. It kicked off with a group shot of Boston's giants: Bill Walton (6'11"), Robert Parish (7'), and Kevin McHale (6'11"). The point of the article was that 7-footers had finally taken over the game. It argued for adjustments: Raise the basket. Make the court bigger. Widen the lane. Field four-man teams. Give the game back to pure athletes.

That was our plan, too. We just hoped to do it without changing any rules of the game.

The next feature in the magazine was a six-page color spread of Twin Tower combinations around the league: Houston's Sampson and Olajuwon (7'4" and 7'). Cleveland's John Williams and Brad Daugherty (6'10" and 7'). New York's Ewing and Cartwright (7' and 7'1"). Detroit's Bill Laimbeer and John Salley (6'11" and 7'). Phoenix's William Bedford and James Edwards (7' and 7'1"). Washington's Moses Malone and Manute Bol (6'10" and 7'6"). Golden State's Joe Barry Carroll and Chris Washburn (7' and 6'11").

Against Houston we controlled the opening tip and went straight into the low post attack: An alley-oop attempt on a pass to Kareem. Missed. A skyhook attempt by Kareem. Missed.

By the time the game was over, Kareem and Worthy together accounted for almost half of all the team's shot attempts. I was grateful for every point they got. But where was the balanced scoring attack we had talked about and drilled? For two long stretches—five and a half minutes early in the first quarter and three minutes late—we couldn't get a field goal down.

I tried a smaller, quicker lineup: Wes Matthews, Coop, James, Frank Brickowski, Earvin. That meant we had to execute the defensive shifts perfectly. Allen Leavell immediately beat Wes at the top of the key with a quick first step. Nobody came to help. I sensed we were in deep trouble. Still, we got out of the first quarter with a one-point lead.

We traded jump shots to open the second period. Akeem blocked Brickowski, then he blocked Matthews. A couple of Kareem's sky-hooks and a 3-pointer from Byron helped us reach a one-point lead by the middle of the period.

Then they ran 15 points to our 4 in a five-minute stretch. Another Kareem skyhook and another Scott 3-pointer meant we were only down six at the half, 60–54. It could have been worse. Earvin was 2 for 7 from the floor. Wes, Frank, and Cooper were each 0 for 1. The Rockets had their hands on most of our passes. Akeem pulled the ball right out of Byron's hands. They were literally prying the game away from us.

Earvin got two layups in the early third period to help us reach a tie at 64. For a couple of minutes we held on to a two-point lead. Reid came in for Leavell and stroked in a long jumper while Rodney McCray stole two straight Laker possessions. Jim Petersen, who only attempted one shot in the first half, suddenly checked in with a J and two hooks. Meantime we managed two more consecutive turnovers. A 12 to 4 run for the Rockets. A seven-point deficit to start the final period.

Akeem Olajuwon blocked three shots in the fourth quarter. First he blocked Worthy. McCray went the other way for a layup. When Michael Cooper hit a long jumper a minute into the period, it was the very first points our bench produced in the entire game. We pulled back within three points.

Akeem's second block, on Kareem, followed a 3-pointer by Robert Reid. McCray hit a reverse layup and a baseline jumper to tie his career best scoring effort at 28. The Rocket lead held at six. The third Akeem block was followed by another Laker traveling turnover. Petersen hit from the baseline and at the line. Our hustle attempts in the last minutes couldn't overcome Houston's determination. Five free throws were the only scoring we could get in the last two and a half minutes.

We actually outrebounded the Rockets in that November 1st season opener—on national TV. However, they out-everything-elsed us. Our moment of truth. We bombed: 20 turnovers to their 11, one blocked shot to their six, 102 points to their 112.

We got on the plane to L.A. as losers. It felt just like when Sampson hit the final shot last year: the bottom of the conference, the bottom of the division. It was our fifth straight loss, over two seasons, to the prototype Twin Towers team. The young and hungry Rockets versus the outdated Lakers.

We had just proved everyone right. Everyone who foresaw the demise of the Lakers. Everyone who said the future of the game lies in domination by big men.

We played tentative. Cooper was tentative. He was cold, too: 2 for 6 from the field, 0 for 2 from three-point range. Byron had better shooting numbers, 7 for 11 and 2 for 2, but he was just as tentative. We had played the same damn way that we had played in the playoffs.

We had a poor effort. Period. That was what dismayed me more than anything else. It was the same kind of effort level that froze us at key moments when Houston took games away from us in the playoffs. It was a carbon copy of those games.

Flying home, Bertka and I talked about that disappointment. How were we going to be able to kick these guys out of their stupor? They were shocked too. They had waited five months to get back.

We gave the players Sunday off. Guys were banged up. And I didn't want to just come back to work the next day. I wanted to give them time to think about it, to let it seep in. We could practice on Monday and then catch a flight right afterwards to our next game. The opponent was Seattle.

I began to think on Sunday about what should be said to the team. Between exhibition and the opener, we had two subpar games against Twin Towers teams. It wasn't so much what the big guys had done against us, although Olajuwon had been fierce, with 6 blocked shots, 17 rebounds, and 26 points. It was more how the team carried itself in those games.

The Lakers had become a team waiting for something to happen to them—waiting for me to devise a strategy, waiting for management to stock them with another big man.

It was, in a way, the same attitude that put them out of contention five months before. They weren't living in the present moment. They were making plans to be somewhere else. Five months ago they were making plans to face the Boston Celtics. It was just a matter of time. Houston would be over pretty soon and we could get to the main feature.

The Rockets were totally in the present moment. They smelled an opportunity and they ran off with it.

Now the Lakers were caught up in projecting themselves into the moment when a big man would come to their rescue.

The NBA schedule grinds on every minute. You handle one challenge, or you get pulled under by it. You go to sleep, get renewed, come back in to steel yourself for the next challenge. Life happens the same way. You never know entirely what it's going to throw at you. You just know that your life is being lived at every moment. You just know you've got to be as ready as possible.

Dyer says that the highest form of sanity is to live totally in the present moment. Be consumed by it, not by what happened yesterday or what you hope will happen tomorrow.

While the Lakers were making plans to be somewhere else, to have somebody give them their key to winning—in the form of another 7-footer—the team's life was going on. They weren't in sync with it, though. They didn't have the right attitude to take care of business. Their inner feelings were, "Why didn't management go out and get a big guy to help us?"

What an irony. All these years people had called us the greatest pool of talent in the NBA. Now, for the first time, the Lakers were feeling sorry for themselves. For the first time they were complaining about manpower. They didn't have the perfect big men to complement the team.

No wonder we had been submarined in previous years by complacency! We were the talent kings of the league! Everything was supposed to be easy. We were living out the worst opinions of our critics.

Right after the Memorial Day Massacre, before we went on to rally our best possible effort and take four of the next five games, *Time* magazine put that view of the Lakers in a nutshell. After praising Boston's legendary toughness, their take-care-of-business attitude, their work ethic, *Time* said of us: "When the surrounding is friendly, and most things go well, the Lakers can be a wonderful team." In other words, count on these wimps to fold once things get tough. That year we made *Time* eat its words. But circumstances had changed.

On the Tuesday following our opening loss to Houston, Peter Vecsey of the *New York Post* updated the same sentiment. "L.A. is no longer larger than life. It has lost its feeling of superiority. Opponents are no longer intimidated."

All of a sudden the surroundings weren't "friendly." Things were not going well. We didn't look like "a wonderful team." Our talent search hadn't come up with an easy answer to the team's personnel needs. Management wasn't going to accept a quick fix by bringing in an average, slow-stepping 7-footer.

When I was in high school, our basketball coach, Walt Przybylo, had a ritual for those times when his words had to sink in deep. He'd say, "All right, men, backs against the bleachers!" And we'd line up against the folded wooden bleachers along the gym wall. Przybylo would go off on his topic of the day. I didn't always listen. But I always knew to look as if I were listening.

It was backs-against-the-bleachers time for the Lakers, backs against the wall.

If your memory is working, some elements of clear thinking will emerge when your back is against the wall. The old voices emerge: your coaches, teachers, parents.

Normally before a practice I'll call the team into a circle and talk for about two minutes. This time I had them put their hands together in the middle. Then I said, "Sit down on the floor. This is going to take a little longer. I want you to be comfortable."

Everybody got into their posture: some holding their knees drawn up, some leaning back with their arms out straight behind them. I looked around the circle and said, "Don't expect a cavalry charge to come thundering over the hill. I'm telling you right now, don't expect that. If you're waiting for your talents to be supplemented with another seven-footer, if you assume that's going to happen in the next month, you've got fifteen basketball games to play in that time. We've got to win. All you guys reading the newspaper reports and believing that you'll soon see some impact player arrive . . . I'm telling you right now that it's not going to happen.

"We are not going to get anybody today. We are not going to get anybody this week. We are not going to get anybody like that in the next month.

"That's why we didn't trade James Worthy this summer. That's why we aren't letting the peripheral opponents select our lineup. That's why we're not giving up core players for people out there that we feel could not come in here and contribute or accomplish what you can. We still have the core together. Our goal is to get a big man and also keep you here. That's the only way you're going to win a championship. If we subtract two of you just to bring in some big guy, we'd just become average again.

"I don't want you to expect somebody to come over the top of the mountain waving a flag and bringing you Twin Towers so you can compete against the Bostons and compete against the Houstons and all these teams that have these new tall lineups. Start thinking about what you do have.

"Change will come quickly for this group if we don't change the attitude. You've gotta play your own games. You've gotta play to win."

We went through the history of the team over the years since the '79–'80 championship. We talked about what we had been through —the players who had come and gone without making a difference, the players who had kept the level up. I said, "There's nobody else around the league who has what you have. Nobody else plays the game the way you can play it. Nobody else has Kareem and Magic and Worthy and Scott and Rambis and Cooper. Your collective experience over the last seven years—no other team has that. That experience is more valuable on this team than any average seven-footer.

"Talent, experience, teamwork, character, winners. You're all right here. Now, gentlemen, it ain't gonna get any better. You guys are going to have to say to yourselves, 'Hey, we're good!' Forget this Twin Towers bullshit. Start getting nasty. Start getting angry. Play the game the way you know how to play it. The way the Lakers play basketball. With tenacity. With single-minded purpose. Believing that you're going to blow people out of the gym with your quickness.

"We're playing from a waiting posture, like somebody is about to arrive and help us. If you hold on to that attitude over the next eight or ten days, then we're going to find ourselves six or seven games out of first place. All you're doing is validating what everyone has said about you. Those writers are saying that you guys don't have the guts or the character right now. You're a bunch of wimps. The Lakers can't deal with a little bit of adversity.

"This is our test. This is the breakthrough we need right now. Management is working diligently to supply us with the right thing. We know we need to get bigger. By the end of the year we will show you that we can make that kind of addition to this team. In the meantime, continue. Except for one Knicks game, you aren't going to see any Twin Towers for about a month. We play Seattle. We play Sacramento. We play Denver. There aren't any excuses now."

We went in and had a great practice, then caught a flight to Seattle that afternoon. Bill Bertka and I went out to dinner at the Metro Grill. We have a ritual when we're on the road, called "fine china, white tablecloths, and candlelight." We get out of the hotel and into a nice, relaxed atmosphere, away from the hassles and distractions of the road. That's where we get into some of our greatest discussions.

Coaches know when they've hit the right chord in talking to a team. Other times they know they missed. Bill and I were buoyed by how the message had sunk in. It was simply this: Stop feeling sorry for yourself. Stop waiting for somebody to come and help you. Just help yourself. We've got a great team. Let's get it done. Let's get started. That's the attitude we took to Seattle.

Later on, Jerry West told us, "I think that Houston loss made your season. Now you were no good. You weren't supposed to beat anybody. All the pressure was off." In a way, we were like the Lakers team when Earvin Johnson arrived in '79. We had had a record of 47 and 35 the year before. Nobody expected any great revolution. It was what I like to call "the innocent climb." Our second game of the season was the first step in the innocent climb of '86–'87.

Seattle had a new spirit. Bernie Bickerstaff, their second-year coach, is an incredibly competitive person. I've known him since the late sixties. He's got a young team and he has tapped into their aggressive instincts. Xavier McDaniel, the X-Man, made the All-Rookie team the year before. Tom Chambers, who later became Most Valuable Player in the All-Star game, is a hard-nosed player. Nate McMillan, a rookie, is another aggressor. Dale Ellis, whom they got from Dallas, spent the whole season hungry to prove he had more talent than the Mavericks had ever realized.

It was an ugly game. They attacked. It was a war. Seattle's talent was astounding, but they weren't meshing yet. They shot less than 40% for the game. Kareem got into foul trouble, but Byron and Coop were hot in the second half. Kurt pulled down 17 boards, which equaled his career best. We ended up winning, 100–96.

Overall, it was a pitiful display of basketball skills and judgment. But it was wonderful. We won the game on effort. Effort makes up for a lot of deficiencies.

Robert Keidel is a Wharton professor and business consultant. He wrote a book about a year ago called *Game Plans*, where he compared sports strategies to business strategies. He said basketball was the most relevant model of all sports for future business effectiveness because it works on flow, process, and chemistry. He also said that basketball is ruled by the constant tension between style and efficiency. There's the pretty way, in which you finesse around the obstacles, anticipate the opponent's moves, and elude them—

basketball artistry. Then there's the brute way. You power through the other team, bang your way into position, get the job done via the direct route.

There was no style, no artistry, in the Seattle game. The opposition just wouldn't let it happen. You couldn't drive the lane without three forearm smashes. The only way to respond was to come back just as hard.

Play like that will take a stylish team right out of its game. Unless that team also has character. Our guys were ready for war. They just kept smashing back. The patterns went to hell. It became a very spontaneous game. Winning by effort gave us a very good feeling about ourselves.

I hate to call the second game of the season a "must win" game, but this one was. It catapulted us into a nine-game winning streak.

On November fourth, one day after Seattle, we got the word on Petur Gudmundsson: out for the season. Just before a game with Denver we signed a free agent off the waiver wire. Mike Smrek had been a backup center for Chicago—a Canadian guy whose first love was hockey. When he showed signs of eventually maturing to seven feet, Canisius College recruited Mike and converted him into a basketball player. As a pro he had some catching up to do, matching six years of basketball experience against guys who had played the game since grade school. Despite that, we liked his quickness and his I-want-to-learn attitude. He had a broken foot in summer league play, but the doctors said he checked out okay. Everyone we asked about his character said the same thing.

Against Denver on the 7th, Billy Thompson was one of seven Lakers who hit double figures. Six Lakers had 10 blocked shots between them. Frank Brickowski had to wear a strange cuff-and-strap arrangement between his left bicep and his left wrist to prevent aggravation of his hyperextension injury. He got 9 rebounds and 13 points anyway.

Denver's center was out. They had a 7-foot reserve, Blair Rasmussen, but Doug Moe decided to match 6'7" Bill Hanzlik against Kareem.

It sounds like a strange tactic, but Moe had already worked it effectively against Patrick Ewing, Ralph Sampson, and Mark Eaton. Sometimes, when you press an advantage, you disrupt your game plan enough to make dumb mistakes. Then you get mad at yourself. You make more mistakes. You get madder and dumber. It's like seeing a pile of thousand-dollar bills in the next room. You rush in to grab them. You're busy figuring which pockets will hold the biggest wads. Then a bucket of water that was propped up on the door drops down, soaks you, knocks you on the head. Lights out.

Instead of working the mismatch, we went straight at the Nuggets with speed. "We like it at up-tempo," Earvin said, "because we're the best at it." The game was ours, 138 to 116.

The Denver game was Kareem's 700th straight double-figure scoring performance. To put that into perspective, Frank Brady at the *Herald-Examiner* got out his record book and his calculator: Kareem had scored more career points than the entire twelve-man roster of six current NBA teams. He had scored about 9,000 more than all of the Chicago Bulls and all of the Cleveland Cavaliers put together.

Jawaan Oldham, the Chicago center we could never acquire, had ultimately gone in a trade to New York. Now they had three 7-footers. The night before we met the Knicks, I watched Seattle beat them in a very tough, aggressive game.

Byron and James fired in six points between them before New York even scored. We led by 12 in the first quarter. Our new defense began to gel. We pressured them into 22 turnovers. I remember A.C., with his cast, and James, pressuring people down low. We were fronting, tapping out steals, then getting out in front and running. We were getting good weakside help on the defensive rotations—constantly communicating, constantly shifting to cover the gaps. We denied every passing lead.

Everyone had at least one rebound. Kareem and Billy got six apiece. We were up 29 after three periods. All our starting players rested on the bench through the fourth quarter. We won by a score of 111 to 88. We now had the Pacific Division lead. Even more important, we maintained our quickness-based style against a physical, grind-it-out team.

"When the Lakers aren't running, the Lakers aren't playing," James said. "We have to approach every game thinking we're going to run."

It takes more than fast wheels to be a running team. It takes tough defense. You rattle the other team into taking the wrong shots, you grab the rebound, and take off. Or you flick out a hand and deflect their pass, then you start your own fast break. Byron Scott came into his own as a defensive force in this game. Every time there was an opportunity to fill the gap in the lane, to help someone who had shifted position, he did it. He always had a hand out to deflect passes. "I've taken more pride in my defense this year," Byron told the reporters who bunched around him in the locker room after the game.

Defenders play a head game with Byron Scott. They get out and crowd him, try to take away his outside jumper. If he misses two or three shots, they back off. They say, "You can't shoot anymore. Hell, we'll give you the shot." In this game he began to put the ball on the floor. He drove the basket, made them pay for backing off.

Seattle came to the Forum on November 12th. They had blown a 27-point lead against the Philadelphia 76ers the night before, so they were mad. We went to Kareem. He set up some left-handed skyhooks with spin moves in the lane: a 21-point performance in the first half.

Lucas got his first minutes as a Sonic against the Lakers and went 1 for 5. He missed a dunk. Later, the rebound off a one-shot foul came right to him. He spaced out and threw the ball to the referee as if there were going to be a second free throw. He hit the referee in the back of his head. The official scooped up the basketball with one hand, rubbed his head with the other, and said, "Laker ball."

Maurice Lucas didn't play in the previous game, up in Seattle. He had smashed an opponent in the teeth with his elbow and received a tear wound that became infected. Definitely an animal-type injury. Our guys gave him a lot of needling for not playing that night. They were merciless after the out-of-bounds mistake. Then he went up for a jump shot right in front of our bench and Cooper came soaring up behind him, totally unseen by Luke, to block the ball into the court-side seats.

The starters got their fourth quarter vacation again. Final score: Lakers 122, Sonics 97. Dallas whipped Houston 114–85 on the same night and we became the first-place team in the Western Conference.

Dallas was looming. They were undefeated at home, and we were reading about the Atlanta Hawks every day. They called Atlanta "the junior Lakers" because they were like a younger, bigger version of our team. They ran like us, pressed like us—thrived on quickness. It sounded like a great matchup and a great challenge on the way.

First we had to face the Sacramento Kings. They stayed close while we played segmented basketball. We got up by 12, then started walking around, and let them right back into the game.

We were down 4 points to them with four minutes to go. Earvin did what we needed him to do: 8 points, the team's entire offense, in the last minute and a half.

He paid the price for the exertion. Both knees had to be iced, along with a shoulder, an Achilles tendon, and an eye. "I'm going to watch highlights of the Rams and Raiders," he said. "I hope I see someone who gets hit as hard as I was."

We canceled the next practice. Nobody's legs had any rebounding drills or any wind sprints in them. It doesn't take a genius to see when a team is beat up physically and mentally. Bertka announced the day off as we rode in the team bus to the airport. All the guys stood up and cheered.

We had a long shootaround on Tuesday, November 18th, taking a full hour of specialized preparation for Dallas.

The Mavericks gave us a totally different set of problems than we had seen yet this season. They execute a great half-court offense. Rolando Blackman and Derek Harper are one of the best backcourts in the league. Mark Aguirre has an unbelievably powerful body to muscle shots from inside and a sharp eye for drilling the perimeter shot.

There were some external situations too. There were ugly verbal exchanges during our playoff series the year before. Dick Motta, their coach, kept going after individual Lakers in the press, even though the Mavericks were behind. He kept saying, "Nothing they are doing is bothering us. We have outplayed them. We have outhustled them. This series should be four to one in our favor." I told reporters, "Motta reminds me of Muammar el-Quddafi. He still thinks he won."

Some writers predicted Dallas was destined to lead the Western Conference. They were considered even more dangerous than Houston—an elite team. They were blowing opponents out by 15 points and more in the first quarter.

We faced the Mavericks in good spirits. The team was together. The bench was into the game. It was like the playoffs—full of passion and fire. Every time I walked from one end of the bench to the other, I stumbled over Wes Matthews. He was on all fours, projecting himself as close to the action as he could.

We missed our first three shots, but we also pulled down rebounds and got second and third attempts. Kurt Rambis stayed close and physical with Aguirre. They ran hard and threw a trapping defense at us, harassing Earvin whenever he brought the ball upcourt. They were up 8 points on us by the middle of the first period.

Kareem got out on a fast break and missed the shot, but Scott and Worthy were there simultaneously for the tap-in. Byron got fouled on a dunk and made the extra point. I tried a Twin Towers ploy to counteract the banging. Kareem and Brickowski doubled on Sam Perkins, their young 6'9" forward, and shook the ball loose. Brickowski came up with it under the Mavericks' hoop. When they double-teamed him, he got it out to Kareem on the wing. Kareem dribbled it the length of the court and finished with a reverse layup. We were within three at the end of the first period.

Coop started us in the second quarter with a 3-pointer. Billy Thompson came in. This was the same building where he had won the NCAA championship a few months before with the Louisville team. He completed a lineup that I wanted to experiment with against Dallas's arsenal of 7-footers: Brickowski and Mike Smrek, whom some clever sportswriter called The Ivory Towers, with Billy at small forward and Earvin and Coop in the backcourt.

Aguirre lit up in the second period: 14 points. But Earvin ran off a string of layups for 10 points. Al Wood, who was trying to guard him, kept grabbing Earvin's left wrist. Eventually they both started laughing. Motta and the official were breaking up, too. It looked as if Wood wanted to take his pulse.

We entered the second half up by 2. Dallas came right back. Blackman began hitting from midrange on the left side. Donaldson, their center, stole the ball from Kareem. Harper took one from Earvin and drove down to get fouled and sink one of two to tie the score at 66. Aguirre hit from the top of the key to establish a lead. They held it at plus three until the end of the period.

Dallas was still ahead, 94–87, by the middle of the fourth. The Maverick fans got real vociferous: "BEAT L.A.! BEAT L.A.! BEAT L.A.!" Worthy got a streak, then Earvin returned and hit a succession of free throws. They were fouling him every time he drove the lane.

Dallas's attempt to run with us came apart at the seams in the final period. They couldn't maintain control and speed both. We won it in the stretch by staying out of foul trouble. Dallas got zero points at the line in the fourth quarter. We got 19. They weren't unbeaten at home anymore. The game went to us, 114–110. "Dallas has come a long way," Cooper told some of the reporters. "But we're a veteran team. We know how to win."

Earvin always comes out of the showers last. He likes to soak his aches before he ices them down. He also likes to give the reporters a chance to disperse. As usual, they waited him out. "They say we're not tall enough," he answered them. "They say we're not strong enough. Well, we'll keep on winning and see where we get from there."

In the next day's headlines we were being seen in a new light: "No Demise in Sight for 6–1 Lakers."

Reunion Arena in Dallas is one of three or four arenas in the league where you get a very special lift when you win. It's always great to win on the road, but wins at Reunion and Boston Garden and Madison Square Garden give you something extra. Dallas is really a classy franchise. They get sellout crowds—highly frenetic, emotional crowds. The team's exciting.

When you go in there and everybody's expecting you to lose, there's an incredible edge to your thinking. My pregame speech was this: "Everybody in Dallas . . . newspapers, radio, television, fans, management, players . . . they all expect you to lose tonight. They've won five in a row here. Undefeated at home, and they expect you'll be their next victim. They expect to rule you throughout this year. They expect to dominate this conference for the next several seasons. It's time to find out who we are and where we're going. So let's go out there."

That was all I had to say. To clip their wings on the first game was a very good feeling. We took care of business in Big Game number one against that team.

We work from the perspective that every single game is important. But we also divide the season up by pointing for certain games—the big ones. There are ten or fifteen in every 82-game schedule. Houston was one, Dallas was the second. Atlanta was the next. We try to build emotional peaks for those games. Sometimes you can win even when you play lousy. Sometimes you'll need all the team's talent and luck and skill on tap throughout the game to battle your way through. Those are the big ones.

The next game, one night later, was against the San Antonio Spurs. We had played tremendous games against them in the playoffs. This year they were showing a new look. Bob Weiss was a new coach, a defensive specialist hired away from Dallas. Mychal Thompson had come in from Portland to augment Artis Gilmore at center. Johnny Moore, a standout guard who missed most of the last year with meningitis, was back. Alvin Robertson, the other guard, was coming off a season where he was named the league's most valuable defense player and most improved player. He had set a new league record for steals with 301.

We had now won six in a row. Bertka and I wondered if the

Lakers might have left their fire in Dallas. You're on the road, you come from behind to beat a contender. Sometimes you look to take a breather. That's when you get knocked off unexpectedly. So you go out and acquire veterans such as Wes Matthews for your bench —insurance policies. Players who have been around a long time. You hope that investment will pay when the team finds itself needing a strong, steady force in relief. You pay a little more for that player than for a promising rookie. You gamble that your veteran won't get unhappy on the end of the bench and become a grumbling, negative presence on the team. We had rebuilt most of our bench to get a positive atmosphere, a sureness of good clutch support when we needed it. San Antonio was going to be a test.

We flew in and decided against practice. We put up at the hotel by eleven-thirty and gave ourselves a good rest. Earvin and Kurt were a little banged up. A.C. still had that cast on his hand. We had been giving him lots of minutes in the games that weren't close. We wanted to keep him in game condition. But it was frustrating for him and for us to see great passes underneath, sure scoring opportunities, go sliding off his bandaged hand.

Robertson had gone crazy the first games of the season. We had to contain him. He led off the game with a short jumper, then an assist to Mike Mitchell after picking Earvin's pocket for his first steal. We came back with two of Kareem's hook shots, a couple of baskets from Earvin, and a jumper and a 3-pointer from Byron Scott. They were hurting us on the weak side. They were sliding into the lane and harassing our entry passes into the post. Wes Matthews came in when we were down by 3 and hit two shots in two attempts. By the time he came back out we were up by 4. Robertson couldn't be stopped, though. He had 24 in the first half and they came out of it with a 3-point lead.

We converged in the second half. Wes hit 4 out of 5 to break up a tie at 82 apiece. We were 6 ahead when he left. It was a well-paced game, very close down the stretch. The Spurs came out aggressive, but we had our best running game of the year so far. We scored well out of our set offense, too, with 10 buckets and 4 free throws in our last 12 possessions. The final score was 117 to 108.

Bertka called it a "character win." Wes Matthews had paid his November rent in full. The reporters asked him if he was driven by wanting to get even with the team that had released him just six weeks before. He just told them, "I was happy as hell when I got picked up by the Lakers. I didn't have a lot of time to be sore at the Spurs."

Mychal Thompson gave the Spurs a lift in the second half: 8 points, 4 rebounds and 2 blocked shots. I picked up a San Antonio newspaper and learned that he had a local radio show to air his opinions on everything in the world of sports. This seemed like a positive step after his Portland broadcasting gig. That was a weekly soap opera update. "Just put a microphone in front of me and I'll do the rest," Mychal said.

We landed back at Los Angeles International at the same time the New Jersey Nets were disembarking. Everybody said hello to each other, but there was a deep look behind it—competitor's evil eye. The Nets had dropped four in a row. We had won seven and were coming off the road. Maybe we'd be tired or complacent. Maybe we could be a stepping stone.

Buck Williams is the kind of relentless, hardworking power forward that A.C. Green is on his way to becoming. We told Kurt, "Stay on Williams at all times. Force him to the outside. Block him out of every rebound." The Nets had backcourt problems. They started a rookie at the point. A rookie capable of flourishing under that kind of pressure might come into the NBA once every five years. This wasn't one of those years.

Periodically we showed an "easy money" attitude. There was an urge to run and dunk in the face of an obviously weaker opponent—cash in quick. We were chomping at the bit to unleash all the powers instead of just playing our game, failing to be in tune with the present moment. We got off to such a big lead early and everything seemed easy. We were clicking. We were driving and backdooring the defenders. It looked ridiculously easy and the guys began to get impatient and to want to have fun. When we stopped playing according to the game plan, we struggled. They played us even up in the second period and stayed close in the third.

A.C. started the game but only played two first-half minutes. When he came back late in the third quarter, we began building again. We exploded to a 20-point lead. The final was 111–95. We finished them off, but we were ugly and it got lousy. I jumped on the reserves, the Blue Team, for selfishness. The sudden nightmare of the Houston loss and all the doomsday predictions were being forgotten. They were ready to let go of the discipline, the connectedness of our play.

The key to success isn't in great talent. The key to success is to learn how to do something right. Then do it right every time. Do it the same way every time. We were frivolous about our method in this game and it pissed me off.

Milwaukee brought a taste of Eastern Conference power into the Forum on November 23rd, a Sunday night. A victory cake was already sitting in their locker room before the game started. If they could beat us, Don Nelson would have his 500th career win. Nellie played on five NBA championship teams and had been Coach of the Year twice.

The Bucks came out strong and efficient in the first half and embarrassed us. We didn't look good at all. I think Nellie could almost taste that cake within five minutes of the tip-off.

When you're playing a Don Nelson team, you've got to be able to react offensively. They had held six opponents under 100 points already, in thirteen games. No one had gotten more than 107 against them. Nelson runs so many different defenses and trapping situations. The Bucks never play you straight up. They always make you adapt and adjust. If you're not into it mentally, they can really make you look bad.

That's what happened to us in the early going. They took us apart—outrebounded us 20 to 11.

We started the second half down by 7 points. The Blues suddenly gave us some great shooting, right about the time we began to rebound the ball. We pulled to a 3-point lead. Then, at the top of the fourth quarter, Wes hit a 3-pointer, James dropped a midrange jumper from the right side, and Cooper bombed in another three. We got off an 11–0 run that broke their backs. The game ended 127–117.

Don't know what became of the cake, but Nelson got number 500 three days later at the expense of the Washington Bullets.

Junior vs.
Senior Lakers

The entire roster of the Atlanta
Hawks—whom the Atlanta papers had called the "Junior Lakers"
—was up in the stands watching us play Milwaukee. Including Mike
McGee, who was able to give Coach Mike Fratello a few extra in-
sights. As we had Wes against the Spurs, the Hawks had an ex-Laker
who was eager to make a statement on the court to his former employers. Even without Geeter's help, we had given Fratello plenty
of weaknesses to analyze.

The best record in the NBA, ours, 9 and 1, was about to meet
the next-best, theirs, 9 and 2. Two teams feeling their powers develop,
both undefeated at home. Definitely a big game. The whole league
was paying close attention.

Our practice was offense oriented. We put in some new options
for the point guard, our off-guard, and our small forward to isolate
on the side. We knew Atlanta was going to double-team a lot. We
wanted the offensive execution to find the shot. The strategy was to

isolate, penetrate, and kick the ball out for an open jumper as the double-team starts to clamp down. They are a team of pursuit. They're so young and aggressive that when you beat somebody on a drive, their whole defense pursues to the level of the ball. We wanted to catch them in mid-pursuit and find the short jump shot. We definitely did not want to find ourselves taking long-range jump shots on a regular basis.

From a purely athletic standpoint, the Atlanta Hawks are the most talented team in basketball. They were the most improved team in the league, sixteen wins better in '85–'86 than the year before. Kevin Willis, their 7-foot power forward, was leading the NBA with 13 rebounds per game.

They lack maturity and experience, but they are quick, youthful, and exuberant. They intimidate with their speed and their dunking. Mike Fratello is one of the best coaches in the league. The Hawks come prepared to take away your strengths.

We reviewed what we call two-up, our power game: two-up regular, two-down singles. They all have to do with cross-picking and posting up Worthy and Kareem. Numbers 52 and 53 are baseline screens for our guards and small forwards to get jumpers on the perimeter. Our defensive plan was to play them straight up, pressure the ball. We had to keep them out of the paint, the lane area between the free throw line and the basket. We had to trap whenever they entered that area. We had to pick up Doc Rivers, their point guard, early and not give him a chance to penetrate and pass. We had to block out their 7-footers, Tree Rollins, Kevin Willis, and Jon Koncak. We had to keep a body on Cliff Levingston and Dominique Wilkins at all times to keep them off the offensive boards. Dominique, the one they call The Human Highlight Film, had to be denied the ball in his favorite spot.

We were going hard in our practice. At the end of a drill, Kurt Rambis came running over to where Gary Vitti stood. He was holding his left hand in his right and yelling, "Put it in! Put it in! Put it in!" Gary looked at the top of Kurt's left hand. He could see that the ring finger was dislocated. He turned the hand over. There was a red wound with a white bone sticking out of it, through the skin. A compound dislocation.

Vitti pulled the bone back into place immediately. Then he dressed the wound, splinted the finger and sent Kurt off to an X-ray lab. It wasn't broken. But it took six stitches and kept him out of action for a week.

After Kareem missed a bank hook to start the game, Dominique opened the scoring with a quick 21-foot jumper off a high post screen. Our next possession was stolen. A Hawk shot missed and Dominique slammed home a follow-up. Byron Scott dropped a 20-footer and then blocked Dominique, who is four inches taller, on the other end. But Wilkins grabbed the ball off the floor and banked in a second effort. You can't stop Dominique, but you've got to slow him down. We weren't getting the job done. All the things we worked on in practice, all the things we knew we had to counter and contain, started happening.

Willis got all alone in the paint for a quick pass from the top of the key for an easy slam. No one was even up in the air with him. On a fast break Dominique whipped the ball into Willis's hands with a wraparound, behind-the-back pass. Rivers hit two outside shots in a row. We were down 18–8 and hadn't made a fast break. They had made 8 of 11 shots to our 4 of 11. They had 10 rebounds to our 2.

Against the Celtics you're concerned that they're going to make you play their style of game: slow paced and deliberate, patiently working for jumpers off screens. That's bad, because they'll always be superior in the context of their own game plan. Against the Hawks we were getting beaten by our own style. That's really bad. That's like Tina Turner coming in second in a Tina Turner look-alike contest. We couldn't rally and say, "Let's just play our game." "Our game" was already in progress. A younger, taller, faster, more hustling team was doing it better than we could.

Atlanta was feeling right. Their only losses were by a margin of two to Chicago on the road and a margin of four against Boston on the road. Three nights before our game they had beaten Boston in the Omni, their first home victory over the Celtics after twelve straight losses.

Spud Webb came in to relieve Doc Rivers. Spud is a tremendous inspiration to every short player in the world. A fourth-round pick, 5'7", he was released then got his break as a free agent. He was a major reason the Hawks embarrassed us 102–93 last February. He has the speed to compensate for his shortness, and he has a vertical lift that's unreal.

With Spud running their attack, the gap widened. After Coop stole the ball from McGee and hit Byron for an 18-foot jumper, we went seriously cold. The Hawks hit us with a 12–2 run that spanned the end of the first quarter and the start of the second.

It wasn't as if we weren't trying. We just weren't doing it right.

We started the second quarter with a greyhound unit: Earvin and Worthy at the forwards, Brickowski at center, Wes and Coop at guards. They showed great defensive pressure on the Hawks' first possession, but Dominique neutralized it by retreating and popping a 3-pointer. They stole our next possession and ran a fast break. Missed. We grabbed the rebound and ran a fast break the other way. Missed. They pulled it in and ran it back at us. Both teams took horrendous shots, but the desire level was incredibly intense. Levingston finally tapped in one of their misses and drew a foul shot.

By the half we were down 60 to 43. Billy Thompson, a reserve, led Laker scoring. Spud Webb finished the period by taking a defensive rebound coast to coast for a layup. Kareem had taken two shots and missed them both. Their shooting had cooled to 45%, but ours was only 36%. They had 31 rebounds to our 16. We were playing lousy against a team that had the skill, the finesse, and the power to keep you locked out once you got down.

I liked the way we came out in the second half. I just didn't know if it would ultimately be enough to make up for the damage already done. Kareem got himself loose underneath with a pivoting move and slammed in his first field goal. Worthy, who had only hit 2 of 9 attempts in the first half, popped a jumper from the top of the key. Byron threw in a 3-pointer, and A.C. had two 3-point plays from being fouled in the act of shooting. Kareem and Earvin worked a nifty give-and-go play, and we were back in reaching distance, 64–61.

From midpoint in the third period we traded baskets, with the lead hanging at one point and two points, Atlanta's favor. Kareem had 6 assists for the period because he was beating their double teams by hitting the open man. He found A.C. beneath the basket and the score evened at 77 apiece. More baskets were traded, until the third period finished with a Byron Scott dunk and a tie at 83.

I rested Kareem, Earvin, and James at the start of the fourth. It's fantastic to make up 17 points in one period, but it's also exhausting. I wanted them to have plenty left for the stretch. I knew Atlanta would.

The key to this game was how they dominated us physically and put us in a hole psychologically. We came back to a tie, but that big hole was still right behind our backs, ready for us to fall in. We took that step backwards in the final four minutes of the game.

A failed big effort play deflated our momentum in the middle of the last quarter. Worthy attempted one of our baseline offensive options. He made a clockwise spin and released a 10-footer. It didn't make it. The rebound crossed to the opposite side of the rim. Frank Brickowski and Tree Rollins went up together side by side, three times in a row, neither one able to gain control. Billy grabbed the ball. He forced up a shot that missed. Worthy found the rebound and forced up another shot, a five-foot jumper. Missed again. Cooper got the ball and jumped into a wall of Hawk defenders. He attempted a push shot from the downward part of his jump. The rebound came off the rim and several players lunged for it. Billy was called for a foul and we gave up possession. Tremendous effort, offset by unfortunate shot selection. Zero points and one foul off four shots.

With six minutes left, our defense broke down and McGee came alone through the back door for a feed from Dominique right under the basket. Then Levingston followed up a McGee miss and we were behind by five. As the game wound down, we panicked with desperation moves and they solidified their lead from the free throw line. Earvin and Cooper both missed 3-point attempts at the end, and we gave it up to them, 113–107.

"Now people can say the Hawks can play anybody in the league," Dominique told the L.A. *Times*. Especially anybody who gives them second shots and open lanes to the basket.

Our first unit was flat and our reserves were outscored 48–17. The first half was the worst I had seen from a Laker team in all my years with the organization, playing or coaching. We went back to our one-man offense. We got paralyzed with fear when we fell behind in the first half. We started dumping the ball inside to Kareem. Luckily he responded to the double and triple teams with some good, opportunistic passes. But not enough players were cutting to the basket to give him a passing target. We never got into our running game.

The next day we had to be ready for a game with the Clippers in their arena. I think the team expected me to read them the riot act. Instead, we just reviewed films of the Atlanta game and I talked about how soft we were on defense. There were no searing comments and no profound searchings for the hidden chord that would undo all our wrongs. All I said was, "Every time we lose a game, no matter what the reason, no matter who we lose to, catch yourselves quickly. Get back on the track with our best performance, our toughest performance. Don't let it slide."

I didn't want to lose a game and then say, "Aw, the hell with it. Let's get them tomorrow night," then lose two, and then maybe get someone in foul trouble and lose a third and suddenly put a lot of pressure on ourselves.

This was a very dangerous game against the Clippers. They were 3 and 11, second from the basement in the league. We had kicked their ass a lot over the years since they moved to L.A. The papers kept talking about how there was no true rivalry in town, how they didn't belong in the same gym. We were coming off a loss to meet a revenge-minded team, a team that needed wins to justify its existence. It was very important not to slip.

The Lakers took that to heart. In our practice I kept the Blue Team, the reserves, out on the floor for two and a half hours. I wasn't very happy with their work over the past couple of games. We drilled them and had them lift weights. Gary Vitti has a conditioning rule: Anyone who didn't play at least twenty minutes on a game night owes him twenty minutes of riding an exercise bike.

We had at least one unhappy bike rider. Wes Matthews was showing an attitude. After his 6-for-7 performance against San Antonio he had gone right back to the bench. He didn't play much in the Atlanta game. His family is from Atlanta and he wanted that moment in the limelight, broadcast by satellite back to the folks at home.

Bench players dream of having a hot game and catapulting into an expanded role. Like the show business cliché—"You're going out there a reserve, kid, but you're coming back a star." The truth is that a reserve has to accumulate a lot of minutes of glory before his role expands. There has to be an attitude of backing up that glory with intense showings in practice. There usually has to be a transition in the making upstairs, too, a starting player whose skills are in decline with age. A reserve has to be patient.

We handed out free Thanksgiving turkeys to everyone. There was still plenty to be thankful about. Our last three games for the month of November were victories, two over the Clippers and one over Chicago. Wes got a lot of minutes in the Clippers games and turned in double-figure scoring performances and started feeling better. A.C. was our high-point man in the Thanksgiving game. The Atlanta whipping was a one-night phenomenon, not a pattern.

"Menmotum" is a word I made up. It means the opposite of momentum. We would be starting December with a tough test: two games against Golden State, a team that always plays us tough, and a rematch against Dallas. Then there was a brutal Eastern trip—New York and Milwaukee back-to-back, one night off, Boston and Detroit back-to-back, then two days enforced rest in Cleveland and a game with the Cavaliers. An eight-day tour, as planned by the Marquis de Sade. We couldn't afford menmotum.

First Eastern
Gauntlet

Just one month after our humil-
iation in Houston, I woke up and had breakfast at home with James.
We spread out the morning newspaper. We were number one at 12
wins and 2 losses, the second-best opening month in Laker history.
Atlanta had slipped to 12 and 3. The Celtics were holding at 10 and
4. Dallas: 10 and 5. Houston: 7 and 7.

A lot of coaches say, "Well, it doesn't matter what happens at
the beginning of the year. It's what you do at the end that counts."
I think it's significant to train your players to get out of the blocks
early. Try to build a four- or five-game lead. Then, if you have some
January and February Dog Days or some injuries, you can absorb
it a little better. So, that Career Best emphasis helped us through
November, even after a shaky start. It was good to know we were
out from the pack, because December started with three tests and a
marathon. At least we would hit that stretch already feeling good
about ourselves.

The press was feeling good about us, too. They were looking for pegs to hang our success on. The *Daily News* ran a special feature on Bertka, about how we call him A.O.A.T.—for Administrator of All Things. Assistant coaches don't always get much recognition, but Bill takes a lot of pride in the job. He also is one of the best coaches for big men. Kareem might not admit it, but I think Bill has even helped develop his game with moves in the post.

Hoop, the NBA magazine, had a story on Jerry West and another one on Kareem. I was named the coach of the month for November.

The big explosion in news was with A.C. Green. There were A.C. articles in everything from the *San Bernardino Sun* to the *New York Times*.

Kurt's compound dislocation had put A.C. back into a starting role. Even with the impediment of a splint on his thumb and the lost playing time, A.C. had 16 steals, 12 blocks, and a greatly improved free throw percentage. It was gratifying to see. At the same time we were committed to keeping our core together, we knew that it was vital to give our younger players some room to grow. You could sense that A.C. was going to do nothing but get better. He added an aggressive, wild, abandoned element to our play. It was a force we needed.

Not all the ink was positive. *Inside Sports* published an interview with Norm Nixon. Three years after being traded away in the deal that brought us Byron Scott, Norm tore up a knee while playing in a softball game in Central Park. Sitting out a season because of a pointless injury seemed to stimulate his bitterness. He took swipes at Earvin, at Byron, at Jerry West, and at me. I just read it as further proof of how important a person's attitudes are in shaping his career.

Our first test for December was a setback. The Warriors clipped us, 116–106. Everybody likes to use the Lakers as a gauge for their own breakthroughs. Houston did it, then Atlanta, then Golden State. They led through most of the game and all of the second half. They came into the game with a 5-game streak going. They were ranked second in the Pacific Division. Beating the Lakers gave them their first 6-game streak in eight years.

It stung us. Golden State has always been an arch-rival. All of a sudden this team that hadn't done anything in years felt they could challenge the Lakers. One win and they've got history on their side. It pissed the team off because Golden State doesn't deserve the right to consider themselves challengers. Dallas deserves it. Houston deserves it.

I call this "woofing." It's like dogs who try to scare off their rivals. "I'm top dog on this block now. Watch out. I'm here to take your spot." The Warriors got carried away with this win and we didn't like it at all.

We left on the same evening. Dallas was waiting for us in Los Angeles on the next day, December 5th. We expected a tough game, and that's what they had in store.

We held a light practice beforehand. The locker room atmosphere was quiet, subdued. Earvin arrived early, about five-fifteen. Kareem sat at his locker and barely spoke to anybody.

Dallas came in as the top team in their division. They jumped out to a 10–2 lead. By late in the first half they were up 17 points on us.

We played tough down the stretch, made big plays. The big difference, compared to the night before, was the attitude on the floor of going hard after the ball. A.C. and Coop pumped life into us in the second half. Kareem and Coop were the offensive spark plugs during an 18–0 run. We took over the game and won 112–104.

This is what the Lakers are all about. After one of our shabbiest efforts we put together one of our most passionate performances. My only worry was getting into an on-again, off-again pattern. Because we're a running team, we can come back and make up huge deficits. A nonrunning team can rarely do that. But if you think that your offense is so explosive that you can nickel and dime them for a while, then come back strong, that philosophy is going to get you in trouble.

It was a very bitter loss for Motta, and it made the Mavericks twice as hungry to beat us in the future.

On Saturday, December 6th, my contract extension was announced. The same one that had been offered back on May 18th, three hours after the Houston series loss. If Buss took as long deciding what horses to bet at Del Mar as he did to decide on the details in my contract, they'd probably have to close the track.

We took that day off. I spent the spare time going overboard on the preparation. I wanted to make a statement to the Warriors.

Earvin came in with a sore Achilles tendon and didn't think he'd be able to play. That meant making some adjustments. We kept them extra long for a game day, two and a quarter hours, and some players got a little irritable.

Once again we started in a hole, down by five. Earvin played, but only half his usual minutes. Byron had some trouble hitting in the first half. In the second half he concentrated on defense and his offense just automatically opened up. At the start of the third period he was a driving force behind a 23 to 2 run. That blew the game wide open. He ultimately scored 20 in the period, 26 in the game. We were moving the ball sharply, and we were hitting the outside shots. Kareem even attempted a 3-pointer, but it rimmed out.

None of the starters played in the fourth period. Billy Thompson went a little berserk and bounced the ball to himself for a reverse, two-handed dunk. George Karl looked unhappy about that play. The next day he was on the phone to Jerry West, saying, "Hey, Pat really rubbed it in last night." But our starters only played slightly more than half of the game.

The only rubbing in was in the locker room afterward, where Cooper tried to massage my scalp with a chunk of victory cake. This was my 300th coaching win. After Coop paid his respects I told him, "I'd probably have four hundred wins by now, if I had any good players!"

In typical NBA run-on fashion, there was less than one day to savor the milestone. We boarded a ten o'clock American Airlines flight for New York the next morning. I was grateful to the Blue Team for making it possible to rest the starters so much against Golden State.

We got in the elevator at the Grand Hyatt, right by Grand Central Station and the Chrysler Building. The elevator doors opened and there was Bonecrusher Smith. He was in town to get ready to fight Mike Tyson. Cooper dropped into a fighter's stance and said to Bonecrusher, "Okay. It's you or me."

Smith looked at him and looked at us. We were laughing like crazy. He shot one more look at Coop and said, "A stiff wind would blow you over."

The Knicks had been facing some stiff winds. They were coming off an overtime loss to Portland on the road. They had just fired Hubie Brown and promoted his assistant, Bob Hill, to the head coaching job. This was Hill's first home game. He tried to rally the troops with a speech and a display of old Knick trophies. Whatever spirit he may have stirred, his team was booed by the New York home crowd even before the tip-off. The reporters, meanwhile, were asking Hill whom they were going to trade and when. A peripheral opponent jamboree.

Ewing hit 20 points and grabbed 15 boards, but the Knicks ended with their lowest point total of the season. We got more cheers from the crowd than they did. Maybe that was because Billy Thompson had salted Madison Square Garden with twenty-five of his friends and family members. They all drove eighty-five miles up from Camden, New Jersey, to see their guy's NBA debut for the area, and he showed them 7 points on 3-for-4 shooting.

This was a game where we honed some of our thinking about how to defend against a Twin Towers team. Every time the ball went into the low post we were down on it—always at different angles. We kept showing them different looks, different traps. Sometimes we'd drop off the wing when their pass came into the post. Ewing would send it back out and we'd close the ball out. If they got it back to him, we'd come down with a double team from a different direction. They got very frustrated. We came away with an easy 113–87 win.

Another factor in our early-season success started to loom in my mind. When the coaches were talking about the New York game back at the hotel, I said, "I think Earvin has a sense that this could be a big year for him. He started off good. He was scoring a little more. He played almost a perfect game. He knows that if you're going to get any kind of support for the Most Valuable Player award, you have to come into New York and play great."

We started to realize that Earvin was putting together the type of year that could win the MVP. When you go into New York, there's more press, and more powerful press, than any other city in the league.

Milwaukee had had five days to rest and prepare for our next night's game. They were 13 and 7, coming off a road win over the Bullets. We had a five A.M. wake-up call. Our six A.M. flight got delayed by an hour, which meant even less time to prepare for the traps and presses we'd have to face.

Travel arrangements such as that always remind me of growing up in Schenectady. In the winters we used to have to get up, leave the house, and wait in the dark for the school bus. I'd be standing out there in the pitch black, watching the snowflakes stick to my face, thinking, "I can't believe this." I got that same old feeling waiting for the plane to Milwaukee.

Nelson got us back for making him waste that 500-win cake in L.A. His team had a 9-game win streak going at home. They weren't going to let us spoil it.

Byron Scott's outside aim got us going early. He scored 7 in the first three minutes and we led them 11 to 4. We played a decent first quarter, but we didn't maintain our pursuit of the ball as the game wore on. You could see it slipping away from us.

They sent Jack Sikma, Randy Breuer, and Paul Mokeski at Kareem. Every single shot he put up drew an in-your-face defensive response. By the time he had fouled the first two Bucks centers out, he was in danger of scoring in single figures for the first time in 715 consecutive games.

During a time-out I told Billy Thompson to make sure he would pass the ball to The Captain underneath. "Do you realize what's happening? He has a streak of double-figure games going back to before you were born." Which was only a slight exaggeration. Tired as Kareem was, I didn't want to be the coach who broke his streak. Finally he hit two layups in a row with three minutes left.

Kareem's shooting record scared me less than Earvin's third-period collision with Sikma. Their knees banged together. Earvin fell to the floor in pain. It happened just as I called a time-out to try to stimulate our defense. I didn't see him lying there clutching his right knee.

Earvin hits the deck more often than anybody in the league. He has tremendous ability to penetrate the lane and draw fouls while he makes uncanny, postcollision shots. Every time he takes a painful knock in the process, I remember the 45 games missed in his second pro season, when the doctors had to cut open his left knee and repair it.

Gary brought him in, loaded up the ice bags, and called for an X ray. We went out of contention when he left the game.

One day of respite and we flew into Boston, having to angle the flight in via Detroit. The talk was low. Boston was snowy and cold with not much to do but walk around. There was extra security at the hotel. Some Boston fans like to throw rocks and bottles and to phone in false alarms and bomb threats and to set cars on fire. Living in "the Athens of America" gives them a special perspective on sportsmanship.

Bill and I always go to a place called Arnie's in Boston. This is one of the great "fine china, white tablecloths, and candlelight" restaurants on our itinerary. We talked about the scouting report Randy Pfund had put together on Boston. The next day we held practice at Helena College. We never get an opportunity to practice in Boston Garden. There's always some scheduling problem. Maybe they don't want us getting familiar with all the dead spots in their floor.

Boston was 13 and 6. They hadn't lost a home game in one year and six days, a 48-game streak. Earvin's knee was badly bruised, but not torn up. After testing it in practice, he decided to play. "This is my big game of the year," he said. "Can't miss this one."

Any Boston-L.A. game is a lesson in basketball greatness. The first few minutes everybody was testing everyone else. Try one offensive matchup, probe another one. See who still has the lateral movement. See who is overanxious, who might be mistake-prone, who can be intimidated. See how close the officials are going to call it. In this case, it didn't take long to find out. They weren't calling anything—at either end. It was force against force, hand-to-hand combat all night long.

They came right at Kareem, hoping to wear his legs down. They hadn't seen him since the strength-building work of the previous summer. He had a surprise for them.

We threw double and triple teams at their big men. They call McHale "The Black Hole" on that team because when the ball goes in to him, it disappears. He hates to pass it back out. We hoped to exploit that trait by making him take forced shots. Instead of feeding McHale at the post, they went to Parish and they popped outside shots.

Worthy and Kareem were getting it done for us. James was blowing by Larry Bird on his first step, and Kareem hit a hook, two free throws, and a surprise 20-footer from the top of the key. However, he also drew a third foul around six minutes into the period. There was no choice but to send in Kurt Rambis.

Earvin picked up our scoring slack. We kept McHale bottled, and their big men began to slow, but Dennis Johnson kept hitting from long and midrange. By the end of the period the Celtics had a 4-point lead. Both teams had red-hot shooting, 64% for them versus 60% for us.

I opened the second quarter with Mike Smrek at the post, Scott and Cooper at the guards, and Worthy and Rambis playing forward. Right away they pressed on Mike's inexperience. Parish took the feed from Bird and spun for a layup. Mike answered on the other end with a baseline hook.

His hook style is totally different from Kareem's. Kareem takes a long time, like a pendulum creating a clear path to swing in. Then he launches with a high lift off the leg opposite his shooting arm. The defense knows what's coming for two or three full seconds, but they usually can't do anything about it. Mike Smrek makes a very sudden flip of the ball, before the defense can react.

Parish came back down at him. He took a low post position, called for the ball, and attempted to spin left around Mike, take one dribble, and jam the ball through the hoop. Initiating the spin, he banged his left thigh against Mike's. Smrek is the strongest man on our team. He didn't give way. Parish went off balance, fell to the parquet, and lost the ball out of bounds. On their next possession he attempted a jump shot over Mike and it went long.

Games are won and lost in skirmishes such as this. Our unheard-of youngster, picked up off the waiver wire, went toe-to-toe with the experienced center of the world champs and held his ground. In four minutes Mike came out for A.C. Green, but Parish only scored two points—on free throws—for the rest of the period.

The score hovered at a slight Boston advantage all through the quarter, except for the brief 56–55 lead we held after Billy Thompson scored on a turnaround. I got excited during one moment and yelled down the bench, "We need Coop!" Somebody yelled back, "Hey, Riles! He's already out there!"

We forced 8 turnovers and Earvin had 4 rebounds and 8 points. But Larry Bird sank a long fall-away from the right sideline with four seconds left. They got to the half with a 6-point lead, 65–59.

Tommy Heinsohn, announcing for the hometown crowd, said, "I don't see the Lakers playing much better than they did in the first half." Earvin opened the period by taking a rebound coast-to-coast for a layup. Might've given Tommy something to think about.

The Celtics went to their frontline scoring. We answered with Kareem and A.C., plus long shots from Earvin and Byron. A.C. blocked a McHale shot. On the Celtics' next possession Kevin tried to bump A.C. out of low post defensive position and he threw an elbow to make the point. Then he scored with a short hook and gave A.C. a fist to the side of his head on the trip downcourt. Green answered back with a 16-footer from the top of the key. Constantly skirmishing and testing.

Right after a Boston time-out, James drove the lane to create a tie at 77. Thirty seconds later, Kareem picked up his fourth foul defending Robert Parish. By the time I was able to get him out we were ahead by 2. But Boston surged with an 11 to 3 run. They closed out the period ahead, 94–88.

Considering they had hit 41 of 65 and had nine blocked shots to our two, I thought it was a blessing we were only down by 6.

Boston opened the fourth period with Kevin McHale and four bench players. We started Rambis and Cooper, Kareem, Byron, and James. Within two minutes they brought in Parish and Bird, rested and ready to lead a charge. But we had Kareem hitting his skyhook. Michael Cooper pegged a 3-pointer from the right side of the key to cut their lead in half. After Parish hit a hook, Earvin drove the lane, got off a running shot, and drew a foul.

Before his free throw they ran in Dennis Johnson and Danny Ainge to complete their starting lineup. Even so, we held them scoreless for nearly two and a half minutes. Heinsohn said, "The Lakers look much better comin' down the fourth quarter."

Cooper and Scott hit consecutive outside shots to give us a one-point lead. They called a time-out. Kareem dropped two free throws after a foul by Ainge. They called another time-out, and Bird finally reopened their scoring with another fall-away shot from the sideline.

In the last five minutes, Kareem scored 8 points to Boston's 6. Earvin added to the cause with four more points, and we cracked their home streak with a 117–110 score. The Garden Party was over.

At last we felt that the breakthrough was total. It was like an instant replay of our comeback from the Memorial Day Massacre of 1985. Kareem had taken over and brought us from 8 points down to a win. He had 26 points in 26 minutes. The new strength was one factor: Parish tried to keep him muscled outside, but Kareem had had no trouble working in close.

The relief play of Rambis and Smrek was another factor. They held the line while foul trouble put Kareem on the bench. James Worthy finished with 25 points, and A.C. had 11 rebounds. Cooper held Bird to one shot attempt in the whole fourth period. Earvin finished with 31 points and went straight into another session with the ice packs.

"They say Kareem is over the hill," Earvin said. "Let them keep thinking that. We knew that the big guy would take over in the clutch. And we kept giving it to him. When you see that sparkle in his eye, give him the ball. Because when he wants it, he's going to go to work."

"They beat us in the fourth quarter," Bird told the writers, "and I don't like to get beat in the fourth quarter."

We flew out of Boston at 8 the next morning, arriving in Detroit at 10:05. We went immediately to our rooms. No shootaround. The players were blissfully happy. They wanted to savor the win, but there was no time. We faced the Pistons that night and the Cavaliers on the next Tuesday.

They had another huge crowd at the Silverdome that night, 33,447, the fifth largest in arena history. This is Magic Johnson territory. He grew up in East Lansing, Michigan, and played at Michigan State. He won the state high school tournament in 1977 and the NCAA in 1979. A guy named Larry Bird was playing for the opposition in that showdown. The people of Detroit tolerate the Lakers coming to town because we always bring Earvin Johnson along.

The Silverdome is one of those forced-air domes built over a football field. I can't imagine how the people in the distant seats can see anything. When you open up any door, the wind blows you back. You have to brace yourself. Five minutes before the game I was walking down a long tunnel where they put all the trucks. There are two doors. One door goes to the outside, and one goes into the arena. I passed Chuck Daly, the coach of the Pistons, as he and his assistants were leaning against a portable metal barrier, talking things over. They caught me out of the corner of their eyes. That's generally all coaches want to do before a game—catch a glance to know where you are, but never talk. They don't want to deal with you; you don't want to deal with them. But I showed my respect and I went over to talk for a second. They had been playing real well. Just dropped a one-point heartbreaker to the Washington Bullets on a last-second Moses Malone shot.

Chuck looked me in the eye and said, "That was one of the greatest games that I've ever seen anybody play last night. I was sitting home watching this game, scouting you, and I got so engrossed in watching that game. I've never seen a game like that in regular season. It was just beautiful." He wasn't setting me up or anything, but I got an instinctive feeling of wariness. It ain't natural for coaches to trust each other too much. "Yeah," I said, "thanks, Chuck."

Then we went out and got our asses whipped. We just didn't have any legs to move with. It was a game of spurts. They stretched out to a 15-point lead on us in the first half, 70 to 55. The most first-half points we had given up in the season. We came back within 3 points in the third period, but we ultimately couldn't get back over the hill. The best we could do was fight back and lose by only 5. Kareem had some exceptional moments, though. Bill Laimbeer, the

Detroit center, was the leading rebounder in the league. Kareem outrebounded him by 11 to 7 and outscored him 34 to 10.

One thing about our annual game in Detroit: If we lose, it's still the least sorrowful postgame scene of the year. Earvin's mother comes down from East Lansing with a barrage of home-cooked food for the whole team. They just set up in a room right there in the Silverdome.

Everyone showers, pulls on their clothes, and hustles over there. Kareem had two plates balanced on his arm. There was chicken, sweet potato pie, greens, the works. She always does it up right.

The way we've lost two years in a row in Detroit, I'm starting to wonder if the food isn't getting in the way of our focus. Coaches hate to see their team acting as if they didn't feel a loss. Still, I'm careful not to saddle the team with unrealistic expectations about winning all the time. We know we're going to lose several. If we're crushed every time we lose, we'll never feel any joy when we win. There are teams like that, where there's no joy in winning. Just an attitude of "So what? This is what you're paid for!"

Still, if you have to lose sometimes, you should use that loss to get stronger. Always catch yourself.

Rest time came in Cleveland. Our flight out of Detroit was canceled by snow and we switched to a later one. We didn't get to our hotel until two in the afternoon. Billy Desser, who runs our video systems, had sent a scouting tape of Philadelphia versus Cleveland. It was lost. Another copy had to come later via Federal Express. Meanwhile, Bill Bertka's silver-colored aluminum suitcase was lost in the flight changeover. So was his briefcase. All his files, his statistics, and his scouting reports were lost.

As far as we know, neither of them has been found yet. Through the rest of the season, we could count on Bill's opening conversations with, "They haven't found my silver case. I don't have my brown briefcase."

He was depressed for three or four days. It was like a circuit-riding preacher who had his Bible and all his sermons stolen. Every day he'd be on the phone to the airlines, cussing and protesting. For all the good it did him.

Cooper and Earvin took Kareem with them to the movies on one of our nights in Cleveland. Usually he stays around the hotel with a book. They went to see *Heartbreak Ridge*, the Clint Eastwood movie about a tough old guy who had to teach the young recruits.

Kareem identified. He stood up and cheered Eastwood throughout the movie at the top of his voice. Kareem, at times, is the funniest, craziest person on the team. "They were trying to tell him he was over the hill too," he explained. Cooper started calling him Sarge after that.

Billy Thompson brought two left shoes to one of our Cleveland practice sessions. Couldn't participate. This was called "pulling a Benoit Benjamin," in honor of the Clippers center, who had taken two left sneakers on an exhibition road trip earlier in the year.

Billy also met some fellow at the Cleveland airport, got into a friendly conversation, and promised to set him up with a pair of tickets to the game. Then he forgot the guy's name. No problem. He just had the Cleveland box office reserve two tickets at the Will Call window for "the guy from the airport."

Just before we went out on the floor, we heard tremendous laughter coming out of the Cavaliers' dressing rooms next door. A couple of minutes later, one of the stadium employees knocked on our door and said, "Excuse me. These tickets were part of the allocation of players' tickets that were sent up. But I don't have a name. I already asked the Cavaliers. Does anybody here know who 'the guy from the airport' is?"

Then we took the floor and beat the youngest team in the league, 121–116. They came out and took a 33–25 lead, but we were able to explode a few times: a 16–2 run, a 26–7 run. It was a struggle, but we found a way to crack the game. Kareem kept us in it with 15 points in the first quarter. Earvin ended with 25 points and another triple-double.

The marathon was over. We lost two, both of them the second game of a back-to-back pair. Of the three we won, the Celtics game counted as a great triumph.

One quarter of the regular season was done. Some dragging was evident—early Dog Days. I worried about our defense. It was getting stagnant. Against Detroit we could never make a definitive defensive stand, couldn't contain their scoring threats. Maybe we weren't doing enough. Maybe we had to trap more, gamble instead of getting back. Add a little more responsibility to the players and give them a new offensive set.

Back in training camp we had put in a shell, a philosophy. It takes time for the new stuff to become natural and fluid. It's like A.C. or any other player working to establish a certain shot that will be all theirs. You get it down, get it so you can do it in your sleep. Other teams react, find ways to stop it. Then you develop little variations. You always want to give them a fresh problem.

The Lakers picked up the new offensive and defensive ideas. They could execute. But they couldn't get to a comfort zone with any of it yet. They could do it, but they didn't have command. We had to learn how to play off the offense. You don't just run an offense. You play basketball off your offense. You've got to be able to react to whatever defensive situation is being thrown at you. If the defense is taking something away, you can't waste your opportunities force-feeding a predetermined attack. In other words, you've got to improvise.

There's always the fine line between pattern and spontaneity. We were becoming sure of ourselves with the pattern. The next breakthrough would be in acquiring spontaneity.

We boarded an early flight from Cleveland. As we walked through the airport, players kept joking: "Maybe that's him!" "Is that the guy?" For the next two or three weeks, until they finally wore it out, "I'm the guy from the airport" was a surefire punch line.

Motivation

How do you sustain your success? How do you stay number one in the NBA? How do you stay one step ahead of the posse in a profession where you're always one step away from the street? People always ask me about motivation. What do I say in the halftime speeches? They want answers they can translate into their own lives. Maybe they're parents or managers or teachers.

You sustain success and you motivate yourself by trying to develop another reason above and beyond the natural motivation of just wanting to be successful. There are 276 players in the NBA. They want to do one thing. They all want to win a world's championship.

The ones who can really separate themselves from the pack are those who understand what it takes to sustain excellence. To get away from a "to have" mentality. "To have" is something we get early in our life. To have power. To have a little bit of prestige. To have position. To have the house and the car and all those things that we feel we need.

And then you understand later on in your career that those things don't mean anything. When you experience them, you realize the only thing left is to be the very best. You prioritize "to be" ahead of "to have." And when you're thinking about being the very best, you're thinking about making sure that you're being a person, a performer, whom you can be proud of.

Once you believe that you want to be the best, you realize that all those other things you worried about for years, such as money, prestige, and power, just follow you wherever you go. Instead of chasing your tail, you realize that your tail follows you, once you stop worrying about it.

The top players on our team make so much money that I just about have to go to them when I need to cash my paycheck. How much more money do they need? How much more fame?

The only thing they care about, ultimately, is separating themselves from the pack. Being the best in the league today. Being the best in the history of the game. It's not that they would want to give away their high-ticket real estate holdings, their superb cars, or their custom wardrobes. But they value their sense of excellence more.

Sometimes I get this kind of attitude from a player: "What are you going to do for me tomorrow?" I tell them, "We have it backwards. We should pay Buss and the NBA for setting this whole thing up here. To give us an opportunity to play a game that we love."

I've been playing this game for thirty years. It's a kid's game. I love it and I get paid for taking part. All of us make enormous amounts of money. To go out and do something we need to do, to earn a living, at something we want to do. And when you can put those two things together, what you need and what you want—there's your motivation. Keep that situation alive. Be so good at it that they can't even think about replacing you.

Earvin
Takes Charge

Right after the Eastern road grind we were scheduled for a first look at the Portland Trailblazers, under new coach Mike Schuler. Then we had a return to Dallas and Houston, a game in Sacramento, and a rematch with Houston at the Forum on the day after Christmas.

It was time for A.C. Green to scale down to a smaller cast on his injured thumb. Gary Vitti and I had mixed feelings. He had gotten to a point of playing so well with it on that we decided not to pressure him about getting rid of it. He tried practicing without it, and the pain from a slight hit made his eyebrows climb up to his hairline.

So we weaned him off the splint, giving him a smaller one, having him play only the latter part of practice with no splint at all. We had confidence in what he could do. We had to develop our confidence in how well the thumb had repaired itself.

When we played Portland on December 18th, A.C. had the

smaller splint on. He hit 26 points, his high as a Laker. Byron came out of a mild shooting slump to score 27. Earvin supplied 18 assists, which tied his season high. Anytime he can feed the other players for scores, he's just as happy as if he'd made the basket himself. Portland had won eight of its last nine games. They were third in the NBA in field-goal percentage. They were the best driving, penetrating, what we call catch-and-go, drive-and-kick team in the league. Their offense is designed to catch the ball on the floor and go into the gap, draw the defense, kick to the open man. That open man either shoots or drives and kicks to the next open man. They're constantly attacking the basket, giving the defense a lot of trouble.

Our game plan was to make sure we got back and got down. Play defense. They like to isolate Kiki Vandeweghe and Clyde Drexler. We had to turn them back into traffic. We had to two-time Steve Johnson, who is one of the best pivot men in the NBA. Block out Kenny Carr and Jerome Kersey.

They hurt us with reverses at the baseline, especially Kiki Vandeweghe. They pushed us out of the low post spot. Kareem's double-figure streak was in danger again. He had 5 fouls and only 5 points. We had a 15-point lead and I gambled with leaving him in. The lead got down to ten and he fouled out, but the double-figure streak was kept alive. A.C. had to come in and try to use both hands. We ended with a 131–115 victory.

The Milwaukee Bucks knocked off the Atlanta Hawks on the same night, so we were ahead of the pack again, at 18 and 5. Only one more extreme road trip left on the schedule, a five-day binge with Washington, New Jersey, Atlanta, and Indiana.

Anyone who wears contact lenses knows how it feels to leave them in too long. Kareem has had his eyes scratched so many times by opponents trying to claw the ball from his hands that now, even though he has worn protective goggles for the last few seasons, he's very susceptible to corneal erosion syndrome. It's like an aggravated case of leaving your contacts in way too long. The cornea dries out, becomes irritated, and small segments can even flake off.

On jetliners Kareem sometimes drapes one of their blankets over his head to make taking a nap easy and to keep the direct blast of the air-conditioning system off his eyes. At the start of our three-game trip, on the way to Dallas, he noticed the pain setting in. He woke up on game day with pain and swelling in both eyes and called an ophthalmologist. He showed up at practice with a patch taped over his right eye.

Kareem was sitting down at one end of the gym, still in his street clothes, but holding on to his gear as if he intended to try to play. "How do you feel?" I asked him. He squinted up at me with his left eye. It was swollen half-shut and obviously very sensitive to light. "What the hell are you even here for?" I said. We sent him home right away. The doctor estimated that he needed at least three days of rest.

Mike Smrek took one look at Kareem and he knew he'd be called on. We worked on some adjustments and told the other four regulars they had to carry the offensive burden. Inserting Mike in his first NBA start, we went out to meet Dallas.

Strange things can happen when you lose a star. Sometimes, in the short run, you even play better. It doesn't mean that the star was a negative force, but it can reveal untapped potential and how people can rally in a crisis. What happened during Kareem's departure was the final emergence of Earvin Johnson.

We practiced a new offensive set: three out, three down. It was a triangle offense for Earvin and for Worthy and for Scott or Cooper, a guard-oriented offense. The plan was to run an isolation set. We'd put the power forward and the center over to the side, in what we call the parking lot, to expose their zone. Force them to play a true man-on-man against our guards. Worthy was at the high post. Earvin handled the ball at the point with an unbalanced set to the right side of the court. Scott would pop out to the wing. We'd enter the ball to Scott. Earvin would cut off Worthy to the low post. At 6'9" and with his ball-handling skills, Earvin can dominate almost any guard in the league from the low post position.

For variation, Worthy would power down and then we'd look to pop Scott for a jumper near the top of the key. Then we'd run flex-cuts: Earvin would cut off Worthy, Worthy would post up, Scott could go down and set a pick for Worthy. It was a pretty versatile offense, based on two guards and a small forward.

Earvin had gotten with the program since the season opened. He was taking about 6 more shots per game and scoring about 3 more points than he did the year before. He still led the league in assists, but he was looking for his shot more.

With Kareem out, with the stock-in-trade of our offense not available, Earvin turned his attack up another big notch. We played a good game and we lost, 130–119. Earvin scored 34. Mike fouled out at the post within 12 minutes. As any team would do, they went straight after the newcomer. Mark Aguirre came at him three times in the first two minutes. First time was a clean block, next two were fouls. But we rotated different post players and finished with the most rebounds and blocked shots.

The game got physical. They were frustrated over our two previous wins. And their center, James Donaldson, was unable to score a single point all night, even with Kareem gone. He and Michael Cooper got into a fracas in the fourth quarter, about the time we were posting an 18–6 run and threatening to get back in the game. It didn't result in any fists swinging, but there was a lot of emotion. I got a little excited about the officiating. I said to the referee, "Christmas is coming awfully early." That tore it. I was ejected with four and a half minutes to go and Bertka took the reins.

With less than a minute to go, Earvin fouled Donaldson underneath and clutched at him to keep the big guy from hitting the floor. Donaldson thought he was being abused and came up glaring, ready to swing. Players from both teams squared off, but the moment cooled as fast as it had started. "Next time," Earvin said, "I just won't hold him up."

I never like a loss, but I couldn't get upset over this one. The sight of Earvin scoring at will was a great antidote. He had finally put the validation on that part of his game. It was okay to score. He was comfortable with it. The team was conditioned to it.

We flew into Houston the same night. This was a survival game. We still didn't have Kareem. The team had to focus in other areas, play more with their quickness, play with a different style.

Our game with Houston was tight throughout, both teams grinding it out. The lead changed several times, but it always stayed around 3 or 4 points. A.C. was phenomenal: 18 points and 16 rebounds. But the remarkable point of the game was the final four minutes.

Earvin had been scoring consistently all night. He was the leading scorer in all four quarters, putting shots down whenever we needed points. With the score 91 to 86, Houston's favor, Earvin led a rampage. By the final buzzer, we had scored 17 to their 5. Earvin either scored, or set up, 15 of those 17.

Akeem Olajuwon reentered to give the Rockets their strongest lineup for the game's closing minutes. Earvin scored a layup, then fed A.C. Green for another. Green was fouled and he converted the free throw to tie the game at 91.

On our next possession he ran our "one-up" set, which is a pick-and-roll with him and one of the forwards. A switch was created where Ralph Sampson had to jump out and defend Earvin. Earvin backed out, started a dribble-drive. Sampson backpedaled off balance trying to match Earvin's speed. Earvin turned his back, picked up his dribble at about 15 feet, and threw in a skyhook. Swoosh. Even though our skyhook specialist was back home with a patch on his eye, our point guard was taking on their biggest player and beating him with a center's weapon.

Dirk Minniefield made one free throw out of a pair. Half a minute later he fed Lewis Lloyd for a dunk that put Houston ahead by one.

Earvin then fed Byron Scott for a long jumper from the baseline. Then he drew a foul from Lloyd and put both shots in.

Houston called a time-out, but we got the ball back before they could score. Earvin fed Worthy for a dunk with twenty-five seconds remaining. Akeem Olajuwon scored their last two points on a layup, then A.C. Green and Michael Cooper went to the line when Houston attempted desperation fouls.

Earvin finished with 38 points and 17 assists for the night. The final score was Los Angeles 103, Houston 96.

Two nights later, Earvin and A.C. played 48 minutes apiece against the Sacramento Kings. We flew straight up there from Texas without a stopover at home. Bill and I got off by ourselves for a great Mexican dinner. We talked about how the plans of training camp were starting to mature. We felt great about the character of the team, the way they rallied with a star player out. Sometimes that kind of situation can bring out the best in a team.

Our practice on game day was loose, good spirited. They were still savoring the Houston win. I threw in a note of caution: "You guys had better be ready to meet a hungry team." The Kings had snapped a four-game losing streak by winning two in a row. We hadn't lost to them in five or six years, but the last game, November 16th, came down to a last-second shot. The papers made a big deal about it. They were looking at this as a breakthrough game.

While we were working out, Reggie Theus and Derek Smith, Sacramento's starting guards, came walking through the gym. We always keep our practices tightly closed, like family affairs. We were talking strategy. When our players noticed the intruders, everyone stopped talking. Derek walked by with a defiant look on his face. All our players stared at him as if they wanted to say, "What the hell business do you have here?"

As they exited, I told the team, "It looks like they want to send a message about the game tonight."

Wes Matthews, Earvin's backup, drew two technical fouls and got himself ejected early in the second quarter. He was reacting to the forearm smashes that Mark Olberding throws when he sets a pick. Cooper got nailed a couple of times, coming off screens. There were a few scuffles. Sacramento definitely had the attitude that they were going to kick our ass.

The game stayed sharp and tight throughout the first half. Byron had a hell of a night. Worthy and Green were operating on all cylinders. After a brief cold streak, we trailed by 13 late in the third quarter. Then Earvin, Byron, and James Worthy connected to create a 14 to 4 run.

The fourth quarter was classic bucket-for-bucket scoring, and regulation ended with Derek Smith banking one in from the baseline to tie it at 112.

Of the 15 points we scored to win it in overtime, Earvin had a hand in 13. He scored a new career high of 46 points. Byron Scott also had a career scoring high with 33 points.

We came back home and practiced Christmas Day. But we didn't ignore the spirit of the season. We told everyone to go out and buy a gift—nothing expensive. Something that would suit anyone else on the squad.

Everybody brought their present in to the Forum and Gary Vitti brought in a tall ficus tree that he had decorated with socks and jockstraps and empty tape spools. We played Christmas music on someone's portable cassette and served cookies and eggnog.

Each player got to come up to the Laker Christmas Tree and select any gift package he wanted. Then they unwrapped the gift and showed it around the room.

The next player had a choice: he could take a new gift or lay claim to the present that had just been unwrapped. There was everything from electric razors to toy trucks to sweaters to X-rated videotapes. Cooper swapped for the toys, to give them to Michael Jr.

Then we held practice until noon. The team concentration was good. But the schedule we had been keeping didn't allow them much time to stray. Nine out of fourteen December games on the road.

We studied some Houston video. Akeem Olajuwon plays the low post with his back to the basket. He needs to physically locate the man defending him before he can begin his offensive moves. His tactic is to bump lightly with his butt, fix the opponent's location, then spin and drive or fall away. He needs to know what he's spinning against. We told our low post defenders, "Don't let him touch you. Make him turn his head to look."

Holidays have meant basketball games and tournaments ever since I was in high school. When I'm away, Chris works very hard to set up our Christmas. But I was in charge of toy assembly. I came home after the Houston practice and we put James down for his afternoon nap. I started trying to put together one of his gifts, a pedal car. I was still working on it when he got up, so the kit went into a closet until bedtime. Then I tried again. Friends dropped by for drinks. Around midnight it was ready.

We woke up on Christmas morning and dressed James in a red outfit. We had our video camera out. The proud parents tracked their son down the stairs and into the living room. He made top speed past the car for Champion, his new rocking horse. He stayed in the saddle all morning. We realized then that there's such a thing as too many gifts. The pedal car went into layaway for next Christmas.

When we faced Houston at home on December 26th, even though Kareem was back in the lineup, Earvin maintained his increased offense: 30 points and 15 assists. The whole team played with a zest that was unusual for this time of the year. No look of fatigue. We pulled ahead by 7 points in the first quarter and held that lead until the half. We extended the lead by one point over the third quarter. Then we hit stride: 44 points to their 29 in the final period. The final score was 134–111.

Again, Earvin was the chief instigator. A lay-in to start the period. A pair of free throws. An assist to Kurt Rambis. An assist to Cooper for a 3-pointer. Another assist to Kurt. Another to Byron Scott. Driving the lane for a shot plus a foul. An eight-foot bank shot.

Earvin finished with 30. Cooper hit two out of two 3-point attempts and finished with 14. James had 22, Kareem 19, A.C. 12, and Byron 21. Adrian Branch nailed 4 points in just two minutes of playing time.

Wins around Christmas and New Year's feel great. Sometimes the guys say, "We want more time off to spend with our families." But going through the holidays on a losing streak is double misery. Traditionally, you take stock of yourself and your surroundings when a year is ending. It's supposed to be the most joyous time of the year, but it's also a time when all your emotions are magnified. You ought to enter the holidays with your self-esteem high. There's nothing like a win streak to make sure you'll feel great.

15

Halfway Home

Dr. J, Julius Erving, made his final visit to the Forum as an active player on December 28th, 1986. We gave him retirement gifts: a high-backed oak rocking chair and a TV. Then we won the game by a score of 111–85.

Charles Barkley is like a Godzilla-sized runaway bowling ball on the court. They list him at 6′6″ and 263 pounds, but he hits like 400. You have to find a way to contain his momentum, make his emotional style of play revert to frustration.

We had run loose-ball pursuit drills in practice. The ball was dropped in the key and 10 players had to scramble for it. This is something Barkley is great at. One Laker was designated as Barkley and one of the others was assigned to keep him constantly blocked away from the loose ball. We emphasized face blocking him, which means to keep looking in his face at all times when you're trying to shield him from the basket. Don't spin around to box him out of a rebound situation or he'll just move you out of the way.

About four minutes into the second quarter he stole the ball from Earvin and thundered downcourt for a dunk. A supreme emotional moment. He attempted a monster two-hand reverse dunk and missed. The ball kicked back out of the hole. Barkley claimed that it went all the way through, hit his head and bounced back out. The officials said it came off the back of the rim.

Philadelphia's coach, Matt Goukas, described the incident as a "momentum-breaker." Barkley stuck to his guns and added a choice word of description for anybody who thought otherwise.

The press loves a scenario like that. Get a hotheaded quote from one guy, go across the room and say, "So-and-So sez that you hurt the team with your selfish play in the third quarter." Instant headlines.

When I played for Adolph Rupp at Kentucky, there was no slam dunking. On a breakaway opportunity, you laid the ball off the glass and let it drop in, soft and sure. If you made a dunk, you'd probably get benched. If you tried one and missed, you'd be off scholarship.

Here's where you see the tension in basketball between style and efficiency. There's a lot of expression in a slam dunk, but there's a risk. Coaches like the primal attack mentality behind dunk shots. They love to see players take the ball aggressively up to the rim. That's the best way to make a shot and draw a foul at the same time. But they get ulcers watching two sure points fly out of the hole. A layup is a certain deuce. Not stylish, but certain.

After Barkley missed that one, we went on a 20 to 6 scoring run. Finished the half with a lead, 45 to 36, and never looked back. With the exception of two minutes for James Worthy and one and a half minutes for A.C. Green, we played reserves throughout the fourth quarter and held the 76ers completely at bay.

We landed in Portland on New Year's Eve to face the Trailblazers on New Year's Day. It was raining like hell. Some of the players arranged to meet their wives on the trip. They wanted to be together when 1987 came in. Bill and I had misgivings. Our philosophy is that you reach a championship with hard work, good organization and a minimum of distractions. But we wanted to appease the players during the holidays. They deserved this consideration. We told them, when they hatched the idea at practice, "Okay. But you'd better win."

Our record was now 23 and 6, best in the NBA. At this time a year ago we began to skid, ran off a streak of .500 ball before we caught ourselves, and never really regained the early-season intensity that had caused people to believe we might be "the best team in the history of the game."

This night, against the Blazers, they came out and played their asses off. The big surprise was Earvin Johnson's 4 points. One field goal from four attempts and two free throws. James Worthy also had a season low at 6 points and 8 shot-attempts.

"This is the new look we have," Earvin told the Portland press corps. "Anybody can do it any night. But you never know who is going to get the job done." Cooper shot 7 for 10 and three for three from 3-point range. Byron Scott had 31, just one bucket shy of his recent career best. He was 11 for 15 from the field, three for three from 3-point range, and six for six from the free throw line.

Usually I only use eight to ten players in a game. This night the bench players all played. Their total minutes were almost one hundred. We buried Portland, 140–104. It was our biggest scoring total and biggest winning margin of the season.

We flew home for a game against the Phoenix Suns. Earvin resumed the scoring load with a 32-point performance. On the second consecutive night we set new season highs in scoring and in winning margin. The final was 155–118.

Bertka had another concern. "I can see now in our offense where things have become instinctive," he said in my office after the game. "The players are reading each other in defensive situations. They anticipate each other's movements. *Please,* Pat, don't add any more offense. They're just getting this one down." Bill knows I love to tinker with things, adding new looks, new counterplays. But at this time we were flying, playing well, running up huge scores. Not trying to humiliate our opponents, just playing so well that the points piled up. Between our December 20th Dallas loss and a loss on January 8th to the Utah Jazz, we won eight straight games and averaged just under 130 points per contest.

The Jazz loss was on the road, at the Salt Palace. Four days beforehand we had beaten the same team 121–113 at the Forum. They made us work hard for it. We played in spurts—just good enough to win. We wanted to coast home, but Utah kept clawing back. Afterwards, Bertka posed the question: "Have we peaked?"

Next we faced the Denver Nuggets at the Forum. This one was

a romp, 147–109. All twelve players got on the court. The bench again had over one hundred minutes of playing time. Nine players reached double-figure scoring. After the game, Doug Moe, the Denver coach, said, "This year the Lakers are lively. Awesome. They've got what they had two years ago. Something intangible, something you can't explain."

Even the peripheral opponents were taking notice. Doug Krikorian, a very opinionated L.A. columnist, wrote a full-page spread headlined: "West Was Right After All. Smart Move Not to Break Up Winning Combination."

Utah plays excellent defense. They're always a tough matchup for us, especially on their home court. Like Denver, they're based high up in the Rockies. Athletes go into those cities knowing they're going to get tired. It's painful when you hit the wall and your body suddenly starts screaming for oxygen. Utah was 13 and 2 at home, 6 and 10 on the road, which says something about how visiting teams are affected there.

What makes the Jazz tougher than the Nuggets for us is how they play. Denver plays our kind of all-out, hard-running game. Utah plays a very defined, grind-it-out game. They work the ball and work the clock; they get us into defensive struggles.

We flew in to Utah on Western Airlines, flight 784. Bill and I took some time to walk around Salt Lake City. The guards split for a movie. Kurt and A.C. went looking for the nearest McDonald's.

The Jazz played a great game. They controlled the tempo. They executed very well against our defensive adjustments. When Utah went on defense they were determined to take away the paint and make us shoot outside. And they pressured the shooters. We shot 32% in the fourth quarter, 39% for the whole game.

John Stockton, a reserve, started at point guard. The usual starter, Rickey Green, had the flu. Stockton tore us up. He kept pushing the ball up and getting them in their offense. A simple pick and roll play with Stockton and Karl Malone, their massive power forward, burned us for 10 points.

We played our best ball when we were down 99–88. James Worthy scored 6 unanswered points. Karl Malone and Thurl Bailey came back with one apiece. Earvin drove the lane and scored a basket plus a foul. Worthy put down two free throws. We were within 4 with less than a minute and a half left to play. But Thurl Bailey sank a 20-footer and a jump hook in the final minute. He finished with

29, his career high. Karl Malone, with 23 points and 17 rebounds, and Bobby Hansen, with 26 points, matched their career best games.

"The Lakers are something special," Frank Layden, the Jazz coach, said after the game. "You get up just a little more for them." This time they got up 107–101 at the final buzzer.

Golden State got up for us, too. We flew into Oakland from Salt Lake City on January 9th and ran through our practice. James was troubled with tendinitis in his knees. Earvin rested on the sidelines, saying he hurt all over. Bill and I went out that night to Francesco's, right next to the hotel in Oakland, for spaghetti and meatballs. We wondered, "Now what are we going to do? How are we going to get them back up there?"

The season is like a single game. You can't play 48 minutes of Show Time basketball. You play as well as you can, minute by minute. There will be four or five skirmishes, when the action flares up into decisive moments. If you can come out on top of most of those skirmishes, you'll win the game.

To win the season, you want to get a bunch of good runs. You want to get out of the blocks well. You're going to have periods of letdown. Even though you're pushing for optimum levels, you're going to get caught. We had breezed for eight games. Then we played the Jazz tired. We had no zip.

I was concerned going in to Golden State because we have played so inconsistently there. We would kick their ass in L.A., then go up to their home court and fail to get the job done. I said, "We have to make a stand here. This is a team that we might meet in the playoffs. We've got to plant our feet, stay out in front, and make them know that when it counts, we can beat them in the open."

The Warriors were ready for us. Joe Barry Carroll always plays his best games at home. We were fighting uphill the whole game. Anytime we drove for a layup, we were pounded to the floor. The same thing had happened in Utah. Karl Malone had taken liberties with Earvin and with Byron. When you're on top, teams measure you for weaknesses. Maybe your motivation level has eroded after a succession of wins. Maybe, if the game is tough down in the trenches, you'll say, "The hell with it. If they want it so bad, I'm not going to fight."

Byron Scott accounted for 8 points in the first quarter. But the team total was only 20, versus 32 for the Warriors. Their physical play forced us into 6 turnovers. Earvin untracked his offense for 12 points in the second quarter, and we were only down 2 at the half.

In the locker room I said, "We're getting measured right now. I don't know if you recognize this, but they're checking you to see how bad you want this game."

We traded one-point leads through the early third quarter. They worked up to 10 ahead, then Earvin scored seven consecutive points. We closed out the quarter still in reaching distance, behind 86 to 82.

About one minute into the fourth we had a tie at 88 each. Then they hit us from inside and outside for 12 in a row. Kept us from scoring for nearly three and a half minutes.

We never closed the gap. We lost our second game in a row, 124 to 109, our first back-to-back losses of the season.

The next night, Sunday, we faced San Antonio in the Forum. They were the last-place team in their division, rebuilding under a new coach. They played a strong game, but we kept a small lead nearly all the way. Two minutes into the fourth period, Michael Cooper blocked a shot and took it all the way down for a score. We were up 99–90, looking good. Then the motivation level slipped again.

For the next seven and a half minutes, the Spurs outscored us 13 to 4 and cut our lead to only one point, 104–103. With the game on the line at 111–109, Laker advantage, only a couple of seconds left, Alvin Robertson of the Spurs rushed a 3-point attempt that bounced away. We were that close to a third straight loss.

It had been a hard stretch: four games in three cities within five days. We took Monday and Tuesday off.

Jerry West called me Monday morning and asked, "Did you hear what happened?" I said no. "Lewis Lloyd and Mitchell Wiggins were just banned for life. They tested positive for cocaine."

It's funny how you spend so much time and effort looking for ways to beat an opponent, then you see them beat themselves. Lloyd and Wiggins were with the Houston Rockets, the team of the future, the defending Western Conference champions.

They say cocaine makes people feel larger than life, as if they can do anything. I understand the susceptibility. People playing professional sports have to keep their confidence level up. Otherwise, they'll get eaten alive on the court or on the field. But cocaine puts things backwards. It lends an illusion of personal power, then it goes on to rob personal power. Now the Houston Rockets were going backwards, and Lloyd and Wiggins were going backwards faster than anybody—from prosperous contracts, playing a game they loved, to not making a dime.

After the league and the players' association agreed to their guidelines on drug testing, a lot of players came forth and went into rehabilitation programs. This was the first time that the league, under the terms of that agreement, followed up on suspicions of "reasonable cause to believe that a player has been using a prohibited substance" and swooped down to test someone. I leaned back in my chair when West told me. I was shocked.

A shudder went through the whole NBA. In the middle of the season, the whole league came to a stop. Drug addiction doesn't understand penalties. It doesn't understand consequences. I went over to my desk and wrote "No Nonsense" on the blue card I was working on to prepare for our next practice. I wanted anybody who would even *consider* drugs to check themselves immediately.

What happens, if you have a player on your team hooked on drugs, is that the other players don't want to turn him in. They'll turn their backs to it and say, "Well, I hope it doesn't affect the team." But there's no way someone can be addicted to drugs and not affect the team. So what you're doing is living a lie. Any time you're living a lie in a team situation, it's going to break the team down—just as it breaks individuals down.

It's the same dynamic that goes on with alcoholism or any other kind of drug abuse in families—denial. "I can handle it. My father doesn't drink that much. My wife only drinks a little. It's just not that bad."

Teams are built on dedication and sacrifice. When you've got people dedicated to their drugs and willing to sacrifice their families and their careers for their drugs, the only thing that can happen is a breakdown of the fiber of the team—or the family.

The layoff after San Antonio refreshed our players, physically and mentally. At Wednesday's practice they were spirited. They weren't looking over their shoulders, looking for doom because of a slump. Golden State was coming into the Forum on Thursday, then we ran the Eastern gauntlet one more time: Washington Bullets on Sunday, New Jersey Nets on Monday, Atlanta Hawks on Wednesday, Indiana Pacers on Thursday, finishing up with the Dallas Mavericks on Saturday. We still had the best record in the NBA, 17 and 1 at home and 10 and 7 on the road.

Golden State was a get-back game. We contested every shot, but still gave them some gaps. We came out soft in the third quarter and didn't run, so they outscored us 38 to 28. In the fourth we came out of the blocks and outscored them 32 to 16. Worthy wasn't hampered so much by the tendinitis, thanks to our days off. He had 31 points, 13 rebounds, and a blocked shot. The team as a whole had 13 blocks, our high for the season. Fresh legs won it for us. The final was 124–109. "Revenge was a factor in a small way," Kareem said.

The win meant Randy, Bertka, and I would be in charge of the West team at the All-Star break. Kareem, Earvin, and James were tapped to play on the team.

Before we left on the Eastern trip, I made a point to the players: "We're two games ahead of Boston. They're twenty-six and ten, we're twenty-six and eight. Atlanta is twenty-five and ten. The Mavericks are twenty-four and thirteen. We have to think about those positions. Because all the teams we're contending with are looking at the schedule right now and thinking, 'Hmmm. The Lakers have a five-game road trip. They'll probably lose two or three of them. This is where we can pick up some ground.'

"We want to go back east and not lose any ground. We want to come back with at least as good a lead as we have now."

The Bullets were pumped up for the game, and they had 19,411 screaming fans, but we pulled out a 115–101 victory. Almost as Wes Matthews had sparked us in his old hometown at San Antonio, Adrian Branch gave us a lift against Washington. He had been born there and was a collegiate star nearby, at the University of Maryland. I had barely played him all year long, but I felt that it was time to give him a shot on the road. We were playing lethargically in the first half. Coming in during the second quarter, he helped us break free, hitting a jumper from the corner and a flying dunk and getting two blocked shots. I was happy for him.

It's really true that every player eventually gets his moment on stage. Adrian has the ability to be a major scoring threat. His one-on-one skills are tremendous.

A lot of people don't know it, but Adrian was very close to Len Bias. They were roommates at the University of Maryland. Adrian graduated and played in the CBA while Bias, in his senior year, became about the most celebrated college player in the country. Picked number one by the Celtics. Then came his death by cocaine overdose. Adrian had come west to try to make an impression on NBA scouts playing in Summer League. His father called him to break the news.

For Adrian, it was like losing a member of his family.

New Jersey was our second afternoon game in a row. We had no time for practice. Not even a shootaround.

There were lots of reporters, lots of chaos. The blackboard didn't work, the video broke down—Murphy's Law in action. Finally I said, "Let's just go out and play it. Get it over with." Earvin scored 22 in the third quarter and 42 points for the game, which tied the record for Meadowlands Arena. He hadn't felt good about his game against Washington. He told me afterward, "I wanted to make up for it." We beat the Nets 126–115 and flew down to Atlanta that same night.

The last time we had seen "the junior Lakers," they had made a strong statement. It was still our only home loss. I'm sure both teams had a lot on their minds concerning the rematch.

Tuesday, January 20th, was a day off. Even though practice was canceled, Gary Vitti took six guys down to a local gym, The Sporting Club. He never lets up on their conditioning, especially for the guys who don't get many playing minutes.

We jumped out to a 5–0 lead, then we went down by 13 twice in the first half. The fans at the Omni were howling.

We outscored the Hawks by small margins in the second, the third and the fourth. With eight seconds to go we had a one point lead. Mike McGee, the ex-Laker, fouled Earvin. He'd already made 7 of 9 from the line. As the officials were herding everyone into place for the free throw attempts, Randy leaned over and whispered something in my ear: "Why don't we put Kareem down on the boards, in case of a miss?"

Like most teams, we usually send our center downcourt during free throws. The idea is that he shouldn't have to run any more than necessary. But Randy had a great point: This was the end of the game. If Earvin missed, a rebound could determine the winner.

Kareem lined up for the rebound. Kevin Willis noticed the switch. He pulled over to concentrate on blocking him out. Now, instead of being flanked by a 7-footer, Michael Cooper was sandwiched between Dominique Wilkins and Cliff Levingston, two guys closer to his own size. Earvin missed both shots. The second rebound went to Cooper's side. Earvin batted it out of Wilkins's and Levingston's hands. Cooper grabbed the ball and tucked it away. They fouled him. He made both shots. We beat the junior Lakers 112–109.

It was the most physical game we had played up to that point of the season, and it took everything we had. Next to winning on the parquet floor, this counted as one of the big ones. They could copy our style, but they couldn't copy our experience.

When we checked out of our Atlanta hotel, the clerks presented Vitti with a $100 limousine service tab. It was for the trip to his workout session. Little Kahuna exploded like Mount Aetna. "We've got 25 rooms here and you're going to charge us for a ride to the gym?"

The Atlanta airport was locked up by a snowstorm, but we had to play in Indianapolis that night. Our flight was supposed to be at nine in the morning. We weren't cleared to take off until after noon. The delay seemed to work out in our favor. Players lounged around the hotel, ate second and third breakfasts, read magazines. We were very rested by the time we got to Indiana and checked into the Embassy Suites around three P.M.

I walked downstairs. There was a big mall and I went into a Mrs. Fields cookie shop. I looked around and saw Jack Ramsey, the Pacers' coach, walking in behind me. "Jack, what are you doing in a cookie shop?" I said. "You're one of those triathlon people, aren't you?" Ramsey is past sixty, but he's conditioned like iron. He keeps himself more fit than most guys forty years younger. "Hey, listen, don't tell anybody," he said. He grabbed two cookies and a carton of milk and disappeared.

We jumped out to a 10-point lead against the Pacers. We pounded the ball inside well, ran well, just put together a sharp game against an extremely young, talented, and well-coached team. Worthy had 22, Kareem had 20, and Earvin had 29. The final score was 118–108, and all of a sudden we were one game away from sweeping the road trip.

Everyone slept late the next morning. This was one of the rare times for savoring. Each player went down to the coffee shop and grabbed the local paper. Spread out the sports section and enjoyed life. There's nothing like French toast and victory. Jawing with your teammates, having some leisure before the next flight and the next battle. We arrived at the airport in good spirits.

Not long after we arrived in Dallas, word came from Lansing that Earvin's sister, Mary Johnson, had died after a long illness. Earvin's father, Earvin Johnson Sr., advised his son to play the game before flying up to attend the funeral.

The Dallas game was nationally televised on CBS. They had

beaten us last time and they were hungry to do it again. It was a hell of a game for the first half. The lead changed twelve times. Every time one team would start to get a significant lead, the other would come back and sink 3-pointers and steal the momentum. The score was even at the end of both quarters.

In the third quarter they went berserk and scored on about 14 of 15 possessions in a row, either with baskets or free throws. With five minutes left in the period we were only down by one, 82–81. By the end of the period the Dallas lead was 12.

Earvin was trying to play his best, but you could see that it wasn't all there. When I get involved in a game, I get so damned competitive that compassion and sensitivity can fade out of the picture. When the game became difficult for us, we all became very frustrated. We wanted it badly and we weren't getting any calls. Our defense was breaking down.

In the last period, Earvin tried to make a run at it. He started driving the lane and he was getting pounded, time after time. There were no calls, and he'd look at the official, or he'd lie on his back in the paint in frustration while the Mavericks scooped up the blocked shot and just hustled it downcourt. Then he started to force up some bad shots. I called a 20-second time-out with six and a half minutes left. They were blowing us out now and I wanted the Lakers to make one last stand. I was exhorting them and I caught his eye in the huddle and I could see that the spirit was out of him. I grabbed his jersey and said, "You're taking it from them and you're not giving anything back." He raised his face level with mine. Suddenly I remembered what had happened in his family. I caught myself and shut up.

Dallas whipped us pretty convincingly, 132–117. Derek Harper picked up the ball and reeled it up at the ceiling at the final buzzer. Motta commented that we were tired and they were rested, but it was a royal whipping. They scored 130 the first time they beat us, 132 this time. Nobody else had scored like that against us. Nobody else had beaten us twice in the season. With their 26 and 14 record, and with the personnel problems over in Houston, Dallas looked like our main competition for Western Conference leadership.

Earvin talked patiently to the reporters, dressed, then caught a cab to the airport, headed for his sister's funeral. I hugged him by the locker room door. Before leaving, he turned to the team and he said, "Stay cool, fellas."

We passed the midpoint of the season three days later: forty-two games down, forty to go. We beat the Trailblazers at the Forum on January 27th, 107–100. Earvin came back on the morning of the game on a red-eye flight. I told him to take as much time as he needed before coming back to the team. He just said, "I'm ready to play. When you're sitting there alone and thinking—that's what makes it bad."

16

First Things First

It was now the exact middle of the season. We were strong, we were out in front, but would we falter in the stretch? I worried constantly about our lack of a true backup center. We had journeymen who were learning and growing and playing their asses off, but they wouldn't stand the test if Kareem had any limiting injuries. I worried about the tendinitis that Byron Scott, James Worthy, and Earvin Johnson all experienced. I worried about the lengthy healing process of A.C. Green's hand, the slow-arriving maturity of Billy Thompson, the hotheadedness of Wes Matthews, the anger of Kurt Rambis over accepting a diminished role.

One thing I didn't have to worry about was the most important team in my life.

The point I want to make is that the first priority of a leader isn't success. Your priority is to take care of your family. Break down the barriers between family and career as much as you can. Don't let them become competing entities in your life. Chris and I are separate people, but we are also aspects of each other. We are a team. Chris and I are the core players and James is a rookie that we're bringing along, teaching him the culture of this team. Whatever we accomplish, it's something we've accomplished together.

When *Sports Illustrated* ran a profile of Michael Cooper, they concluded by observing how much Coop and Wanda, his wife, functioned as an interlocking unit. The writer said, "You get the feeling that these two people have rubbed off on each other in some important way." That's exactly how Chris and I aim to be. The career of Lakers coach is a shared experience. She is connected to me and to the team.

She invests energy in a Lakers wives' organization—whose members include Marilyn Baumeister, Karen West, Linda Lombardo, Anita Scott, Angela Worthy, Wanda Cooper, and Linda Rambis—that brings together the players and their families to accomplish some great goals.

A year ago they pulled together a charity cookbook whose proceeds fight drug abuse in the Inglewood area, the community where the Forum stands.

This year, with a maximum of input from Wanda Cooper, the wives arranged for the team to record a rap single—written by Angela Worthy—and a video, with proceeds again going to antidrug concerns. Instead of the "We are number one" stuff that other teams have done after winning a championship, our project was called "Just Say No." We had tremendous fun doing it and the reaction has been great. It just might prevent some kids from getting hooked on drugs.

All of this comes from this wonderful sense of family involvement, something Chris has made her priority. When individuals are down, she lifts them up. She has remarkable instincts for people, and she has all the skills she developed when she got her marriage and family counseling degree and certificate. That's what the Lakers are: a family. The dynamics that go on are family dynamics. There are predictable ups and downs that have to do with the cycles and rhythms of a family's life. Some family members get selfish and they need to be brought back to a team-first attitude. Some members get hurt and alienated and they need to be reminded how important they are. Chris keeps the environment positive with her direct involvement. That kind of involvement is only possible when your number one team, your family, is connected spiritually.

A lot of coaches, a lot of business managers, don't like to see their wives enter the picture. I've had discussions with other coaches and some of them say, "Oh, you've got to keep the wives out of it. Get the wives away from the team." I tell them, "What do you mean? The wives have more impact on their husbands than I can."

Managers like that recognize the power of the family, but only in a negative way. They are afraid of it. They see it as something unmanageable, something that will bring chaos. They need to take a different attitude: respect the family connections that orbit around your team and strive to keep them positive. Those connections are always going to be there. We all need people to love in our lives. The crux is that the love and the life have to work together. They have to be one set of interrelated forces.

You have to be aware, because the wives and families can become the team's allies or they can become the greatest Peripheral Opponents in the world. When jealousies build up, when unhealthy dynamics are at work, the families can rob power and distract players from their goals. Wives might envy the dedication that has to go into being a winner. They could grow to hate the sport for absorbing their man's attention. They might envy the stardom and acclaim given their husbands, especially if their husbands are so foolish that they won't share the glory. Wives might envy the position that another player has on the team, versus the glory they believe their husband should be receiving. All of a sudden, you've got someone in the inner circle who is cheering for failure. Success is the most fertile soil for resentment.

I know the dialogue that goes on after games. Somebody didn't get as much limelight as he believes he deserves. A bench player saw a starter faltering and thinks he should get that man's position. A starter saw the score shift negatively when the reserves were in and thinks those guys are a bunch of stiffs and he deserves better support.

Chris and I used to hit the freeway after games, back when I was a struggling player, and the verbal diarrhea used to flow out of me. I was angry one night, overexcited the next—tremendous mood swings. Chris was always a sounding board. And she'd be very objective. Some nights I'd be spewing venom and she'd say, "Hey, c'mon now, grow up. That isn't true. You're just angry."

Am I saying that my home life now is always perfect? No. We can disagree. We can feel frustration. We can assert our individual selves without feeling as if the marriage and the family are instantly at risk. Our child can behave like something less than an angel. But as the Lakers have to, we catch ourselves. It's easy to do because we have a commitment to ourselves as a team.

That kind of commitment has a lot to do with the success of an individual. When the Lakers won a championship in 1980, then fragmented in 1981, it was because we weren't a together team. Being a together team is more important than winning. If you're not together as a team, any success you taste is not going to last. Achieve togetherness, achieve unity of purpose, and success will come into the picture. It will come through attraction, not by force.

Picture a guy who takes a leadership job in a struggling company. He knows his work well. His home life is bad, but he compensates for that by putting all his energy into keeping the company afloat. Things might turn around. Success might show up. But will it be sustained? What happens when the core of the family no longer holds? Picture this guy looking at his great new title, his terrific car, his fat bank balance, and saying, "This doesn't mean anything. I'm hurting and I'm lonely."

Family is vital to the Lakers. Most pro basketball players are unmarried. They're young, in a profession that takes incredible time and energy and involves constant travel. They're thoroughbreds, sometimes with high-strung temperaments to match, always under competitive pressure. A lot of the women they meet are drawn by the celebrity and riches of NBA life, so it's hard for players to initiate and develop lasting relationships.

We happen to have a high percentage of married players. And even the bachelors are typically from families that have stayed intact. They all have a profound sense of how important it is to hang together.

Michael and Wanda Cooper are a great model. They have the whole team over for a gumbo party every year and you can see the younger guys checking out how happy and close they are. Coop also sees the link between family stability and championship performance. We were talking about our families one time and he told me, "The only way you can play basketball at this level, to the maximum of your ability, is if you go out feeling loose. You can't compete with stress or worries tightening you up. It works on your concentration. It makes you second-guess your instincts."

In midseason, Wes Matthews had troubles within his family. He missed one of our team flights and expected to get chewed out royally. First he called Kareem to seek advice. The two of them usually sit and talk together on the plane. Kareem told Wes, "Hey, you're all right. Just go ahead and talk to Pat. He's gonna be real. Just let him hear your side of the story." Wes called me at home and said, "I understand I haven't been 100%. I'm having a little family problem and it's taking me away from my game." I told him, "Wes, the main thing I want you to do is get your family stuff together."

Earvin told a reporter who asked about the character of the team, "When they draft or look at a person being traded to the Lakers, they look at the individual, how good a person he is. And we have some great individuals. Everybody has great family lives. And that helps, it really does."

Mychal Thompson established himself as the chief jokester and storyteller on our team. As such, he opened himself up for a lot of teasing in return. After he had been with the Lakers for a couple of months, Mychal told me, "These guys are great people. If you're down about something, they'll be the first ones to come and put an arm around you and try to pick up your spirits. But in the same breath, they'll crack a joke about you. It's like, you can tease your brothers and sisters all the time. But don't let someone from the outside do it."

James Worthy calls the Lakers "a small family." He says, "Everybody's shooting at us. It's important to have a close family as an asset."

Sustain a family life for a long period of time and you can sustain success for a long period of time. First things first. If your life is in order, you can do whatever you want.

Surprise Package

One night after our win over Portland we were in Seattle. We'd won two from them in November, including our first win of the season, holding them below 100 points each time. Each game was a barroom brawl.

This time we got pounded by the Sonics, 125–101.

Our flight was delayed and we arrived in Seattle at one P.M. on game day. The Seattle fans knew something was up. They set an attendance record of 14,634 at Seattle Center Coliseum, a building that dates back to the 1962 World's Fair. The Sonics played inspired and we played tired. Two statistical comparisons tell the story: the Lakers were outrebounded 57 to 38, and we shot 29 free throws to their 45. Seattle's forwards, Tom Chambers and Xavier McDaniel, went off on us like we had never seen them do before—37 points for Chambers, and 28 for the X-Man.

Later, when we faced Seattle in the third round of the playoffs in May, a lot of fans wondered what they were doing there, how this bunch of little-known players from the far northwestern corner of the league could be in contention for the Western Conference title. We didn't wonder about it. This night the Sonics proved that they were for real.

This was the biggest point differential against us all season, and one of the most animated and aggressive opponents we had faced. Houston and Dallas were supposed to be our competition in the West, but Seattle had a maturing, explosive team on their hands.

Back in Boston, the Celtics were on a 5-game winning streak. Our league lead held at one game. We would see Dallas again on the first Tuesday of February, and Boston would show up thirteen days afterward.

We flew straight to Phoenix from Seattle, with one day to prepare for a game on January 30th, our last contest for the month.

We arrived and immediately went to practice. I drew them into a circle for pre-practice comments. I talked passionately to the group. I challenged the frontline players, saying, "We're getting to the point where we've become very inconsistent in our rebounding. We got killed by the Hawks on the boards. We got killed by Dallas on the boards. Seattle pounded us on the boards. Even though we can win during the regular season, we're not going to be able to win in the playoffs unless we're consistent rebounding the ball. Our mentality, when the ball comes off the rim, has to be concentrated mayhem. We have to root it out, scratch, do whatever it takes to get position and get the ball."

I looked at A.C. Green. I looked at Kurt Rambis and Kareem. "You guys aren't getting the job done on a regular basis. Guys are getting career high numbers—thirty-five, twenty-seven, twenty-five points—against us at the power forward spot. People are going away from their main point of attack on offense and deciding, 'Well, let's exploit them at power forward.' We've been outrebounded in the last six games. If there's one area where we know we got beat last year by Houston, one area that we broke down in and one reason why we lost our championship, it's that we could not control the boards. And if we can't do that, we ain't going anywhere. We're bleeding in front of people and they smell the blood. If it doesn't improve quickly, we're going to have to do something."

We had a great workout at Phoenix College in the early evening. We concentrated on moving the ball, defensive fundamentals, blocking out. I showed the team our efficiency numbers, the downslide in effort. It was proof enough. We finished with drills on fast breaks after made baskets and filling the lanes after misses, getting the center to take the ball out of bounds so our power forward could run the break quicker.

Byron came out in the Phoenix game and did a great defensive job against Walter Davis, the Suns' off-guard. With some help from Cooper, he held Davis to 16, about 7 below his average. This had been one of the sore points in the last few games: heavy scoring from the opponent's off-guard position. Dale Ellis had 25 in the Seattle loss. Rolando Blackman had 20 when we lost to Dallas.

Against Phoenix, our containing, protecting, and contesting defense worked to perfection. Every time Davis caught the ball in the first option of their offense, Byron Scott and two or three other people were looming in his face. We didn't let people get into their comfortable shooting spots.

Mike Smrek hit three out of four shots in five minutes of relief time for Kareem at the end of the game. A.C. had 25 points. Shot 9 of 11 from the floor and 7 of 7 from the line. His best offensive output in weeks.

A.C. had been below double figures in scoring for eight out of the last twelve games. Teams had made some adaptations to him and he hadn't reacted right until Phoenix. They were ignoring A.C. to double-team Earvin, especially since the offensive surge that he had begun in December with games of 34, 38, and 46 points.

The double teams created offensive opportunities. A.C. was not capitalizing. Instead of taking the open shot when the ball came to him, he kept swinging it out to the weak side. He reverted to some of the deferential behavior of his rookie season. You could see him thinking through each offensive decision: "I've got a shot! Should I take it? Maybe I should! What if I miss? Will they think I'm selfish?" By the time he balanced his shoot/don't shoot impulses, the defense was up in his face and he had to pass.

I always tell my players not to stop and think. Because if they do, they'll never start again. Basketball requires a high intelligence level, but the thinking has to be automatic. They say football is a game of inches. Basketball is a game of microseconds. Timing advantages are crucial. The players that last, like Kareem, are the smart players, the ones who learn how to play with perfect economy, who know what they want to do before the situation opens up, who know what their opponent is going to do even before the opponent has it figured out.

We flew back home. It was time for our last regular-season meeting with the Dallas Mavericks. February 2nd—a big, big game for both teams. Our season series was tied two to two. For the first time in the history of the Dallas franchise, they had a clear shot at owning the bragging rights for the Western Conference.

We had two days between the games, and our preparation was extensive and excellent. A.C. drilled on fronting, denying and contesting Mark Aguirre. Kareem focused on keeping his body on James Donaldson and taking away his left-hand hook. Worthy prepared to trail Rolando Blackman close and contest every shot. We knew we needed to dig in with our defense, continuing to stress containment, protection and contesting. We had to be relentless. There could be no gaps. Offensively we had to move out quickly, execute the plays, never force them.

Dallas was coming off a road loss to Portland the night before.

The first quarter was played tight. We controlled the tip. Kareem scored first, a layup off a great pass from Earvin. We held the lead throughout the period, but they dominated the boards, 14–8. A bad omen. Especially at home.

We gave up the lead briefly in the early second quarter. Then we rebuilt a three-point advantage. We traded them score for score, free throws and field goals, on every possession over a three-minute stretch, until they evened it at 46 apiece.

Green sank two free throws. Aguirre hit a bank shot. Tied at 48.

Kareem swung up a hook shot from the lane. Derek Harper tipped in a Dallas miss. Tied at 50.

Byron fired a 3-pointer from the corner. Worthy finished a fast break with a slam dunk. Earvin swatted the ball away from Aguirre, who then stole it right back. At the end of the first half we were up, 55–50.

The rebound situation was bad. They kicked us, 26 to 14. The talk we had before our Phoenix game suddenly looked very temporary.

Rebounding is the epitome of effort areas. The team that fights for position and aggressively pursues the ball off the boards is eventually going to be the team that wins. You can be outrebounded and still win a game or even a series of games, but the toll will be taken somewhere along the line.

The third quarter was horrendous. Ironically, we started to match them on the boards. But four minutes into the period they tore off a series of shooting streaks: 6 to 2 over one minute, 6 to 2 over one and a half minutes, 6 to 2 over one and a quarter minutes. They cleaned our clocks for the period, 28 to 18. Aguirre and Blackman combined for 17.

We tried to surge back in the fourth quarter. Scott fed Worthy for a score under the basket and then hit another 3-pointer with under two minutes left in the game. But we were forced to foul in the last few seconds and the Mavericks made all their shots from the line. We lost by four, 103–99.

Dallas got something they needed. They beat us 3–2 in the season series. Their general manager called it the most significant game in the history of the franchise. Derek Harper told reporters, "We definitely feel we can win here. We had control of the game all the way down to the last couple of seconds."

A reporter carried that news to me. He said, "The Mavericks say they have a psychological edge on you." I said, "Bullshit."

"You don't think they have a physical and a psychological edge on you?"

"The reverse," I said. "They're going to be so confident now that they can't be beat, they'll be flat."

I've always sensed this with young, talented teams that are emerging and challenging the Lakers and the Celtics. They don't keep their mouths shut long enough. They win a significant game, such as the Golden State Warriors did, or a series, such as the Mavericks did, and all of a sudden they start running off at the mouth.

They just don't understand the length of the season. And they don't understand the nature of the NBA from season to season. You've got to do it night in and night out. And if you're that good, you don't feel much need to brag and posture. Talk doesn't hold confidence together. Consistent performance does.

Those teams ride the roller coaster. They boast and they feel good. They thump and pound their chests. They talk about how they're going to dominate you, how they can match up with you. "We know we can play with this team now. We've got the confidence, we've got the coaching, we've got the offense."

The next week they're down and they don't know how to deal with it. That's what Dallas was all about last year. They were a team that was talented, that was coming, but they weren't mature enough and experienced enough to deal with a full season of high expectations.

They beat us on February 2nd and it was the most significant game in the history of the franchise. To us, it was game number 45. That was our psychological edge. They knew, and we knew, that this one game wouldn't mean anything in the playoffs. Assuming they could get there.

The morning of that game, a story broke about Jerry West's ongoing conversations with Bob Bass, the general manager of the San Antonio Spurs. The trade deadline was February 15th, less than two weeks away. Mychal Thompson was the man we wanted. Thirty-two years old, 6'10" tall, he was a character, but a superintelligent ballplayer.

We had done wonders all season long. Brickowski and Rambis gave great-effort performances, trying to hold position with Kareem out. But they were forwards matched up against true centers. Smrek was a project—lots of heart, learning fast, showing flashes of substantial promise, but not yet a big-game-caliber player. We knew we needed another piece to the puzzle.

Coop and Magic used to talk about Mychal Thompson back when he was a Trailblazer. "Man, wouldn't it be nice to have a big guy like that. Someone who could run the floor, could shoot the basketball from the perimeter. Doesn't have to play with his back to the basket, can pass the ball."

"Last week we were making a little bit of progress," West told the press about the negotiations for Mychal, "but I can't say that's the case today." San Antonio hinted that Boston and Houston were willing to deal for Mychal. San Antonio was insisting on Billy Thompson, our top rookie, in trade.

"We'll continue to talk with them and see if something can be done," West said.

Shortly after, Jerry said to Randy and Bill and me, "The Mychal Thompson deal is dead." Then he said, "Even though I'm telling you it's dead right now, I think we're gonna get him. If we stay calm and in the right posture. I think San Antonio definitely wants to move him."

Sacramento came into the Forum on February 4th. The Kings were having a losing season, but they had played us tough twice and had won against the Pistons, the Warriors, the Trailblazers, and the Supersonics.

We had drilled hard after the Mavericks loss. It was predictable that the Kings would find us fired up. But nobody could have predicted how that game was going to unfold. History was made that night—the embarrassing kind.

Kareem controlled the opening tip against LaSalle Thompson, and A.C. Green scored right away on a feed from Byron Scott. Earvin scored a layup. Byron hit a jumper from the right, then a jumper from the left. A.C. scored on a follow-up shot.

Sacramento called time-out. Then A.C. dunked. Kareem dunked. A.C. sank a jump shot.

Sacramento called another time-out and substituted Eddie Johnson for Terry Tyler. Then Byron scored on a break. James Worthy dropped in his first points on a short push shot. Earvin passed to Byron on another break and Byron dunked it.

Sacramento called another time-out. A minute went by and no one scored. Then A.C. Green broke the ice with another dunk shot. Sacramento substituted Jerry Eaves for Reggie Theus. Byron Scott put a 17-footer in from the baseline. Sacramento substituted Mark Olberding for Otis Thorpe. A.C. sank two free throws. The referees called a technical and Byron made the shot.

The score was now 29 to nothing. If it had been a playground game, somebody would have said, "Let's choose up new sides."

In the final half minute, Reggie Theus was fouled by Michael Cooper and got both free throws. The score at the end of the period was 40 to 4.

The previous record for fewest points scored in a first quarter was 5. That was set by the Syracuse Nationals on November 13th, 1954. The New York Knickerbockers tied the record on November 21st, 1956. Those were the days of no shot clock, when teams would run deliberate slow-down offenses.

The odd thing is that we weren't out to administer Sacramento a whipping. They just got snakebit and their condition kept getting worse. Every time they'd come down and try to pull the trigger, you could see them squeezing harder and harder. They started forcing shots, forcing offensive situations. The ball got heavier and heavier for them. Around 20 to nothing they started to isolate on the side of the court and try to draw a foul in one-on-one play. Nothing was working.

I have tremendous respect for Phil Johnson, who was the Kings' coach, and Frank Hamblen, who was his first assistant. I say "was" because Kings management fired both of them four days later. Phil is a former Coach of the Year award winner.

There are certain coaches with whom, whether you win or lose, you can sit down and talk after a game. You go out for food and drinks, enjoy and respect each other's company. Johnson and Hamblen are like that.

Other coaches you don't even want to be around.

I started to feel for them. I was hoping somebody would score, just to break this embarrassment. But the harder they tried, the worse they choked. Our players were jubilant and high-fiving. They wanted to shut them out for the whole quarter. I tried to tone that down. You're always going to meet someone again down the road.

The Blue Team played almost half the minutes of the entire game. They ran well and played good defense. We were ahead 36 points at the half, 71 to 35, and we finished with the same margin, 128 to 92.

Chick Hearn has a favorite rap that he uses when a game has been put out of reach. In any Lakers broadcast, somewhere late in the fourth quarter, fans will hear his pronouncement, "This game is in the refrigerator. The door is closed. The lights are out." On this night, he made the claim at three minutes and forty-seven seconds into the first period.

We had an away game in Portland on the following night, a layoff for All-Star weekend, a return match with Sacramento, and our second Indiana Pacers game. Then we faced Boston—Game Two of the regular-season series—the last meeting until the playoffs.

I was concerned about one small detail on the way to Portland. Three players would leave afterward for Seattle, scheduled to play in the All-Star game there. The other nine Lakers had a midseason holiday and were ready to scatter for all parts of the country—some back to L.A., some to points east.

Instead of just thinking about the game, they were packing bags, calling their hometown friends and their families, making travel arrangements. They were anticipating getting home and not anticipating playing in the game. They were together in the flesh, but mentally they were completely scattered, not living in the present moment.

You can never overlook the mental aspect of basketball. Any good athlete is ready to play a game, soon as they can get their legs into a pair of shorts and sneakers laced on their feet. But are they prepared? That's a different matter.

Ask a bum on the street if he's ready to take a million-dollar-a-year executive position. He'll usually say "Yes!" But would he be prepared?

I didn't hear one person talking about the game against Portland. Not on the plane, not on the bus, not when we arrived at the hotel. Everyone was asking Gary Vitti about their connections. "Should I check out of the hotel early? Do you have the tickets? What time does my flight leave?"

I entered the locker room that night seething mad. "Shut up!" I said. "Stop being concerned about your travel plans and let's get focused on the Portland Trailblazers."

Lack of focus cost us that game. I hate the pain of losing, but I really can't stand the misery of giving one away. We came into the fourth quarter with an 84 to 76 lead. Within four minutes they drew up to an 88–88 tie. We stayed within one or two points of each other to the very last.

At nine seconds left we were ahead by one. Then we fouled Terry Porter. Defensive switches weren't made quickly enough. He was allowed to turn the corner and Kareem bumped him with a hip. Porter went to the line and made both shots. Portland was up 105 to 104.

We called time out and ran a play with four seconds on the clock. James Worthy got the ball at the top of the key and had an open wing to the basket. He took the ball in, ready to jam it. He would have dunked it, would have sealed the game at 106–105, but the ball just slipped out of his hands when he squeezed it for a one-hand grip as he launched toward the rim. A.C. had a brief chance for a follow-up shot and missed. In twenty-four hours we went from setting records for dominating an opponent to losing.

The All-Star weekend was a nice break. We had Kareem and Earvin and James representing the Lakers, plus Byron Scott and Michael Cooper competing in the 3-point shootout. Randy and Bill were there. So was Chris.

She flew up with Steve and Holly Chabre, two of our closest friends. On Friday night I led the four of us in search of an important NBA reception. We tried one hotel after another with no luck. Holly and Chris didn't seem to enjoy battling the steep streets of downtown Seattle in their high heels. I was positive we'd find the right place eventually, but the troops were starting to doubt my leadership. Finally, someone checked a schedule and learned that the reception was on Saturday. Steve pictured the next morning's headlines: "All-Star Coach Lost, Last Seen Walking to Tacoma." He offered to help me find the Kingdome on game night.

Even with a letdown against Portland, we still had the best record in the league. We had come back from all the gloom and doom about losing to Houston. Nobody considered that news current anymore. We wouldn't look at Dallas again until the playoffs—theoretically.

My only worry on All-Star weekend was whether the West players would stand up and boo me when I entered the locker room. This was my fifth All-Star game in the last six years, thanks to the Lakers' having had the best record in the conference. But I had won only one and lost three. I was starting to feel like the All-Star jinx.

It turned into a great All-Star game—went right down to the wire. Ralph Sampson had had arthroscopic knee surgery and was replaced by Tom Chambers of the Sonics. Hometown hero gets a chance. He ended up the MVP of the game.

We were behind with three seconds to go. We ran an out-of-bounds play for Rolando Blackman and he drove the baseline and drew a foul. When he went to the line Isiah Thomas was talking in his face, trying to make him crack up.

Blackman didn't blink. He sank both free throws, the game went into overtime, and the West team won it going away.

Right after the All-Star break we flew back to L.A. and re-grouped the team to visit the Sacramento Kings at their home court.

Sacramento was now coached by Jerry Reynolds, the former second assistant, when we arrived at their arena on February 10th. He had been the head guy for twenty-four hours.

Jerry's from deep in basketball country—French Lick, Indiana, the hometown of Larry Bird. He has a great sense of humor. He was going to need it. The Kings got behind right away and were in a struggling posture the rest of the game. The game was another blow-out. Tamer than the last one, but very definitive. We won it by a score of 114 to 98.

The moon was full on Friday, February 13th. Jack Ramsey had brought his young Indiana Pacers team into town.

Early in the morning I mused over two related stories in local papers. The *Daily News* reported, "Lakers Look for Backup." The story focused on Petur Gudmundsson's rehabilitation work since his back surgery in November. He was lifting weights, riding a bike, and running in water. His biggest recent milestone was running a half mile. But any hope for his return this season in fighting condition was very remote. The other story said the NBA trading deadline was two days away. The writer wondered if there was still time for the Lakers' general manager to produce a miracle.

Earvin sat out the shootaround that day with a sore Achilles tendon.

Indiana used Herb Williams, their 6′11″ forward, to jump at the start of the game, instead of Steve Stipanovich, their 7′ center, a guy we had inquired about in the preseason. Kareem controlled the tip to Byron Scott. A.C. Green hit a free throw, made a steal, and blocked a shot on Chuck Person, their Rookie of the Year candidate. Kareem, Earvin, and James scored quickly and we had a 7–0 lead.

Indiana regrouped behind a time-out and scored twice. We surged again—a run of 9 to 2. Our veteran talent and game wisdom drew them into committing several fouls. Their rookie talent and young legs kept them coming right back into contention. Indiana closed to within 4 points by the end of the period.

But the most excitement was being generated above the court, by an unknown. Up at the press tables, halfway to the rafters, a Forum assistant passed down the press rows and handed each TV, radio, and print reporter a bulletin. The news was brief: we had finally acquired the missing piece to our puzzle. Mychal Thompson was now a Laker.

West and Bob Bass, the Spurs' general manager, had finally set terms. Our 1987 number one draft pick, some cash, Petur Gudmundsson, and Frank Brickowski were exchanged for Mychal. He would come to town, receive a bare-bones introduction to the Laker system, and be available for our game against Boston on the 15th.

Down on the floor, Indiana closed the second quarter strong. They were up 55 to 50 at halftime.

The third quarter turned into the Earvin and Byron show. Our guards scored 21 of our 30 points, and they actually outscored Indiana for the period. We took a 5-point lead into the fourth quarter and maintained it to the end for a 113–108 win. Earvin finished with 40 for the night.

Down in San Antonio, Mychal Thompson turned in his silver and black San Antonio Spurs uniform to the equipment manager. Over in Boston, Larry Bird was heard to say, "If San Antonio needed money, we would've sent them money. But to go and help the Lakers like that is just terrible."

Celtics at
the Forum

Back in November I had told the players, "You've got to do it on your own," and they took that attitude. But without one more exceptional player on the squad, they would have to be perfect, and no team can be perfect across a whole season.

The team learned about the trade in practice, before the Indiana game. They were ecstatic. Earvin was being advised by the doctors to rest his sore Achilles tendon, but he was too excited to stay off the court.

Mychal was probably the last person to know about the trade. It was a game day in San Antonio and he was resting at home for the Clippers, watching the afternoon soap operas. His phone was unplugged, so none of the calls from Spurs management could get through.

He drove in to the HemisFair Arena and walked down to the

June of 1987 was a time for savoring. Earvin and I celebrated with a Caribbean fishing trip. Mychal Thompson was right: Folks in the Bahamas love the Lakers.

Earvin always has a positive attitude. Look how happy he is, even though he caught the smallest fish.

This trophy from the ocean was exciting, but the ones we take from Boston are the ultimate thrill.

Chris and me following the rules of the Bahamas. Eight days of sweet relaxation.

My basketball coach at Linton High in Schenectady, New York, was Walt Przybylo. Walt was always trying to make a few profound ideas stick in our heads. We didn't always listen. But nowadays, when my back is against the wall, some of those messages come back. My teammate is Ben Winslow.
(© SCHENECTADY GAZETTE)

Adolph Rupp was one of the true legends of college basketball coaching. He was stern and he kept us thoroughly drilled. No distractions allowed, just hard work and lots of it. We made it to the NCAA finals in 1966. My teammates are Cliff Berger (45) and Thad Jaracz.
(© TIME, INC.)

With the help of Bill Bertka *(foreground, holding basketball)* and Randy Pfund *(background, white shirt)*, I emphasize an offensive point at our Palm Springs training camp. No other NBA team has such great assistant coaches.
(© John McDonough/ SPORTS ILLUSTRATED)

Fire-breathing time. The practice plan in my back pocket shows hours of detailed preparation. The rant-and-rave expression on my face shows immediate reaction. You need both. Once the game begins, you cannot stop to think.

Coach Bertka, the Administrator of All Things, checks in for preseason strategy sessions in Montecito, near Santa Barbara. Bill has held every job you can get in basketball, from ticket-taker to General Manager. One of his particular strengths is coaching big men.

My video room at home. There are always tapes we have to review, our own and our up-coming opponents'. Every year we put together a highlight tape. I want the players to remember how much work it took to get on top, and how great we felt when we made it.
(© *John McDonough/ SPORTS ILLUSTRATED*)

Earvin Johnson and Kareem Abdul-Jabbar. Two of the greatest in basketball history. We've worked together so long, sometimes our communication is almost telepathic. I totally depend on their leadership within the team.
(*Andrew D. Bernstein*)

June of 1986. We lost to the Rockets and the grass wouldn't grow in our yard for months. Fortunately, I had my buddy, James Patrick.

James always believes we are Number One. Or else he's telling me what play to call.

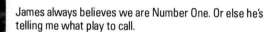

Christmas of 1987. The Riley team with their top rookie. We have a busy household, but we put a high priority on staying connected. We try to keep a family feeling within the Lakers, too.
(© Cliff Kramer/Nathanson's Photography)

One name could never be enough for this guy. Earvin is the everyday good-hearted friend. Buck is the energetic, tough-as-nails player who is all over the court. Magic is the center of fun at every party and an amazing, unstoppable force in every game.
(© Malek Abdul-Mansour)

Michael Cooper, the pride of Albuquerque and the '86-'87 Defensive Player of the Year. Earvin, who won NCAA and NBA championships in consecutive years. Byron Scott, one of the most dangerous shooters in the league and an elite off-guard. They're a tight trio on the court, and off. *(Andrew D. Bernstein)*

Kareem stuffs emphatically in Game Six. In spite of early foul trouble, Kareem's performance in our championship game was his most awesome of the year. In a life-or-death game, he's the first person I'd choose.
(© Malek Abdul-Mansour)

The ultimate moment: Winning the '84-'85 championship at Boston Garden after being humiliated in the Memorial Day Massacre. The big question: How do we top it? Gary Vitti, the best trainer in the league, is at my right. *(© Barry Chin/THE BOSTON HERALD)*

Coop climbs James Worthy at the final buzzer of Game Six. James cracked it open for us with his incredible steal and full-extension dive to create a third quarter fast break. *(© Malek Abdul-Mansour)*

(Page following.) Earvin and Kareem in the background, me and team owner Jerry Buss in the foreground. Champagne on everybody and everything, including the trophy that says we're the top team of '86-'87. Our goal is to go above and beyond. That's what Show Time means. *(© Andrew D. Bernstein)*

locker room thinking he'd spend the evening on the bench, waiting
to relieve Artis Gilmore in the low post. He slipped on his shorts
and sat up on the trainer's table, waiting to have his ankles taped.
The trainer walked into the room, took one look at Mychal, and
said, "I don't tape the enemy."

He arrived in Los Angeles the following morning. One local
paper greeted him with the headline: "Thompson May Not Be the
Player Lakers Need."

The writer of that article, Mitch Chortkoff, wondered why we
went after a player that two other Western Conference teams had
traded within a single season. He said that although Mychal was the
first player taken in the NBA draft nine years ago, he had had only
a mildly successful career. He said Mychal had the reputation of being
a soft player, not physical. He questioned the price we had paid, not
because it seemed too high, but because it seemed too low. We didn't
give up our number one rookie, yet we were still able to outbid
Houston and Boston for Mychal's services.

Now, playing devil's advocate is one way sportswriters sustain
their careers—but wait a minute. Two of our toughest rivals, Boston
and Houston, also wanted Mychal Thompson. Why would they be
interested in a "soft . . . mildly successful" player? Check the Portland Trailblazers book and you'll find several team records connected
to Mychal's name. Mildly successful players don't score in double
figures for eight consecutive seasons.

This year Portland had a new coach, Mike Schuler. They had
gotten into a rebuilding frame of mind. They were looking to go with
Sam Bowie at center, so they traded Mychal to the Spurs in June.
Then Bowie broke a leg five games into the season. If Bowie would
have broken his leg earlier, Mychal would probably still be a Trailblazer today. But scenarios shift.

Sometimes it simply becomes time for a player or a coach or a
general manager to move on. Jack Ramsey left the Portland coaching
job in 1986, going on to Indiana. The Pacers won 41, exactly half
their games. A year before they had won only 26. There's a 15-game
improvement. But look at the chemistry. Indiana was a real young
team—tremendous rookie talent combined with one of the toughest
disciplinarians around. Coach and team matched up well. In the
meantime, Schuler took Ramsey's old team and made it perform
better. Portland improved by nine games. Schuler, deservedly, was
named Coach of the Year.

At San Antonio there was another first-year coach, Bob Weiss. He also wanted to put together a younger team. Mychal's salary could be used for some young players who might possibly be two or three years away from star potential. Larry Krystkowiak, a 6'9", 220-pound rookie out of Montana, was showing potential. He could take over some of the playing time initially earmarked by the Spurs for Mychal.

Meanwhile, the Lakers needed a developed, versatile star player. Right now. The Spurs were looking at a long-term development program. We were looking at a championship drive in progress. Mychal was a prize for us. We can see him serving three or four years, at least, switching between center and forward. He brought in tremendous intelligence, conditioning, and discipline.

Four months after the acquisition, at seven in the morning, June 15th, the day after we won a world's championship, Mychal Thompson was in the weight room, pumping iron. He knows he has a chance in Los Angeles to be a vital part of a winning team over a span of years—something that had eluded him for nine years. He has the skills and the character to make the best of this special moment in his life. That's why we gave up a lot for him.

It's chemistry that makes basketball teams great. You have to look at whether a player can meld into your situation, not whether somebody else decided to trade him.

Boston came into the Forum on a hot streak. Their record was identical to ours: 37 wins versus 12 losses. They had won 10 of their last 11 games. The Celtics' only loss in that stretch was in overtime to Atlanta on the Hawks' home court. They had ripped through three straight Western Conference opponents on the road. McHale scored their first 11 points against Denver. An article headline in the L.A. *Times* asked, "Is Celtics' McHale Unstoppable?" There was talk they might sweep the whole trip.

We were coming off that shaky win over Indiana. It looked like a ripe moment for Boston to assert some dominance.

Saturday, February 14th, the day before the game, was James Patrick's second birthday party. At first he was happy to see the other kids playing on his slide and playing with his toys. But after about an hour he started to get territorial. He bit one kid on the shoulder. Then he smacked another kid with his little plastic guitar. About the time we got all that cooled down, he wanted to shove a girl off his slide. Like most any two-year-old, James needed to learn more about sharing. But he was displaying the kind of attitude that I hoped the

Lakers would have against a hated opponent. The Lakers needed to stake out their territory.

Bill Bertka met with Mychal on the morning of the game. The two of them spent an hour going over the basics of the Laker offense. Bill told him, "If you remember half of these plays, you're a genius." After the game Mychal said, "You're looking at a certified genius, 'cause I remembered them all."

Normally I don't like a guy we just acquired to play immediately. Maybe they'll get some time if the game is a blowout, but never any significant minutes. This was different. We were confident that Mychal could already play our style.

We came out playing like we had in our home game against Atlanta: we were playing to hold them off. Boston was playing to win. By the middle of the first period they were 10 points ahead of us. Earvin collected six free throws driving the lane, plus three buckets, to score 12 of our next 16 points. We closed to a four-point deficit at the end of the first period.

Mychal Thompson opened our scoring in the second quarter with a short hook from the right. James Worthy dropped in a finger roll from Mychal's assist, then Mychal hit another right-side hook. Earvin stole the ball from Kevin McHale and fed James on the break. We were tied at 36 with nine minutes left in the period.

Boston edged ahead over the next six minutes. McHale was connecting in the lane. Instead of matching his baskets, we committed turnovers. Danny Ainge capped the period with a 3-point jumper from 25 feet out in the final second. We were behind 58–50 at the intermission. Byron had shot 3 for 12. Kareem was 1 for 4. Coop was 0 for 3 from the floor and 0 for 2 from 3-point range. Defensively, A.C. was nonexistent. McHale had scored 7 of 11. We were lucky to be that close.

Boston is a team that can paralyze you—like a fighter who comes out and lands a couple of quick right hooks. They were so flawless in executing their offense in the first half. They made it look simple. We were embarrassed by how inept they had made us look. But the slow, deliberate style of the Boston offense makes them a team you can always get back at.

The second half started out as the Larry Bird/Kevin McHale clinic. By mid-period they had combined for 12, and Boston had us down by 17 points, 75–58. Then we got aggressive. We started to assert that this was going to be our party. Cooper, James, Earvin, and Mychal tore off a 14 to 2 run over a five-minute stretch. After nearly three scoreless minutes, Boston got back three points with a free throw by Bird and a driving lay-in from Dennis Johnson. We inbounded with only four seconds left. When Earvin crossed the midcourt line, there was only one second left in the period. He pushed the ball at the basket from 45 feet out. The buzzer sounded. The ball nestled in. We were within four.

The fourth quarter was a war. In three minutes we took a one-point lead. They took it back until the final minute and a half. At that point, Coop came sprinting up the middle, running our fast break. He dropped a soft bounce pass to Earvin on the right wing as they crossed midcourt. Danny Ainge turned to defend the right side of the key as Earvin started his dribble and turned up his speed a half-notch with each bounce of the ball. When the two players were almost touching, Earvin threw a shoulder fake to his left and then bent at his waist, put his head down, and lunged to the right. Ainge shifted his weight to keep Earvin forced outside. At the instant their bodies brushed together, Earvin spun a full circle clockwise and accelerated, gathering up the ball. He took a long step and delivered a soft, underhand layup. Ainge, with his hands up in the air, spun around in Earvin's wake like a traffic cop on a turntable.

At the final second, Bird missed a desperation 3-pointer that could have sent the game into overtime. We won, 106–103. We had swept the season series.

"I had a terrible game," Kareem said afterward in the locker room. "A couple of other guys did, too. But we just kept playing hard. We just kept coming."

Kareem's streak of scoring in double figures was in serious trouble, until free throws at the end gave him an even 10. Mychal got 10 of his own, plus 4 rebounds and a couple of deflected passes. He proved it was possible to learn a new offense overnight.

Bertka told me, "I've never seen anybody come in off the street like that and do so much in a first game."

Jerry West had proved what he could do. After months of careful waiting and watching, he landed the deal of the season. Now we had all the parts. Mychal had proved what he could do. Now the Lakers had to prove something. That they could be champions again.

Salt Palace Explosion

Two events took the luster off our Boston win right away. First, the Utah Jazz whipped the Celtics by 20 points on the following night, 109–89. Either the Jazz were better than we realized, or we weren't as great as we thought. Then, on the 17th, two days after our nationally televised win over the defending champions, Moses Malone handed us our heads.

The Washington Bullets came into the Forum as 12-point underdogs. They were just five games over .500 for the season. Malone had failed to start against Phoenix the night before, suffering from flu and dizzy spells. We were coming off a tremendous confidence-building win. I told the team at our Monday practice, "We've won our glamour game with Boston. Now we have to get down to normal business."

The Bullets are a power lineup, with Moses doing most of the damage inside. It's the M and M show—Moses Malone and Jeff

Malone. They take about 57% of the shots on the team. Our game plan was to never leave Moses alone in front of the post—take away his spot, double-team every pass in to him. We needed a tight rotation because of their great rebounding. Offensively, we wanted to jump out and run on them.

With 8:25 left in the game, Moses took a spill in the lane and stayed down for a long time. He got up, looked a little groggy. Put in one of the two free throws. Then he cut loose an inhuman display of rebounding and scoring. While we were held to 15 points, Moses Malone scored 5 and pulled down 12 rebounds. They whipped us solidly, 114–99. Our third home loss and also the worst one.

I don't think there was any doubt that we played flat after our Boston win—just like the post-Boston loss to Detroit in December. We had played one game as if it was for a world's championship. Then we played the subsequent game like an exercise we had to get through. Against opponents who, if you don't have your game together, can absolutely kill you.

Sometimes, when you augment a team, everyone else decides it's their chance to take life easier. We needed to maintain our effort level and add Mychal to it, not take the attitude that he had arrived to carry the burden.

A year before, we added Maurice Lucas to augment our rebounding. He became our leading rebounder, but other players actually declined in that area. I didn't want to see our effort-area play go down just because we had brought in a great player. We still had to play disciplined. That aspect of our performance was slipping away. We hadn't played well in seven of our last ten games. We were cruising. It felt like that "We'll turn it on for the playoffs" mentality.

I had another concern relating to Mychal. He was making an impact, which we needed. I found myself writing in a game summary: "We don't win games without Thompson." But there are only so many minutes in a game. His time came at the expense of Kurt Rambis and A.C. Green, the other power forwards.

Even though our players welcomed Mychal with open arms, Kurt's attitude began to change. His contribution was lessened and I think he felt down. And I think A.C. was looking over his shoulder, too.

Kurt had already had to accept A.C. Green's starting. It was easy to see how it benefited the team. A.C. became a more solid contributor and Kurt's role, as measured in minutes played, actually changed very little. He was still the first power forward off the bench. His minutes were almost as high as Green's.

Now, Mychal Thompson took away that part of the rotation. There were games where we didn't play Kurt at all in the second half. We had the potential for a really negative situation within the team. Fortunately, Kurt showed class.

I thought back to when we made a reserve out of Jamaal Wilkes, in order to bring James Worthy into a starting role. Jamaal had been one of the greatest forwards in team history. Coach Paul Westhead once described his elegant jump shot as descending "like snow falling off a bamboo leaf." Everyone deferred to Jamaal. Even though his skills were in decline with injuries and age, the transition hurt his pride. He still had three years left on his contract, with two and a half million dollars guaranteed. You could see him sitting there wondering, "Why are they treating me like this?" It hung like a veil over the team. He got to where he wanted to be traded. He had to go through half a season with the Clippers before he realized for himself that retirement was the right choice.

Kurt's greatest asset has always been his fire. He brings a level of exertion into the game that gets multiplied as it rubs off on the other guys on the court. He not only achieves points and rebounds and blocked shots in his own right, he also inspires everyone else to kick themselves into gear. But the coming of Mychal Thompson put him, for the second time in the season, at a crossroads. Could he keep feeding his essential positive qualities into the team while he dealt with feeling alienated? It was a pending question. I think everyone on the Lakers was wondering.

We flew into Denver for a game on the 18th. The first of four consecutive road games. I called a team meeting as soon as we arrived, wanting to sound a warning.

"We have become a perimeter team," I said. "I still want all of you to feel free to shoot the ball when you're open. But we can't win games from the outside. We are going to win championships going in to the low post. Going to Kareem. Going to James. Going to Earvin. The perimeter shots should come off of initiating the offense from the inside out."

In other words, I wanted the ball constantly going inside. Make the defense react. Make them go down and double team. Now, if Kareem or James sends the ball back outside, it's fine to take your shot. Just don't treat the outside jumper as your first option. You've got to be a post-up team in this league to win championships.

It's the same thing as a great football team. The best way to establish a good passing game is to run the ball. The best way to be able to run the ball is to open up the passing lanes. Create balance. Keep the defense loosened up.

The players gave me a dubious look. I read in their eyes, "Oh, we're going to go back to the way we were last year. We're going to go back to being predictable."

Kareem hadn't been as involved in the offense recently. His average scoring in the last six games had dropped to 14 points. I said, "Fellas, you've got one of the greatest centers of all time here. Don't take this too far. What we did in training camp didn't mean that Kareem wasn't going to shoot the ball anymore, you know. Just keep in mind where our top gun is. He's not the only focus of our offense, but we still need to get him the ball when he's got a good shot. Two thirds of our shots have been coming from long range. Two thirds. That won't get it done, fellas."

Our timing was going bad. Kareem would get position, but before the ball could be delivered, defenses would shift. Or three seconds would elapse and he'd have to move out of his spot.

So we made some commitments prior to that Denver game. We were going to drive the ball and pound it inside a little more. We'd make certain that Earvin brought the ball upcourt in critical situations. Pressure the wing to high post passes in Denver's offense and double team Alex English inside twelve seconds on the shot clock.

We won at Denver 128–122. Kareem had 25 points in 35 minutes, plus 11 rebounds. But we also let them back into the game three times. That's not unusual against the running, gunning, passing game of the Nuggets.

It was a beautiful ride out to the airport. A clear, crisp, tranquil day. Deep snow all around. We read the reviews of our performance in the newspaper and felt very satisfied.

Out at Stapleton Airport, getting ready to fly to Chicago, I heard Bertka say, "Goddamnit! Another three hundred dollars down the drain!" I said, "What did you do?"

"I left my glasses in my room."

"Call the hotel. Have them send the maid up. They'll have the glasses sent to you in Chicago."

Bertka got his glasses back. He spent his day constantly on the phone with Rick Weinstein, the Lakers' computer analyst. Rick was giving us constant updates on our shooting charts. Bill compared the last ten games to ten from the same period last year and confirmed his point: we were becoming shot happy. Our offense was becoming undisciplined. Bill always keeps a finger on the pulse of the team and lets me know the trends, good and bad.

I dropped an idea on the team that caused them to believe NBA pressure had finally ruined my brains. Every time you play Chicago, the first order of business is to contain Michael Jordan. He's the leading scorer in the league and one of the most dangerous guys to try to defend. I said, "Push Jordan to the ball." They looked at me cross-eyed. I said, "I'll pass that by you again. Let Michael Jordan catch the ball. Let him get the first option pass, then stunt designated players to him. Make him see five Laker uniforms. Make him give up the ball. Retreat. Deny him position for the second pass. He likes to go to the low post. Make him have to constantly go to the second and third effort to score."

Michael Jordan is such a talented, creative, explosive player that people don't see how much of his game is based on pure effort. He is always in a crouch, ready to spring, like a jaguar stalking its prey. His head is down, his knees are bent and his butt is down. He moves slowly and intently, then he uncoils powerfully towards the basket. Jerry West gave him the ultimate pro compliment when he said, "I'd pay to see him play."

Jordan was averaging 37 points per game, which accounts for exactly 37% of the Bulls' offense. We restricted him to just below his average. Earvin said, "You know it's going to be 'The Michael Jordan Show.' What you hope to do is not go out and let him make it 'The Michael Jordan Spectacular Show.' " We won, 110–100. We were the first team to win 40 games in the season. We started to think we could sweep the trip.

We flew into Philadelphia on Saturday and put up at the Hershey Hotel. Our practice was scheduled for the gym at the Philadelphia School of Pharmacy and we gathered in the lobby to go over there. But first I heard Bertka yelling, "Goddamnit. I lost my glasses again. I left them on the airplane this time."

I said, "Why don't you get a string and keep them around your neck?"

"I've had a hell of a year, for Christ's sake," Bertka said.

Stories broke on the morning of the Philadelphia game about

Kareem's financial misadventures. Alex English had had him served with papers after the Denver game. It was a repercussion from the multimillion-dollar suit Kareem had filed against his former business manager, who was also the manager for English and a few other NBA players. Allegedly, money from various players was combined in some restaurant and real estate ventures that weren't very closely managed.

It wasn't my role to pry into it. The press had that covered, anyway. There were long, detailed stories in the *Times* and the *Herald*, which were picked up all around the country. They made it look as if he were broke, down and out, begging. Which was definitely not the case. It hurt me tremendously to see Kareem going through this nightmare, but he handled it with class, dignity and strength.

It's a necessity in this sport to be able to focus, to have tunnel vision. Kareem showed no sign of becoming distracted or fragmented or out of sync. He didn't act frustrated. He didn't take it out on the team. He didn't come to any of the games unprepared. The story was all through the papers for weeks, but his character and his every-day demeanor never changed.

I asked him a couple of times, "Are you okay?" He said, "I'm fine. Everything's cool and it's being taken care of. It's not the easiest situation, but we're gonna be okay."

The Philly game was on CBS, Sunday at noon. In the first half there was no anticipation on defense. We just let Andrew Toney and Charles Barkley do whatever they wanted. By this point in the season, Philadelphia had broken down into an isolation-oriented team. They'd set up Toney one-on-one against Scott, or they isolated Barkley against A.C. Green.

We were down by 3 at the quarter, by 6 at the half and by 11 in the early third quarter before we took control. A.C. lifted us with 9 points in the period, 6 of them off the offensive glass. We finished with a 94-point tie and went into overtime.

With six seconds left in the overtime period and the game tied at 110, we called a time-out. We set up a play we call "line."

Cooper handled the inbounds pass. He's our most reliable passer for these situations, tall enough to see over defenders and quick enough to exploit any opening. Everyone else formed a line in front of the ball between halfcourt and the top of the key. Kareem was at the high post on the left side of the basket. James Worthy was at the back of the line. He looped around the first two guys. Earvin stepped out high, and Kareem set a solid pick for James. Coop got the ball and sent it right where it was supposed to go, directly to Worthy. James was supposed to send it inside to Kareem, but he saw an opening. He put his head down and made a running, right-handed hook shot off his left foot. A leaping leaner. There were only three seconds left on the clock. It was a great win.

A reporter asked me after the Philadelphia game, "Are the Lakers the best team in the NBA now? You just beat the Celtics and the Seventy-sixers on national TV, two Sundays in a row." I told him, "We're on the brink of greatness or disaster." I looked around at the players. They were getting dressed, joking with each other, talking into microphones for the media. I said, "It's up to them."

There was still a long road to go. The playoffs still seemed distant, just like finals week in college always seemed distant when you were finished with midterm exams. The Lakers could go on to be recognized as truly great. Or they could go off the end of the earth.

The last game of our road swing was against the Phoenix Suns. We were set to play them back-to-back, once in Phoenix and once in L.A. Earvin sat out both games to rest his legs. Earvin's a tough player. He always plays banged up and hurt. Every opportunity, The Little Kahuna treats him with ice packs and ultrasound to take the bruises and the inflammations down. But the reporters, especially this time of the year, start asking me, "When are you going to decrease his minutes?" And they're asking him the same thing: "When are you going to take it easy?" That's a peripheral opponent talking. All players have to watch out about listening to this kind of talk.

Here we were, a couple games in front of the Celtics, lined up against a team we could probably beat without him. Meanwhile, I was pushing to take our concentration off the fatigue and the injuries. Everyone else has those factors, too. If we handle ours better, we can maintain an advantage.

Nobody knows better than the player himself whether he ought to stay out. Vitti and I have debates from time to time about specific cases. There are some injuries that create risk. You've got to lay out or you're taking a chance on having a worsened condition or a permanent impairment. With other things, it's best to play through them, not allow them to restrict you.

Michael Cooper got his chance to run the offense. He piled up very good numbers and we won both games, 97–93 and 99–91. But it was obvious we were missing Earvin. Michael can run the offense just as well as Earvin when it comes to calling plays and getting the ball to the right people. But when it comes to beating pressure defenses, Earvin can create unlike anyone else. Stress time, for Earvin, is simply opportunity time.

Coop got a new understanding of the stress that goes with running the point. "Thank God you're coming back," he told Earvin. "I'll never bitch about playing time again. I don't want to play forty-five minutes a night with all that pressure on me."

Phoenix came right at Coop. They saw a big opportunity in playing the Lakers when their star playmaker and scorer was out. They did a hell of a job pressuring us out of our offense. Both games came right down to the wire. If Phoenix had not had so many injury problems of their own, they could have won both.

With Earvin on the bench, more of the offensive focus returned to Kareem—and not just skyhooking. In the last minute of the first half, Cooper missed a jump shot. The ball took a hard bounce and went deep into the left corner of the court, right in front of our bench. Kareem was closest and he chased it down. Then he spun back to the basket. I heard voices: "Do it, Cap!" "Throw it down!" "Go for it!" Meantime, Larry Nance, the Phoenix forward, figured Kareem would be working to get the ball inside, so he failed to come out and harass defensively. So Kareem calculated for a half second. He squared to the basket and stretched up full height into a soft jump. Then he arched a 25-footer. Nice backspin. Dropped straight into the hoop. His first and only 3-point shot in eighteen years of NBA basketball.

I looked down the bench and said, "Who told him to shoot it?" All the confession I needed was the grin on Earvin Johnson's face.

In the second Phoenix game, Kareem stole a pass with one minute left in the game. Then he dribbled on the run for 70 feet and slammed it.

Earvin came back for our next game—February 27th against the Golden State Warriors. Chris Mullin had 14 first-quarter points and they maintained a lead on us until the middle of the second period.

Earvin scored our first 8 points for the second period and assisted on the next 4. That was enough to start a rally that had us ahead 60 to 57 at the half. In the third we scored 11 straight points and stopped their offense cold for three minutes. The Warriors never got back in the game. We finished 121–109. Billy Thompson got eighteen minutes of playing time. Still a little mistake-prone. Picking up fouls that could have been avoided. Turning over the ball. But the talent package was still exciting, the quickness and the leaping ability. I wanted to see him keep coming along. I hoped Billy would be a surprise piece in the arsenal when the playoffs began.

We flew into Salt Lake City on the next day, the 28th. The team's attitude was hangdog. There was a sense of subconscious disrespect: "We've won six in a row. What do you want from us? You're overcoaching us. This is the last place in the world we want to be."

We dumped the game. It was a miserable effort and I absolutely exploded, as I explained in chapter 2. When I yanked open the locker room door to make my exit, Frank Brady of the *Herald* almost fell into the room, ear first.

The last resort is getting angry. I had to do something, though, to rebel against what was happening. Peripheral opponents were intruding on the team's mentality. Dissension loomed on the roster. A Dog Days attitude threatened to cost us our position as league leaders and the homecourt advantage in the playoffs.

New Commitment

Let the locker room situation hang for a while, I decided.

The last step in our responsibilities to each of the games on our schedule is filling out the Final Look. This is a one-page summary of key material such as matchups, reminders about our game plan, and ideas for the next time we'll face the same opponent. When you review the Final Look pages for a season, you get a barometer of the team's performance. Even more so, you get the coaching staff's frame of mind.

Here's what Bill Bertka wrote in the Final Look after the Utah game: "Not getting back . . . Very indifferent attitude . . . Nightmare . . . ATTITUDE . . . WHY? . . . Hate success? Hate winning?"

In any classic story, you've got somebody going up against the odds. Think of Humphrey Bogart and Katharine Hepburn in *The African Queen*. They make up their minds to torpedo the German gunboat that rules over Lake Victoria. To get the job done, they have to pilot their leaky old boat through vicious rapids and past hillside gun emplacements. Then they have to pull her through stagnant waters that are full of leeches. Finally they have to experience some luck, when the Germans blunder into their torpedoes.

At the start of the season the Lakers had a mission, just like Bogart and Hepburn. The big lake was the playoffs and the gunboat was the Houston Rockets.

Everything grew out of the fact that we were underdogs. That was the realistic view of most expert basketball observers. The team used their underdog status to develop some toughness. The more that Twin Towers stuff got rubbed in the Lakers' faces, the more they took the attitude that those guys were like big redwoods. We were going to start chopping and chopping. When the time was right, we were going to take our saws around to the other side of those redwoods and say, "Which way do we want them to fall? To the left or over to the right?" The whole Lakers team was stoked by that vision. Every time someone called us "too short," every time we read the stories that said "the aging Lakers" must trade so-and-so, we strengthened our attitude.

We had been running roughshod over the league for years. People loved to see us get buried. They wanted us to be so bad so quick that they weren't using good judgment. They painted a picture that the Rockets were a dynasty in the making. In truth, the Rockets were a young, hungry team with plenty of talent but also plenty of problems. Dissension between Sampson and management. Drug use. Unreasonable expectations.

Like the Lakers in '79, the Rockets submerged their problems long enough to win a championship. But that didn't make them a championship team. Management didn't help foster their growth as champions. They gave Akeem Olajuwon a $25 million contract, and they renewed the coach's contract, but they slighted Ralph Sampson and Rodney McCray. Even before the drug problems hit, I told a journalist, "It'll be interesting to see what happens to Houston this year. I have a feeling they might fragment." I said that because I know what subconscious sabotage can do. I've seen it in action. I've been part of it.

When I was a player I sat on the bench nearly all the time. I was just as eager as anyone else to be a star, but my physical skills were those of a bench player. I used to see Gail Goodrich out there, starting every game, averaging around 25 points. When the coach brought him out to rest, it was as if his career were threatened. "What'd I do wrong?" he'd say to me. "Why the hell did he put me on the bench?" One night I went off on him. "I never play! You think I want to listen to you complain about sitting down for a few minutes?"

I would sit there, some nights, watching him play and thinking, "Make a mistake . . . turn the ball over . . . make a stupid foul." My attitude was even more immature than his. An attitude of subconscious sabotage is like an accident waiting to happen.

Were members of the Rockets subconsciously hoping to create failure? Were there factions on the team who felt McCray and Sampson were being disrespected by management? Was there an undermining of trust? Why did two significant guys on the team, within sight of a great and lasting pinnacle for their careers, risk everything for a brief, ecstatic rush from a line of cocaine? I don't know, but I'm sure that those things couldn't happen on a true championship team.

At the time we lost to Utah, Houston was maintaining a 30 and 25 record. Not bad, but not the standards of a contender. Their fade subtracted something from the Lakers' motivation picture. We no longer were troubled by people who called us chokers and who tried to rub salt in our wounds. We were the big gunboat now. Article after article appeared: Kareem's redefined role makes us contenders again. The coaches are brilliant. Byron Scott has truly come of age. Earvin Johnson is a shoo-in for Most Valuable Player. The chains have been taken off A.C. Green and he has become the secret ingredient in restoring Laker greatness of old. Jerry West has made about the most brilliant trade in league history. Mychal Thompson provides the missing link to league domination.

The Celtics were still champs, but hadn't we beaten them twice already?

Dallas scares a lot of people, but we weren't convinced. One of their three wins over us came when Kareem was out. The other came at the end of a five-games-in-seven-days road trip, right after Earvin's sister died.

More importantly, they were jiving themselves into a losing posture. They were so intent on reaching the top of the hill that they lost the attitude of respecting their opponents. They weren't at the top yet. They weren't dug in. But they started thinking and acting as if they had it made. In the words of a gospel song, they got what they wanted but they lost what they had. And everyone on the Lakers could see it coming. We didn't talk about it because it was smarter to let them go ahead and overinflate themselves.

You've heard it said that every man is his own greatest enemy. Every team can also be its own worst enemy. The Lakers, like the Mavericks, were building an attitude that they had it made.

My blowup at Utah was the culmination of a battle against that got-it-made attitude. We were playing bad and still winning. To some people, that meant subconsciously that there was no penalty for playing bad. We were trending back to the position that we had the most talent and our talent would always carry the day. We were practically begging to get our asses kicked.

As I said, anger is always a last resort. I know I can't totally be a friend to the players, not as intensely as they are friends to each other. There's always love and respect between us, but there's also a certain kind of distance. They may make more money and get more recognition, but I'm still an authority figure. The dynamics of any boss/employee relationship apply. But I want their good feelings and their respect. I don't fly off the handle indiscriminately.

One time, five seasons ago, I staged a big dramatic blowup because I needed to make a point. Our effort and concentration had been slipping for several games. We had lost five games out of eight. It was time for something drastic.

Next to the door that separated the training room from the locker room is a table. Cokes and cups of ice are set out there after every game. I scoped out the location of the table and I tested the door to make sure it was solid core. They were going to be my props in a Temporary Insanity act. Before a game with San Antonio I told the trainer and the team doctor, "If you hear me yelling in the locker room after the game, stand clear on your side of the door. And if my foot comes through the door, push me back out. Don't leave me standing there on one foot!"

With two minutes left in the game that night we were down by five or six points. I called a time-out and gave the team a play to run. While I outlined the play, a couple of our players were looking in a different direction. They were staring at the dance moves and the curves of the Laker Girls. Now, the Laker Girls are paid to be a distraction—but only for the paying customers. I was furious.

When we went back on the floor, one of those players didn't

know where he was supposed to be at a crucial moment. We lost the possession and we lost the game.

When everyone was in the locker room, I ripped into the guy who had blown his assignment. I said, "The next person to pull something like that is gonna wake up in *Cleveland*." Then I kicked the door to the training room as hard and as high up as I could manage. The casing splintered. The top hinge pulled loose. The whole door sagged back.

Then I made a swipe at the tray of Cokes. Instead of slapping the drinks into the shower area as I had intended, my blow hooked the whole tray into the center of the room. Bob McAdoo, Jamaal Wilkes, and Kareem, three of the most valuable players on the team that year, got soaked from head to foot. Kareem was so surprised he was actually quivering.

The next day we flew to Dallas and had a practice session as soon as we got off the plane. When the players got on the bus to the gym, they avoided eye contact with me. I didn't say anything to them either. They were sure it was going to be a big punishment session.

I called them into a circle, and then I finally softened up. I had to let them know that I still loved them. But I also said, "This doesn't mean that I won't do it again." We beat Dallas and our next six opponents in a row. Nobody had to go to Cleveland. They just had to get back on track.

In Like
a Lion

Three out of four games, including Utah, we scored less than 100 points. I was on a tirade. The team thought they were in a comfort zone. Ahead of the pack going into the last seven weeks of the season, they were outfitted with the reserve center we had wanted for so long.

It was a dangerous time. My chewing out was a dangerous response.

We flew back to L.A. on Sunday, March 1st, and went straight to the Forum for a 35-minute shootaround. Usually there's a lot of banter during the stretching exercises, just before we start to drill. Billy Thompson might get abused about the yellow Corvette he drives. Mychal Thompson might get kidded about being an illegal alien. A.C. Green gets the stick for being addicted to Big Macs. New nicknames emerge, such as when Mychal hung the name "Diesel" on Mike Smrek.

I used to insist on quiet during practice. But then I figured out that the jawing was important. People get a sense of where they stand with their teammates. Like in a big family, a certain amount of teasing indicates a level of love. If the old pros give a rookie a nickname, that really means they like him. He has a special identity. The respect is inverted into a joke, but it's still respect and it's still a ticket to belonging.

I also like to listen. I learn a lot about the mental state of the team.

This time there was nothing but silence in the gym. When the stretching was over, Earvin looked up and said, "Uh, Riles, could the team have a meeting by ourselves?"

I said, "Sure."

They went off to the side of the court, out of my earshot. I don't know what message Earvin gave them, but it must have been a positive one. They practiced hard.

When we played Golden State on Tuesday night, up in Oakland, we came out playing Laker-style ball. We faltered a little at the end, but held them off for a 114–109 win. It was a big game, and we approached it that way.

The very next night we demolished Seattle, 138–124. They had beaten us by 24 points in our last game. They were hot this time, too. They answered everything we did. In the third quarter we scored 43 points on 84.2% shooting. They scored 44 and shot 69%.

It was one of the best spectator games of the year, a beauty to watch. Both teams were showing the depth of their talent. Patterns gave way to spontaneous and beautiful play. Two teams getting after each other with incredible efficiency. Players breaking each other down in one-on-one games, making all kinds of shots. Seattle played about as well as they can play. We had to play even better. If we hadn't knocked the complacency out of our attitudes, the Sonics would've eaten us alive.

After the Seattle game I called Earvin into my office. I always try to keep the lines open between myself and the leaders and top producers on the team. They're my greatest allies. "What did you think about what I said in Utah?" I asked. "Was the approach good or was it bad?"

Earvin said, "It was good and it was bad. It was good because you really got us thinking. We really needed it. It was bad because you scared the shit out of half the guys. You've got to remember that there are seven new players on this team, and they don't know you like Kareem and James and Coop and I know you. There were a couple of guys whose jaws hit the floor. And they're wondering, 'Why me? How come he's blaming me?' "

The fact is, in that chewing out I had not pointed at any one individual. Never. But the guys who were not getting the job done thought I was talking straight to them. Because they knew they had been playing poorly. And they knew that I knew.

Our efficiency rating shot up 200% over the next few games. I found myself writing Final Look comments such as "Fast break has improved . . . Team really loose and jabbering at the shootaround today . . . The environment less oppressive."

I had been telling the team that they would like the scheduling for March: fourteen games, only four on the road, and only two back-to-backs. It was, as Earvin calls it, "Winnin' Time."

We kept breezing through the month. We were two games better than last year at the same time. We led Boston by 1½ games. Beat the Cavaliers 122–118 in a tough game. We were supposed to win easy, but they had three great rookies—Ron Harper, John Williams and Brad Daugherty—and all of them were hard to contain. We had them down, then they got right back in and we had to win the game a second time.

We took Sunday off. When we came in for a shootaround on Monday, the team showed a sense of fun, a lot of camaraderie. My only message was, "Let's take advantage of the opportunity. We must get a lot of wins in the last weeks of the season. We must have homecourt advantage all through the playoffs. It will be pivotal. Don't lose your concentration just because things have gotten easier. In the past, we have never really taken to putting out the effort needed for the best record in the NBA. This year we must."

Frustration makes for ugly games. The Clippers decided that they were going to kick our asses, even if they didn't stand much chance of winning. We have been beating them regularly for a long time. The pressure of losing was beginning to mount for everyone. After their starting center, Benoit Benjamin, was ejected, the rookie reserve started mauling Earvin. Steffond Johnson flagrantly fouled Billy Thompson. Byron Scott scored 30 and we won it 136–114.

Against the Nuggets one night later, all three of our frontline starters went over 20 points. Earvin had 20 assists and we outscored them 143–107. Doug Moe said it was "the most insignificant loss of the year."

Moe is unique. He's like the character Red Skelton used to do,

the mean little kid who always said, "I calls 'em the way I sees 'em."
He coaches the game of basketball exactly as he sees it, and he talks
about it the same way. There is no bullshit. But there is also no
diplomacy. He'll chastise his team publicly in the paper, he'll rail at
them right in front of the fans. He'll say exactly what he thinks about
any opposing player or coach.

He's an excellent coach and a good man, enjoyable to be around.
But he might be too honest. You don't have to expound every thought
in your head. Sometimes being too frank can give fuel to the opposition or demoralize the troops. Sometimes you can create unnec-
essarily big issues out of small items.

It's always fun to play the Nuggets. Instead of a lot of tactical
preparation, you just get ready to play a wide-open, wild-ass game.
They come in and run hard. We try to throw 24 seconds of tough
defense at them on every possession. Then we run right back at them.
The Nuggets run all the time, not just in the transition, but in the
passing game too. Moe always says, "The Lakers may be the best
fast break team in the league, but we're the best running team."

There was lots of chatter in our next practice. We had the Portland Trailblazers scheduled at the Forum on Thursday night, March
12. Kareem was a complete motormouth in the locker room on the
night of the game. He arrived before anybody else and took a seat
where he could see everybody come walking through the door. As
each guy entered, he worked them over like Don Rickles.

Between his physical presence and his philosophical demeanor,
outsiders tend to see Kareem with a big "Do Not Disturb" sign
pinned to his chest. Within the team, he can be extremely funny.
Only the inner circle gets to see that aspect.

Against Portland, his old team, Mychal Thompson had one of
his best games as a Laker. He was more aggressive, more determined,
more active on the offensive end. We won, 125–116.

It was our fiftieth win for the year and the eighth year in a row
to go above fifty. That's a generally accepted cutoff point for the elite
teams. Only six clubs reached 50 wins in '86–'87. We were the first.

Game number 65, versus the Clippers, was Kurt Rambis's game.
He had 18 rebounds in 31 minutes, a career best, and 12 points and
a blocked shot. He had an aggressive posture every minute he was
on the floor.

At the first of the season, when we switched on the green light
for everyone to shoot more, Kurt was thinking offense too much.

The very first time he'd get the ball in the low post, he would try to score. Or he'd take the first wide-open jump shot opportunity and maybe throw up an airball or a boinger. I wanted him to shoot, but I also wanted him to use good judgment. This was a night when he put together a really complete game. He made all the coaches happy and gave himself a confidence boost.

Since the Utah blowup we'd won six straight and averaged 129 points a game, shooting 57% percent. I started giving the team time off. I wanted to get them away from the court as the season wound down, to dispel some fatigue and be in better playoff condition. On most road trips the Gold Team got to head for the local movie house while the Blue Team, which doesn't get as many game-time workouts, would have a practice or weight training session. The Blues know they need the extra conditioning and they're spirited about the workouts.

At the same time, we were making a conscious effort to push all of them mentally and keep them challenged with Career Best statistics.

Our rematch with Utah came on the 18th. Our posture on offense was to take it right at them—take it straight to the hoop. We'd set the tone early and, on defense, make every one of their shots tough. Earvin got his fifth triple-double of the season and we won it 111–97. Billy Thompson blocked Mark Eaton, who is a whole foot taller, and then went downcourt for a two-handed reverse dunk. We were ahead 31–22 at the quarter, and they made a comeback in the second half. But we tattooed them pretty good. We won it by driving the lane and going to the free throw line.

The next day at practice we talked about maintaining concentration. While the rest of the team was all ears, Billy absentmindedly took a shot from the corner. From his angle, the ball should have either gone through the hoop or bounced off away from the group. Instead, it caught the edge of the backboard and came down and hit me. There was nothing to do but laugh. Billy had his spectacular dunk the night before, but he also had a lot of mental lapses. He missed defensive assignments. He got suckered into committing unnecessary fouls, right when the referee was on top of him. He wasn't always in the right place for our offense. That had been his pattern: six or seven good games, followed by big holes in his concentration.

Billy was a two-time All-American, probably the most recruited high school player in the nation. Then he went on to win a national championship with Louisville. His potential is phenomenal. He makes you drool to think about what he could be.

He has a problem, though, that is peculiar to a few of the most gifted athletes. He's what coaches call a floater. So much of his game comes easily that he didn't need to maintain a high level of concentration against the people he faced in high school and college. Dean Smith, James Worthy's college coach at North Carolina, advised us to watch out for the same tendency in James's rookie season. The challenge for a floater is to stay in the present moment at all times. Otherwise, they become victims of their own talent, of their potential for greatness.

It isn't a question of intelligence. Billy was an honor roll student in high school and on the dean's list in college. It isn't a matter of bad attitude. Billy is easy to like and also deeply religious. It's strictly an effort area, a mental effort that has to increase with maturity.

Two nights later it was a 147–115 win over the San Antonio Spurs, then 129–121 over Sacramento. The 10-game streak, our longest of the season, made us 19 and 2 since the All-Star break.

I've always thought that Josh Rosenfeld, our PR man, was an exceptionally smart guy for the job. After the Spurs win I had proof. A big cake was waiting for me in the locker room. It said "HAPPY 39th." Josh said, "The best ten years of your life will be between 39 and 40, if I have anything to do with it." The team broke into singing "Happy Birthday." Kurt gave me a shower with ice water. Cooper dumped a bucket full of popcorn on my head. He called it "a Laker birthday."

Two years before, on my 40th, Chris planned an elaborate party at a club. Everyone came dressed fifties-style. We had tapes of Motown and doo-wop. Everybody was dancing. All of a sudden, Michael Cooper screamed and fell down in the middle of the dance floor. He grabbed his knee. He contorted his face. Everyone gathered around him. Somebody started crying. I ran over and said, "Mike, Mike, what's wrong?" I was thinking, "My God, it's one month to the playoffs!" The team doctor bent over him and said, "Get an ambulance. We've got to get him to the hospital. This is major surgery!"

I turned around and buried my head against the wall. When I looked back again, Cooper was up on his feet and moonwalking backwards out of the room. Grinning like the devil. Got me good. I chased him all the way out into the street and halfway down Beverly Boulevard. I yelled, "Someday, sometime, I'll get you, Coop!"

After fourteen days at home, we actually welcomed a road trip.

The team bonds get renewed on the road. We're together for more hours. We're away from friends and family and other priorities. The focus sharpens. After our Sacramento win, Earvin said to a reporter, "It will be good to get out of town. We've been here too long. Sometimes when you have a long home stretch you relax too much."

On Tuesday, the 24th of March, the same day his fourth Player of the Week award was announced, Earvin dropped to the floor in the early first quarter of a game at Phoenix. He and Jay Humphries were both racing toward the sidelines after a loose ball. Humphries's knee hit the back of Earvin's calf like a big rock. Earvin crashed down and grimaced. Vitti eventually got him up, then Wes and Adrian supported him while he limped off the court. The injury was more painful than it was serious, but he was done for the rest of the game.

Phoenix had come out hammering us—physical as hell. As a result they had, at one point, eight team fouls to our one. So Jerry Colangelo, the Suns' GM, went over to his public address guy and had him announce the fact—embarrassing the officials and inciting the fans. I was infuriated. I went down to Colangelo and yelled, "This is bush! You'd do anything to win! You're supposed to have class!"

A few days later, the league fined him something around $1,000.

We had planned on using a lot of guard post-ups and two-man games. Our plans weren't as effective without Earvin. I juggled the lineup to try and jump-start some speed, but we stayed slow as molasses. We had 38 fast breaks, versus 50 or 60 in a typical game. They outscored us 28 to 12 in the second quarter. We didn't score a single basket off our set offense that whole period. No execution. Struggled for every point.

Scoring was even in the second half and we finished with a 108–93 loss.

I hate to say things like this, but this was a game to wash away and forget. I told the team at practice, back home in Los Angeles the next day, "It's okay to lose some. Losing is just as much a part of NBA life as winning. But don't get on a slide. We win a few in a row and our attitude gets funny. We get mental slippage. What's wrong with winning more than ten in a row? Why not thirty?"

They came back strong, making some noise against the Pistons on the 26th. We clinched the Pacific Division title with a 128–111 win over the team that had beaten us last December. They were playing tough, packing in the middle and trying to force us into perimeter shooting. But we had our stingers going. Byron Scott had been unconscious throughout the first half. He had 9 of 14 drop, plus 3 free throws, for 21 points. "It was one of those nights," he said. "Some nights you know you just can't miss."

Cooper hit two of three from 3-point range. James blocked 5 shots. The Lakers and the Atlanta Hawks were now the only two teams that had beaten everyone in the NBA at least once.

The Pistons are a lot like the Hawks. When they're pushing the ball and hitting from outside, they're unbeatable. Isiah Thomas is a master at breaking down defenses. Detroit's weakness is to rely too much on the perimeter game. Bill Laimbeer constantly floats around the upper key. They needed to add some consistent post-up play. The more Adrian Dantley becomes a primary part of their offense, the more they'll have it.

In '81–'82, my first year as coach, we popped champagne when we nailed down the division title. Not this time. Our attitude was, "This is not enough. Let's continue to work. We'll be swigging on the magnum later."

We flew down to Houston on the next day, the 27th. The Gold Team took the day off. The Blues scrimmaged hard.

The first quarter of the Houston game, Kareem played some of his strongest minutes of the year. We ran off 14 straight points early and finished the period at 41–21. Earvin said afterwards, "He's been king of the hill for so long. And here comes Akeem ready to join up with him and get ready to take it over. Kareem, he doesn't want to relinquish the whole hill."

Akeem is virtually unstoppable, but our new defensive techniques gave us more control than we had a year ago. The Rockets enter the ball from the left side of the court, Rodney McCray to Akeem, ninety percent of the time. Last year we had only one defensive tack. We'd come down and double-team as soon as he caught the ball. Now we mix it up. On the flight of the ball, the man guarding McCray double-teams Akeem. So we force a pass back out to McCray. We close him out and he sends the ball back to Akeem. Now we drop down a third defender from the elbow, which is the free throw line extended across the width of the court. We force Akeem to pass over to the weak side. Now there's ten seconds left on the shot clock and the ball is out of the hands of their first option. Somebody else has to attempt the shot.

We beat the Rockets 123–109 and went home to prepare for our last regular-season game against them, March 31st. I usually run with eight or nine players, but the entire bench got into the games in this Houston series. I was definitely thinking of having them tuned up for playoff action. Billy Thompson went 16 minutes in the second Houston game. It was his 17th straight appearance. We got another victory, 111–96.

Our 13 and 1 record for March matched the best March performance in Laker history. But someone else got named Coach of the Month and that drove Bertka crazy. "Where's the respect?" he says. "I don't believe it."

"Don't worry, Bill," I told him. "We got it in November. They got us out of the way early."

The regular season closes April 19—three weeks left.

James Worthy is playing the best basketball of his career. Byron is playing a complete game, rebounding and defending as well as scoring. A.C. has improved in almost every facet of his game. Kareem, in a diminished role, still ranks statistically as one of the elite centers in the league. His offensive rebounds are up 16%, which is the area we most hoped to see improved. Earvin is compiling MVP votes in every sports page in the country. He still takes over the game when we need him to.

We had that need on April 2nd against the Sonics, our first opponents on a short three-game road trip. The intensity level was high enough for a playoff game. We were tied at 100 in the fourth quarter, and Earvin threw down 13 of our last 17 points for a 117–114 win. We learned a lot from this game. The tapes became our study material for facing Seattle in the playoffs.

In Portland on the next night, Earvin and Mychal Thompson put on a two-man basketball clinic—a little evening of pick and roll. Earvin got his third straight triple-double, and Mychal scored 22, his best total to date as a Laker. Most of them came off assists from Earvin. Mychal still lives in Portland during the off-season, when he isn't back home in the Bahamas. He wanted to show the Oregon folks that he was still a player. Portland had a strong third quarter and took a 4-point lead, but Mychal scored the first three buckets of the final period and we closed them out at 127–121.

Bertka and I have an ongoing debate about practices. He thinks I call too many. We didn't practice before Seattle and we didn't have a shootaround before Portland, so he claimed a philosophical victory. "They know the system. They don't need practice anymore. They just need playing." I said, "Bill, please don't tell anybody that."

We loaded into the bus, ready to head out to the Portland airport. "Where's Billy?" Vitti asked everyone. Nobody had a clue. It turned out that Billy Thompson arranged for a friend to drive him to the airport. Then he forgot to tell anyone. Every time a player is late for a bus or a practice or a game, there's an automatic fine. The fines double during the playoffs. By the end of the season we have a great party fund put together. Billy was going to be making a lot of people happy, one way or another.

We usually keep disciplinary things, even the minor ones, within the family. When word gets out to the beat writers, a small problem could grow out of proportion. But it isn't easy to conceal the fact that a player isn't on the bus—not when reporters are also riding with the team. Frank Brady and Gordon Edes started asking me, "Are you going to suspend him?"

That's the last thing I want to do. My philosophy is to apply the fines and hope that peer pressure will do the rest. I don't think it's smart to create a big melodrama with suspensions and threats. The team doesn't have time for that kind of distraction.

The last game of that trip was in Denver—a CBS Sunday afternoon broadcast. By now it was obvious that we'd be meeting Denver in the playoffs. This was their chance to show how competitive they could be. We flew in on Saturday afternoon. The Golds left for the movies, the Blues worked out.

Denver played us the best they had all year. It was tied at the end of one quarter. We were up two at the half and just one at the start of the final period. The big difference was in free throwing. We drove the lane and drew fouls, especially in the second half. The final score was 126–118.

Kareem scored his 15,000th field goal off a hook shot, early in the third quarter. If you look in the NBA record book, you'll see Kareem at the top of the list for games played, shots attempted, shots made, blocked shots, All-Star appearances, and minutes played. At UCLA, he was the most important player during the only real dynasty in collegiate basketball. The freshman squad he led whipped the varsity, which was the reigning national championship team. The NCAA outlawed the dunk shot just to try to negate some of Kareem's domination of the game. When the press crew asked him about his most recent accomplishment, he just said, "If you stick around long enough, I guess it'll happen."

We came straight off the road trip to play the Clippers. Billy had a brilliant stretch in the last of the fourth quarter: four baskets, three of them dunks, and a pair of free throws. Ten points in four minutes. He had been riding the bench for three games and was going all out to prove he could maintain his concentration. We hoped he could keep it up. We beat the Clippers 135–112 that night, then played them again on Thursday and won 118–100. The starting team rested throughout the fourth quarter.

Five games were left in the season. The first Clippers win cinched the best record in the NBA for us. We now had homecourt advantage for the playoffs.

On the morning of the second Clipper game we all drove down to Manhattan Beach for our annual team poster shot. Last year we posed around the Forum snack stands like customers and attendants. We had players and coaches loading mustard on hot dogs, serving soft drinks, and eating popcorn. Jack Nicholson stood right in the middle, wearing his lemon-yellow sport coat from *Prizzi's Honor*. Anything to get away from the stock shot of twelve guys in two lines on the gym floor.

This year we all climbed on a yacht and posed with fishing poles and rubber sharks and swim fins. I said, "Why don't we take the team picture with hard hats and lunch pails and thermoses full of coffee?" I got shouted down on that one.

We fought off San Antonio on the next day, the 10th. The Lakers led all the way, but when there was about six minutes left, the Spurs pulled within a point. Then Cooper lifted us with 7 straight points. Kareem, Earvin, and A.C. did the rest. We won it, 121–111.

In our practices we began reviewing the passing game Denver would use against us in the first round of the playoffs. To toughen the defense, we had the Blue Team come down and play 24 seconds of offense without shooting the ball. When the 24-second-clock horn went off, they were free to take a shot. This way we kept the defense concentrated for 24 seconds and more on each possession. It was a drill we'd used before, especially in getting ready to play great passing teams.

There were a lot of questions being asked by the media about resting the players. Of course, we didn't want anybody getting hurt or becoming physically drained. But if you take away too many game minutes from your starters, you risk their losing some of their edge. After spending eighty-two games getting into top shape, they can't afford to lose their conditioning. We also wanted to deflect the idea that we were going to coast to the playoffs. We got in enough trouble thinking that way last year.

I had a team meeting and said to the guys, "I don't want anybody in here to say, 'Yeah, we're gonna rest. We're gonna relax. Then we'll play hard when it counts.' "

I was not being totally truthful to them. But they understood we wanted to rest them in the last two games, because there were only three days beyond that to prepare for Round One. But it had to be the coaching staff's decision to rest, not the team's, not the media's.

We played the Phoenix Suns on April 12th, when their drug probe was just coming to light. There was more to it than drugs. There were also allegations of gambling and throwing games. Every night for the rest of the season, I heard our players and coaches from the other teams talking about the Phoenix situation. It was about the worst example anyone had ever seen of a team's getting defeated off the court. It put a pall over the whole league, like the suspensions of Wiggins and Lloyd from the Houston Rockets.

Nevertheless, the Suns were the last team to have beaten us and they were riding a seven-game streak. Worthy tore up the first quarter with 14 points. Mychal closed it out with 4 points in just over half a minute. We held the lead to the end, 119–104.

Byron Scott and Michael Cooper celebrated late-season birthdays. Scott was twenty-six on March 28th, and Coop was thirty-one on April 15. But the lion's share of attention went to a guy who turned forty.

We flew into Salt Lake City on Cooper's birthday, a Wednesday. We practiced in L.A., then caught the flight. Now, our last trip to Salt Lake had been pretty eventful. I decided to have some fun with this one. As soon as we got to the hotel, I announced a team meeting within thirty minutes in my room. I said, "We're going to discuss the game plan for tomorrow and set the attitude straight." They all looked apprehensive as hell. They were figuring, "Coach is about to go off again. Another ass-kicking meeting about how we've got to beat Utah. How we've got to make a statement."

We tipped everyone but Kareem to get there early and bring along any presents they might have. When he opened the door, everybody yelled "Surprise!" and the party was on. Billy Desser made up a nice video of career highlights. He used the theme from *Top Gun* and the song Levi Stubbs sang in *Little Shop of Horrors*, "Mean Green

Mother from Outer Space." Every time Stubbs sang "I'm bad," Billy cut in a shot of Kareem dunking or blocking somebody.

There was a waitress, wearing one of the standard hotel uniforms. Only hers was a little bit shorter and tighter than usual. She was really a stripper. Vitti hired her on a recommendation from Don Sparks, the Jazz trainer. We told her, "Don't get raunchy on these guys. It should be something subtle." When she served slices of the cake, she was supposed to bend over a little farther than necessary, or get her legs bumping in between somebody's knees. Then, later, she was supposed to say, "Isn't it hot in here?" and unbutton a little bit. From that, she was supposed to go into a dance routine in her bra and G-string. Just something to spice up the old guy's fortieth birthday.

Instead, as soon as the cake was served, she hauled out a tape player, cranked up some bump-and-grind tune, and started getting down to the nitty-gritty right now. She was throwing each piece of her clothing on a different guy. Most of the players were very uncomfortable, and they moved over to the other side of the room. But one of the guys who didn't move started encouraging her: "Okay, honey, show him what you got. Let's get right down to it." By the time she was finished, half the guys had gone out the door.

The whole thing bombed. She put on her stuff, grabbed her tunes, and left. I looked at Bertka. He looked at me and said, "Bad choice." We both turned to The Little Kahuna and said, "Vitti, you blew it."

I pulled Earvin aside the next morning at our shootaround. I said, "What about last night?" He said, "We don't need that. The guys are cool, but it wasn't such a good idea."

The Jazz opened the game with a 10–4 run and we came back with a run of 24 to 8. We took them 110–97. The win gave us an 11-game streak, which was our longest of the season, and the longest Laker streak since a 14-game run in '78–'79.

Eleven turned out to be our limit. We decided to reduce all the starters to short minutes against San Antonio on the 17th. I said, "Bill, I know where they are mentally. This is Friday night. We have a game on Sunday, then we go into the playoffs on Thursday. I don't want the team going out there playing half-speed and maybe getting hurt."

So the starting five only played half of the game. Kareem had a painful quadriceps tendon, so we only used him for 19 minutes. The

Spurs gave it a great effort, scored 54 against us in the paint, and came away with a 115–103 win.

We closed out with Seattle at the Forum. A win would give us a new team homecourt record. Kareem didn't play at all. Coop had a night where he missed every shot he tried. A.C. could only score from the foul line. Mychal picked up some slack and finished with 24, his high as a Laker. Earvin's shot percentage went down the tubes, but he tried to rally us at the end. He hit a driving layup to tie it at 102 with three minutes, twenty-three seconds left. Then, except for two free throws from James, we went scoreless. Seattle won the final season game, 110–104.

Even if we had won, I wouldn't have been happy. We were offensively out of sync. We were slow. Our shots were forced. It was the fourth game in five that we were outrebounded.

The playoffs opened in three days. It was time to clean out our closet and focus on our best stuff.

Every so often I ask players a simple question: "What do you get when you squeeze an orange?" They look at me like I'm crazy. They wonder what the trick is. Then I tell them the answer: orange juice.

You get orange juice because that's what was inside the orange. Put anything or anyone under pressure, and you'll bring out what's inside. NBA playoffs are maximum pressure time. They call it "the second season." Lots of fans who ignored basketball all winter suddenly tune in to every broadcast. Every game is sold out. The fans rock the house. Lots of prize money is at stake. Most of all, the privilege of calling yourselves champions is on the line.

Last year, Houston squeezed us. Complacency came out, followed by humiliation, followed by shame. It was time to see what this year's pressure would bring.

The Setup

We finished the year soft. The postseason had to start with a training camp mentality. We met on Monday and walked through the Denver game plan. I wrote on the chalkboard "W H O A." I said, "Let's stop and gather ourselves, okay? Let's get in the right frame of mind for this challenge.

"Even though I rested some guys, we shouldn't have the attitude, 'Ah, this is gonna be fun.' Sure, you can have fun. But take your fun seriously. You were unconsciously sabotaging six months of hard work in the last two games. Thank God for the losses. We proved that we're not ready. We proved that we're setting up adverse situations. We have become undisciplined and complacent.

"Kurt, A.C., Billy . . . every time Bill or Randy or I said something to you in those games, you hardly responded. When a coach says something, he's trying to help you. And goddamnit, you pay attention.

"We all have to center on a routine for the playoffs. Inform your wives, inform your friends, that you are not going to be a husband and you're not going to be a friend for the next two months.

"This is going to be like a fast. We're going to fast on ticket requests, friends' requests, dinner requests, celebration requests. It's not a normal life. But if you want the ring, you have to sacrifice. You have to educate the people around you: 'I'm just like this for the playoffs. I'll see you in two months.' And hope they understand.

"Keep interviews to a minimum. There will be media people from all over the country. Don't get inundated.

"We haven't looked connected. From now on, we all stay in the locker room until it's time to hit the floor. We go out as a group. After the game, we come into the locker room. We bring our hands together and we sit down." Kareem backed me up. "We have to all be pulling in the same direction with all our strength. Whatever we do, we have to do as a unit."

We held ass-kicking practices on Tuesday and Wednesday. The mood was great. We told them: Don't feel pressure. Feel excitement, feel anticipation of something good that's going to happen. Remember who you are. You should be confident. You have prepared diligently over the past three and a half days. That's what confidence is all about, preparation.

On Thursday night, just before the game, we reviewed the keys: Take care of the ball and the boards. They have the best rebounding guards in the NBA. They're the fourth-best rebounding team in the league. They force the second-highest number of turnovers in the league. Defensively, we had to disrupt their passing game, keep them from igniting the fast break and taking the open jumpers.

The Lakers were fired up. Somebody said, "We know what we have to do!"

I said, "Yes. I know that. But I want to make a point. They're calling this a mismatch. The best team in the West versus the worst. Well, we are better. I'm not going to sit here and lie to you. I'm not going to tell you that they're a better team. We won sixty-seven games this year. They only won thirty-seven. We're thirty games better than them. But are we gonna play better?

"Denver is a very gritty team in big games. They had to work their asses off in the late season to clinch a playoff spot. They have momentum. They will kick, scratch, and bite to stay in it. They have the ability to beat you. If you're not ready to play and you lose one game of this mini-series at home, you're in trouble."

I leaned on this angle even though Denver was without Calvin Natt, because Doug Moe had been poor-mouthing the Nuggets' chances to win even a single game.

Frank Brady, from the *Herald-Examiner*, after listening to Moe's "no hope" rap, tried to pin down one of the Denver players. "Really, what are your chances?"

"Not too good. Bad."

"How good, how bad?"

"Slim."

"C'mon."

Finally, the player cracked a smile. "That's what Doug told me to say."

I recognized the psychology. If the Nuggets didn't think there was any shame in losing, the pressure would be off. If the pressure was off, they might play great. There was nothing they could do but be heroes. And if they managed to win one, there was nothing we could feel but demoralized.

The 24-second defensive drill we'd been working paid off. After Denver took an early 10–5 lead, we scored five fast-break baskets in a row—mostly off blocks and steals. They tried double-teaming Kareem and we found A.C. Green open under the basket.

With four or five seconds left in the first half, Bill Hanzlik tried a desperation 3-pointer and missed. Earvin got the ball in the corner. He took one dribble and threw the ball on the stride, like an outfielder trying to peg a runner at home plate. The ball crossed halfcourt with the buzzer sounding. Then it nestled perfectly into our hoop—3 points from 80 feet out. I grabbed both sides of my head and bent over double. Kareem's jaw dropped to the floor.

Earvin's 3-pointer made it 82 to 53 at the break. We had tied the league playoff record for scoring in a half.

We added 10 points to the lead in the third quarter, then we inserted subs in the fourth. We had great balance on our break. The ball movement was sharp. James Worthy finished with 28 points in 29 minutes. Alex English, the third-hottest scorer in the league, had averaged 28.2 points per game in the regular season. James, with some help from Coop and A.C., held him to 14. The final score was 128–95.

"We played awful," Moe said the next day. "But had we played sensational, we would still have had zero chance."

His attitude was beginning to annoy me and the players. I didn't care anymore if it was sincere or if it was a ploy. We were not going to let him make our team complacent. Anytime you make the play-offs, you should think that you have a chance. You should present yourself that way.

Between Game One and Game Two I told the Lakers, "They're discounting your greatness. They're discounting what you did all year long. You worked hard to be where you are. They're turning it into a joke with this 'we can't win' attitude. I'd want to kick somebody's ass who had an attitude like that!

"You're gonna have to make them pay for not wanting to be here, because they've insulted your intelligence. And you can bet they're gonna try to catch you off guard. Be as great as you can be, no matter who you play and what the score is. Let's be above the verbal garbage. Let's have a peak performance.

"They say they don't belong here? They don't want to compete? Well, let's send them home."

I think some of the Denver players were just as upset, because there were times out on the floor when they looked totally beaten, even when the score was close. I didn't see what I normally see in that team. Two years ago we beat them 139 to 122 in the first game of the Western Conference Finals, then they came back and walloped us 136–114 in the second game. It wasn't going to happen again.

Our practice session between the games was upbeat. Everyone was talkative. We had some concern about maintaining focus, and it wasn't just Doug Moe. The whole town was saying, "This series is over. Let's move on."

Bertka said, "We have to keep the attitude of being the hunter and not the one who's hunted. We're hunting—moving, looking, hungry. The mission is to get back where we were."

We jumped out to a 40–23 lead in the first period of Game Two, then we coasted in the second. We lapsed into more of a set game instead of running. They cut our 18-point lead to 12 before we regained momentum.

In the last five and a half minutes they mounted a 24 to 12 run, but we held on to win it, 137–127.

Kareem finished with 28 points and 4 blocked shots. English finished with 17 points.

I was upset. When we came together in the locker room I said, "We shouldn't have had to battle them at the finish. We let them get some back, let them start feeling good about themselves. Maybe start thinking they could win Game Three."

One of the reporters saw after the game that Kurt Rambis had a big circular bruise in the middle of his forehead. Was it a pounding from some Nugget's elbow? "No," Kurt said, "the Cookie Monster did it." He had been playing that afternoon with Jesse Rambis, his fifteen-month-old son. Kurt picked up a Cookie Monster doll attached to a suction cup. He stuck it on his forehead. Every time he shook his head, the Cookie Monster wobbled and Jesse laughed. But when Kurt went to remove it, it wouldn't budge. Finally, after a big struggle, he pried it loose. A big purple ring developed. "That's no bruise," Kurt said. "That's a giant hickey."

One preplayoffs newspaper article had said, "Dallas Mavericks —This is the team the Lakers should fear the most." Dallas was matched against Seattle. They had swept the Sonics 5–0 in the regular season. A 55-game winner versus a 39-game winner. They annihilated the Sonics 151–129 in their first playoff game.

The Dallas papers had a field day ridiculing the losers. They called Clemon Johnson "Lemon" Johnson. Then, on the same day as our second game with Denver, Seattle squeaked out a 2-point victory, 112 to 110.

We took Sunday off. I read the morning paper in the backyard, having breakfast with James and Chris. I saw Kareem quoted about how he hated going to Denver. "The altitude is worth fifteen points," he said. "I don't like playing there because I can't sleep at that altitude."

Game Three was scheduled for Wednesday, the 29th of April. We concentrated on hard defensive work in Monday's practice, the Blues acting out Denver's passing game, and the Golds working a 24-second defensive drill. I told the team, "Anybody that's bothered by the altitude in Denver, we'll get you a humidifier for your room." The guys had complained about this before. We're always a little tired in Denver. I have a hard time sleeping there, too. It's dry. You can't adjust the air-conditioning in your room, because they've got big windows that don't open. You feel confined. So, when four or five of the players requested humidifiers, we went out and bought them.

It seems like a small thing, but professional athletes need quality rest. They have to be confident that their bodies will respond to every demand. In Denver it's excruciating because they know they're going to hit the wall at some point, and then they're going to have to keep on going. We always have to grind it out there. A win in Denver is always a fatigue win, which was all the more reason to come at the Nuggets hard. If we won it in three, we could devote more time to resting and honing ourselves for the next opponent on the schedule. At this stage of the season, any edge you can get is invaluable. Utah had already whipped Golden State twice, as expected. One more win and they would be our challengers in Round Two, starting immediately.

We flew in to Denver on Tuesday and held a workout, plus a shootaround on Wednesday morning. The team had a great, self-motivated enthusiasm—the best I've seen since I started coaching. They were into it. They were up. When we ran layup lines, Earvin got everybody chanting in call-and-response cadence, like a little military unit.

"One two—"

"—three four."

"One two—"

"—three four."

"One two three four, one two—"

"—three four!"

Alex English came out in the papers with an attitude contrary to his coach's. "I think we're going to come out and play hard, and I think we're going to win," he said. "There might be some blood on the floor, but maybe that's what it will take."

There hadn't been any skirmishes in the games, so everybody wondered where in hell that comment came from. I said, "That's just the blood cry of an athlete who is about to get beat. They're going to play tough. You know as well as I do that they're professional athletes. When it comes down to trying to win a game, they're gonna come out and play in spite of Moe. I want you to hit the hardest. Don't start thinking, 'We just need one. If we lose this time we're still okay.' Expect the worst and be ready to fight through it.

"Alex isn't going to be about teamwork the next time we see him. His pride is on the line. His attitude will be to get back at us. He's going to go after us. He ain't gonna be passing to anybody. He'll be trying to get his shot off quicker. We've got to squeeze him quicker."

There was also a lot of angry talk in the press from Moe and from Vince Boryla, the Nuggets' team president, about the referees. "They get away with bloody murder out there," Boryla said.

"It may have been one of the worst officiated games ever," Moe said.

I stayed out of that dialogue. I didn't want any con job in the picture. The calls went good and bad, and they went both ways, as they do in 99 out of 100 games. A coach can always see what he wants to see in the officiating. I try to see it as impartial. I can't always maintain that view, but that's what I shoot for.

The day before our third Denver game, Seattle shook Dallas another time, 117 to 107.

Nobody saw blood flow, but Denver played a much more competitive game, as teams will often do when their backs are against the wall. Mike Evans hit a 3-pointer near the middle of the second period to pull them ahead 42–40.

Michael Cooper answered with two consecutive 3-pointers from the top of the key. We outscored them 15–2 over the next few minutes. By the end of the game English had gotten his scoring touch back for 25 points, but we restricted their point production from the low post. Kareem had 5 blocked shots. James and Mike Smrek had 3 apiece and the team had 14 altogether, which established our record for the year. The final was 140–103.

Billy Thompson had played significant minutes in the series: eighteen in the first game and six in the second. After playing three minutes in the last game of the series, he went up high to jam on a breakaway and Maurice Martin knocked him to the floor. He landed with his knees flexed, but got up limping. We sent him in for X rays and there was no damage. The diagnosis was hyperextension.

Back in California, Golden State had surprised Utah in their third game, 100–95, while we were beating Denver. So we could count on some rest and preparation time. Utah just needed one more victory, while Golden State needed two more in a row. No team in history had ever managed three straight playoff wins after being down two to zero.

Decorum at
the Forum

With the three-game sweep of Denver completed, we flew home on Thursday, April 30th. That night, the Sonics whipped the Mavericks 124 to 98. In three straight games "the team the Lakers should fear the most" had vanished from the playoff picture. Five weeks later, a new head coach was in place for Dallas.

We held intense workouts on Friday and Saturday, but we still didn't know our next opponent. Randy Pfund worked double time to complete scouting and matchup reports for both teams. I told the team, "This is your biggest challenge: waiting, patience. Our biggest challenge is to stay focused while we're waiting for our next opponent. The other teams are playing in more games. We have the luxury of more time off. But we cannot afford to lose our edge, mentally or physically.

"What happened to Dallas? They got full of themselves. They

got cocky and they got caught—maybe like we did last year against Houston. That's what you face. We must never let our guard down. There's no place for arrogant statements, puffed-up pride.

"What we're talking about is just taking care of business. It starts here in practice today. Did we learn last year how you can get caught? There are no guarantees but your attitude and your hard work. There's nothing else.

"If you watched that game, and all the celebration, it was like Seattle had just won a world's championship. You saw the character they had in beating the Mavericks. They're an 'innocent climb' team, like we were when we took the championship in 1980. Nobody expected much of them. They were supposed to stay on the bottom rung of the ladder. You've got to acknowledge the strength, the power, the determination, and the character. An innocent climbing team is dangerous as hell."

I told them to put the Denver series behind them. The competition was going to get stiffer. But first there were some compliments due. We set some records in rebounding and in assists. We set a record for blocked shots in a three-game series. Our field-goal percentage, steals, and turnovers were at a high. I complimented Kareem for his last game: 9 points, 5 blocked shots, 6 boards, and 7 assists. Finally, I told James, "That was the best defense you've ever played against Alex English. The best defense you've ever played, period. And your offense was even better. You were awesome at both ends of the court."

We scheduled Sunday's practice late. We wanted the team to watch the final Utah–Golden State game together. It came down to the final seconds. We thought Utah would win, but the Warriors scored the upset. We finally knew what team to prepare for. We distributed the Golden State reports, talked them over, and then held a light workout.

Our scouting reports start with a little synopsis of each player, their strengths and weaknesses and the best way to contain them. Then there's a page of X's and O's, showing their key plays. Randy assembles video on the key plays with a voice-over. First he explains the mechanics of their play sets, then he gets into each player's individual tendencies. This material is the backbone of our preparation.

After the workout Mychal and Byron got into a playful dispute over who was the best boxer. Everyone on the team is competitive to the extreme. They compete on shots from every corner of the floor. They argue about who plays the meanest game of Ping-Pong, who swims the fastest, who can kick whose ass on Pac-Man. Mychal claims he's killed the most sharks of anyone on the team. The guys who grew up in New York, Michigan, and L.A. will generally concede that point, but not always.

Once in a while I look in the locker room and I see five hundred pounds of muscle with four legs, four arms, and two heads, bouncing off the chairs and the walls. They scare me sometimes. This time it was a boxing match. "I outpointed him in the first two rounds, ten to eight, ten to nine," Mychal said.

There were two days to concentrate. Tuesday, May 5th, was the first game of the series.

Our locker room was very quiet before the game. I thought back to the Houston series of one year ago. This wasn't going to be the same. Attention was sharp throughout the video and the blackboard work. The Warriors were much more to them than just a second-round opponent. They were the team that beat us and crowed. They were an old rival announcing themselves as the new force on the West Coast. And they had done an impressive job against the Jazz, sweeping three after being two games in the hole. Last year they were the basement team of the Pacific Division. They hadn't been to the playoffs since losing to the Lakers in the second round ten years ago. Just like Seattle, they were a team on an innocent climb.

"They will wage war," I told the team. "They are a belligerent team. You'll have to be prepared for it. They'll constantly ride a hand on you on defense. They'll hold you coming through screens. They'll smash you on your cuts. They'll try to root you out of the post.

"Being physical is the only chance they have. You have to respect that. So we're not going to come out, play the game, and get hammered all over the place. We're not going to respond. We're going to be the instigators, especially here at home. We can't give 'em one at home. Our strength, our mental strength, is going to be a factor. Because we have the experience. We have four guys—Kareem, Earvin, Coop, Kurt—who have each been in more playoff games than the whole roster of Golden State."

We matched up Earvin defensively against Rod Higgins, a small forward. Kareem started against Larry Smith, their power forward. A.C. took Joe Barry Carroll, the center. James started on Chris Mullin, the off-guard, and Byron took on Sleepy Floyd, the point man. We knew Mullin would be guarding Earvin, so he would have to chase Earvin down at every transition. We'd have a timing advantage with our outlet passes.

Offensively, we had to be aggressive about getting position. They rotate their defenses well, so we had to drive the gaps. Ball movement had to be sharp. On defense we had to swarm Joe Barry Carroll and play him physical, take away his hook shot. We had to challenge Sleepy Floyd, but also contain him. He likes to launch to the basket on a long last step, like a broad jumper. Smith had to be blocked out at all times. Mullin had to be crowded so he couldn't get into his catch-and-shoot rhythm. And we couldn't slack off when their bench came in. The Warriors have a very effective bench. Purvis Short and Terry Teagle are dangerous scorers. Greg Ballard can hit the perimeter jumper all night. We had to keep our 24-second defense mentality. We were going up against a very explosive team.

"Don't be careful," I told them just before we took the floor. "Play full out, with faith. Don't be provoked. They will be emotional and their tactics will show that. Be contained, intense, filled with confidence of your collective power as a unit. Stay focused. Stay efficient. Stay strong. You're prepared. You have no limitations. You won't give up what's yours. Just work with diligence. Work with one collective mind."

Joe Barry had an outstanding first half. He hit from the baseline on both sides, hit from underneath, made the tip-ins. He was 8 for 10 from the floor and a perfect 4 for 4 at the line. The perimeter game was killing us. They were making over 57% of their shots, more than half of them from long distance. We were down 62–55 at the half, but we looked good in the effort areas: 26 boards to their 16, four blocks to their two.

Up in the press row, Lowell Cohn of the *San Francisco Chronicle* asked Jerry West if he thought the Lakers still had a chance. Jerry said, "I think we'll win." When he said it, according to Cohn, "His voice was as casual as a man asking for a refill on a cup of coffee." I wasn't as casual down in the locker room. I jumped all over Mychal about working harder. I said, "We didn't bring you here to play like that. We need much more." Mychal and Kurt both had to come in with better effort. "Our execution is terrible," I said. "They're taking us out of our running game. We need three things: judgment, execution, and patience."

Our defensive intensity was down. We went to a four-man

rotation. We put Kareem on Joe Barry and double-teamed the post. When one guy came up to double the post, the next guy would rotate over and cover the first one's man. We kept it tight. We got to the shooters quicker and it frustrated the hell out of the Warriors in the third period.

James and Earvin started the second half strong. We reached a tie in three minutes, then we steadily pulled ahead. Our defensive pressure was tremendous. It took Joe Barry seven minutes to score. Two points was all he got for the entire second half.

Earvin scored 8 straight at midpoint, then James had a tip-in and two consecutive breakaway jams. When they tried to tighten the lanes in the last three minutes, Cooper set up behind the 3-point line and made a 25-footer, a 24-footer, and another from 25—plus a 20-foot jump shot. Coop was on fire. The crowd went insane. There was so much noise the Laker Girls couldn't hear the music to do their dance routines.

We scored 49 in the third quarter to Golden State's 23. It was a new playoff record for third-quarter scoring, and only two points shy of the playoff record for any quarter. Within twelve minutes, Earvin had 13 points, 7 rebounds, and 7 assists. "I couldn't believe the fans," he said. "Only when we play Boston do they react like that."

George Karl, the Golden State coach, even told reporters, "It was beautiful basketball. That's probably as much as I've enjoyed watching a team that was kicking my butt. They just ran right by us."

Golden State made up some ground in the fourth quarter. Teagle got a 10-point streak going. But the noise that started with Coop's 4 for 4 long-range shooting exhibition didn't stop until the game was over. The final score was 125–116.

"Your effort was good," I told the team at Wednesday's practice, "but one period is not enough. Don't make it disjointed."

Game Two had me concerned. Mychal and Kurt came in near the end of the first period and didn't make the kind of effort we need from them. The Warriors were again disrupting our running game. Both teams scored 21 buckets in the first half, but we got to the line more often. Free throws gave us the halftime lead, 58–51.

A little drama started to build between Cooper and Sleepy Floyd. They collided in the first half. They started jawing at each other. When Coop went to the line, Floyd walked up and continued the lecture. Coop just turned away and ignored him. Then he made both shots. At the end of the third, when we were up 84 to 78, Floyd creamed Cooper right in front of the Golden State bench. He left him lying on the floor.

Early in the fourth period they came within 3 points. Kareem went to work with his skyhook, then Coop, Mychal, and Byron scored inside. We built a 16 to 4 run. Nine of those points came from the Captain. He finished with 25 and we had a 116–101 victory.

A playoff series doesn't really get started till a team loses one at home, or until the seventh game. We had a 2–0 series lead. That's the way it's supposed to be. You've got to win the home games. Now it was their turn to try. The Warriors have great crowd support at home. The game was set for two P.M. on a Saturday, so we knew the fans would be ready to roar. Golden State usually puts together their best efforts at the Coliseum. On the other hand, we haven't played well up there the past couple of years. Unlike Doug Moe, George Karl kept saying he believed his team could hang tough and win. Even after our big third-quarter explosion, Karl told a reporter, "I leave with some optimism. Take away eight minutes and we win the game."

Houston and Seattle were the other two Western Conference teams still competing. The Sonics took the first game by five in overtime and the second by just two points. Then Houston came back strong to win their third game by 18.

The Oakland Coliseum is a lightless, depressing place. The dominant color is concrete gray. They've got a black ceiling and a black curtain that goes all the way around. You can walk into some arenas and get uplifted. Not here. The Coliseum looks as if it were designed by the same people who did the Berlin Wall.

We flew up Friday for a Saturday game. I told the team, "Great job. The intensity has been good. Half-court defense has been superb. Coop, Byron, and James have done an excellent job containing their shooters.

"But we can play better. We had one really good period. That's good enough for home. But it's not going to be good enough for here. Why are we erratic? We've had seven erratic periods and one great period.

"In three games against Denver we committed thirty-two turnovers. In two games with Golden State we've already had forty-six. Denver, in the three games, only had twenty-three layups. Golden State, in two games, has already had twenty-five. We must get back quicker, we have to handle the ball better. We've gotten sloppy. We're throwing the ball away in the lane."

Scott and Earvin were pretty banged up. Billy Thompson's knee injury still wasn't responding to treatments. For my money, Vitti is the best trainer in the NBA. But some injuries respond and others will not. Sports medicine knowledge has grown tremendously in the last ten years, but there are still plenty of unknowns.

The first half of Game Three was like a clinic. We shot almost 60%. James had a 14-point first quarter. He's usually so cool and reserved. Newspaper writers were calling him the Silent Assassin. This time he was yelling, encouraging the other players, calling for the ball. "When he does that," Earvin said, "all you can say is 'Yeah! Keep it going!' " Our halftime lead was 73–56. We only had three turnovers.

Kareem picked up personal foul number four right at the start of the third quarter, so Mychal Thompson entered the game. He came out ready to play. Mychal got down the floor for a lot of dish-off passes and layups. He lifted us with 22 points and 9 rebounds in the second half. Kareem only returned for two additional minutes early in the fourth quarter.

James finished with 28. Cooper, who continued his jawing, bumping, and shoving war with Sleepy Floyd, scored 19. Kurt had 6 rebounds and 7 points. We won it, 133–108, because of the fire James showed, getting off early and quieting the home crowd, and because of the intense play from our bench. Sometimes it does some good to get on people about their performances.

There was an effusive feeling in the locker room after the game. Though not boastful, it was lacking in reserve, lacking in discipline. They were letting loose after a 25-point win. Everything was great. We were playing great. The Warriors would have to come back and win four straight to take the series away.

Bill and I went to Francesco's for a spaghetti and meatballs dinner. We ran into Chick Hearn and all three of us talked about how good we felt. The next game was at two on Sunday afternoon. There was no time to practice. Bill asked, "How are we going to get them up for tomorrow? Let's get this thing swept." We were concerned, but we also had a great feeling of relief—six straight playoff wins.

I read the *Chronicle* in the morning, Mother's Day morning. One of their columnists said, "The Warriors aren't going to beat the

Lakers if they play until the Fourth of July. . . . This isn't a basketball team. It's a steamroller."

Before Game Four I asked the Lakers, "Do you think they're gonna fold? This is going to be their easiest game to play. Everybody's expecting it to be over with, so it's the most dangerous game. They're not going to show any weaknesses.

"Larry Smith has had eighteen offensive rebounds in three games. He's gotta be blocked out. We aren't doing any kind of job on him at all. We've got to continue to squeeze Sleepy Floyd. We haven't allowed him to get off so far." Then I wrote "NOT NOW" on the blackboard and drew a circle around it. "Don't let it happen today. Keep squeezing. Chris Mullin hurt us with back cuts and reverses. We've got to contain him better.

"On offense, we just have to get there. Like Mychal did yesterday. You're going to get a lot of layups. I want to be strong with our passes in the post. Don't force the offense, just let it happen.

"Don't give them room to produce any miracles today, fellas. No daylight. All business. Let's get it done and get home to Los Angeles. You've earned the right to be effusive, but haven't we learned about that? Let's catch ourselves. We need the intensity. Keep the edge. Continue to stay together in single-mindedness. We had a clinic on offense yesterday. Let's put one on in defense today. This will be the toughest test."

You could read the test results in Monday morning's headlines: "Sleepy Floyd's 51 Points Turn Off Lakers' Lights."

The game started funny. We edged out to a 4 to 1 lead and then they scored 10 straight. We took a time-out and answered with a 12–0 run. It was like we were trading cold streaks and the Warriors stayed coldest longest. The Lakers were ahead 34–27 at the quarter.

The second quarter was more balanced. We had a 65–57 lead at the half. Floyd wasn't hot, but he kept putting the ball up anyway. He had 12 points at halftime. Kareem, Byron, and Joe Barry each had more.

We added 6 points to our lead in the third quarter. Sleepy hit for 10 of their 31 in the period. He already had his best numbers for the playoffs.

All his frustrations from the first three games came to a head in the fourth quarter. Sleepy hit 12 consecutive shots—underhand lay-ins, spinning lay-ins, driving lay-ins, dunks. There was no stopping him. "I can't describe the feeling," he said to reporters afterward. "The basket felt like it was ten feet wide."

It was a once-in-a-lifetime display. Sleepy Floyd scored 29 in the quarter, 39 for the second half, 51 for the game. The Warriors spread the floor and just let him go. No one had ever scored that much against the Lakers in the playoffs. He broke Elgin Baylor's 33-point halftime-scoring record. He broke Gus Williams's 23-point quarter-scoring record. We seemed to be standing around, waiting to see if he could miss.

We played as if our basket were about ten inches wide, scoring 19 to their 31. Our 14-point lead was erased in four minutes and we lost the game 129–121.

We left the Bay Area after the game and reconvened on Monday in Los Angeles to talk things over. All through the flight I wrote on everything I could get my hands on: napkins, travel-guide packages, airline magazine covers, stat sheets. The effusiveness had gone over the line. We had become diffuse, spread thin, caught up in the image of being unbeatable. The Warriors had busted right through our wall of arrogance. Game Five was Tuesday night.

At the team meeting, I started talking about the arrogance problem. Our emotional displays were getting carried away. It was Cooper and it was the rest of the team as well. It was dunking the ball and pointing at the guy they had beaten to the basket. It was too many high fives and too much woofing. I said, "Something has entered this series that shouldn't be part of the picture. It's just going to hurt us as we go further. I'm not saying I don't want you to have fun, that I don't want you to support each other. I want to see the high fives. I want to see the emotion. But let's keep it in the proper perspective. You keep barking so much and you'll get your head bitten off.

"That's the importance of decorum. You're professionals. You prove what you're worth with your actions, not with your mouth."

Kareem seconded that. And when he talks, it makes an impression.

Then I started talking about Show Time. Reporters had been asking the Warriors about the displays and the jawing, and they said, "It's going a little too far. But that's their trademark. They're supposed to be Show Time and Hollywood." I said, "Everything we do is minimized when people perceive us as lacking substance. We're always being dismissed as a team that lacks character—a flash team, not hard workers. And what people perceive us to be is exactly what you've been showing them. You're showing them this arrogance, this display of emotion. People think that you're Hollywood. You know, self-centered, fragile, big-egoed people. That when it gets tough, you'll crack, just like you did in the fourth period. And that's what people want to see.

"What I want, for the rest of the playoffs, is to convince people that we're blood and guts. If we're ever going to shake this reputation, now is the time."

Bruce Jolesch was the PR director of the Forum in my first head-coaching year. He moved down to Dallas and started his own PR and marketing firm, Jolesch and Company. He sent me all the articles from the Dallas Mavericks and Seattle Sonics playoff games. I read each headline to the team. I said, "A team that's supposed to beat us and win a World Championship this year. In the space of five games. That's how fast it happens.

"It happens with Sleepy Floyd getting twenty-nine points in a quarter. And you say, 'We'll get 'em at home in Game Five.' Before you know it, five days later, you're kicking yourself. Do you remember last year after Game One against Houston? That within a short six days we had lost our World Championship and it was over with? I can bring out the same headlines from the L.A. *Times* last year. You remember that, fellas? This is how quickly it happens."

We were four weeks into the playoffs, with four weeks left. The key was going to be our mental durability. We came in to practice on Tuesday and I said, "No ass-dragging today. I want everything sharp, efficient. I want to hear the sneakers squeaking on the floor. Have we plateaued? We'll find out. We're four weeks away from what we want."

We nailed down our game plans. Purvis Short had done a hell of a job containing Earvin in Game Four. I told Earvin, "Purvis Short playing you? He has the reputation of being the worst defender in the league and you're making him look like an All-Star defender. He's guarding you and he's gonna start tonight. He's gonna pressure you full court."

Golden State had blown past Utah by shooting 3-pointers. We expected them to come out shooting everything from the perimeter, trying to jump on top quickly. "Keep pounding the boards," I said. "Let's keep our turnovers down. Be ready for half-court presses.

"Right now is exactly what's supposed to happen in a seven-game series. We've won the first two at home. We went up to Golden

State and we split. You're supposed to win in Game Five. And that's what we have the opportunity to do tonight. We have the homecourt advantage, so let's get it down. Let's break through to the next level."

We looked a little weary in the first half. Larry Smith had 18 rebounds. He's one of the best board men in the league, and nobody was blocking him out. Cooper came in late in the first quarter and gave us a big lift defensively. He woke everybody up with a couple of awesome plays—blocked Sleepy Floyd, blocked a Chris Mullin shot out of bounds. He and Purvis Short got into a tussle and they both took a swing, so the officials called a double technical.

We took a 7-point lead into the second half. Larry Smith only got 6 more rebounds, and we built a 99–77 lead. They surged in the fourth quarter, but couldn't catch up. At the final buzzer it was 118–106. We had made it successfully out of the second playoff round. Two more were on the way.

Down in Texas, Houston hammered out their second win over Seattle, against three losses. The winner of that face-off would be our next challenge.

Seattle
Slamdance

The same day we eliminated Golden State, *Sporting News* named Earvin as Player of the Year, based on a balloting of NBA players. Out of 184 votes, 136 went to Earvin. Michael Jordan was second with 36, and the remaining 12 were split up between Akeem Olajuwon, Larry Bird, and Charles Barkley. Recognition from your peers doesn't get much stronger than this. Earvin had already been Player of the Week five times and Player of the Month twice.

He led us in scoring and had the highest average of his career, 23.9 per game. He led the league in assists for the fourth time in five years, and he set a new Lakers record for assists with 977. It's wonderful enough when an average player improves. For a long-established superstar to improve so much is like having the Rocky Mountains grow taller.

The sixth Seattle-Houston game was going to be played on

Thursday, May 14th. If Houston won it, the series would go to a seventh and deciding game, and we'd face the winner on the following Tuesday. If Seattle won it, we'd meet them on Saturday, just two days away.

On Thursday morning, after a day of rest, we met in Pauley Pavilion at UCLA and ran through an all-out practice with Seattle in mind.

The first segment was a talk. I complimented them on their attitude breakthrough, which helped us close out Golden State. Then we gave some thought to our opponents. Houston was our tormentor of one year ago—the team that gave us a nationally televised whipping on opening day. We might have an opportunity to get back at them. Seattle, on the other hand, was something different from what we had ever experienced.

Houston had used Lewis Lloyd and Mitchell Wiggins and Robert Reid last year to pound Earvin full court. They were very physical with us from end line to end line. I said, "Seattle uses the same tactics Houston beat us with a year ago. But Seattle does it twice as hard. They do it better and they're quicker at it. How are we going to beat the tactics that beat us last year? We can do it by being tougher and by being less predictable."

Seattle's defense is the most aggressive I've ever seen. It's constant full-court pressure, trapping, harassment. Not dirty or out of control, it's just plain hard defense, every second you have the ball. Our philosophy was to have the Blues play an extreme version of it. Bobby Knight uses this same tactic at Indiana: Make practice five times harder than the game will be.

We called it the "pit bull" practice. The Blues were instructed to be overly aggressive, to bang the Gold Team hard. They were to reach in and claw for the ball, root people out of position, foul them every time. They loved it. I said, "Earvin, there won't be a single moment that you won't be bumped and blocked and knocked down and hacked and pressured."

We worked on the initial part of our fast break, starting with our regular five-man outlet drill. It's geared to getting our fast break off in a hurry after an opponent's shot. Three guys are under the basket, and two guards are at the elbows of the free throw line. The drill is to shoot, rebound, and make an outlet pass to one side, do it again to the middle, and then to the other side. We have to make the rhythm of the outlet pass second nature.

Every team in the league except Seattle lets us rebound and outlet normally. The Sonics, with their speed, run up and molest the rebounder with two guys. Then they pressure our point guard full court to deny him the outlet pass.

We ran the basic drill five or six times. Then we put the Blues in on defense. When the shot went up, two guys came up hard against the rebounder. As soon as Earvin got the ball on the outlet, I wanted forearm smashes. I wanted him knocked to the floor.

It was crazy. We couldn't get the ball from under the basket to half court without throwing it away or stumbling or looking as if we'd never played the game before.

The Golds didn't handle it well for the first half hour. They looked at me like . . . "What are you doing?" I stopped the drill and told them, "I'm telling you something. This is how it's going to be. You've got to recognize that these tactics are going to be allowed. Maybe this drill is more severe, but I'd rather have you face it here.

"You're not being strong enough. We have to be strong and alert enough to make the proper moves to clear the defense in the back court."

Eventually they started to get it. They started to anticipate, coil up, and bounce off the contact. They made quicker outlet passes. They made quicker cuts to the outlet areas. Instead of trying to dribble out of pressure, they made two passes. They started to instinctively pick up ways that they could beat the pressure.

Seattle finished off Houston that same night. So we ran the same type of practice on Friday, getting ready for a Saturday afternoon game.

Seattle was finely honed. After Dallas had humiliated them in their first playoff game, the Sonics lifted themselves to another performance level.

What happened with the Sonics is they started to build stronger and stronger individual reputations for their defense, and so, as a team, they created enough confidence to start taking more liberties. They had the second-highest foul total in the league. But they compensated for the fouls. Their aggressiveness held opponents to low scoring percentages. And it created turnovers that the Sonics converted to scores.

The officials also allowed them to get away with a certain style of play. Rule enforcement changes in the playoffs. There's a "let 'em play" mentality. You have to be ready for it.

We had two offensive objectives: one, to be ready for a karate-style, hand-to-hand combat series; two, to keep up our floor percentage while we also score from the line.

Seattle is a very predictable team on offense. Xavier McDaniel, Tom Chambers, and Dale Ellis score sixty-five to seventy percent of their points. They're the only team in league history to have three guys averaging over 20 points per game. They're the fifth highest scoring team in the league. So our defensive philosophy was to shut down one of those guys each night. When all three of them get off, Seattle is going to win. If we can hold two of them to their averages and the third one down around 10 or 11 points, we're going to win. They don't get enough scoring punch from their bench to make up the difference.

The guy we zeroed in on was Dale Ellis. He's an explosive perimeter shooter who can rip off 8 or 10 in a row. Most players have to catch the ball, bounce it, get their rhythm, and then shoot. Ellis is one of the great catch-and-shoot guys of all time.

The Sonics are a tremendously superb rhythmic team. Every time Ellis comes off a baseline pick, the pass lands right in his hands. He has it fired to the hoop before his man can fight through the pick. We had to give him no daylight at all. None. We had to make Ellis put the ball on the floor every time he caught it. Every single time he came off a screen, one Laker would be trailing him. Another would stunt into his passing lane. We had to contain him with sliding and shifting and stunting.

Chambers would be double-teamed in the low post. McDaniel is a great athlete and a very emotional player. Our plan was to prevent him from getting the turnaround jumper in the post.

The first game was low scoring and close. You have to play carefully against a swarming defense. We won it 92–87, which was the lowest point total of any game we played all year.

Seattle is a running team, but all their running initiates from their defense. They don't run after an opponent makes a shot. They walk it back up and execute the maximum time in their offense. But they will run like a bitch on long rebounds and steals. The Sonics are the best offensive rebounding team in the NBA. That's where their quickness comes into play. We had to compete for every rebound, prevent them from getting fast breaks and second shots.

Our shot percentage was just over 45%, which is a borderline performance. They beat us on the rebounds, but only by a margin of six. Our field-goal shooting went to hell in the fourth quarter.

The big difference was we got to the line 40 times for 30 points, versus their 18 out of 26. It was similar to the way we won in our first contest with Seattle, the second game of the season. It was ugly, but still a win. That's how Seattle makes you play. I'd rather win ugly than lose pretty anytime.

"Pit bull" practices made the difference.

Bernie Bickerstaff took his team back to Seattle after the game. He wanted them to lick their wounds and retune their strategies in familiar surroundings. I liked that. With him out of town, we didn't have to share our practice facilities. Best of all, the writers didn't have any Sonics to interview from Saturday until the next game, which was on Tuesday. It quieted the whole thing down. The focus was on work instead of woofing.

"Okay," I told the team, "the first one is under our belt. We concentrated on stopping their offense and fending off their defense. I think that made us a little tight. We're going to attack more. Now they'll see our game—fast and precise, aggressive on all first options. We've got to do a better job on the boards. Kareem, Kurt, A.C., James, Mychal, Buck: Get your ass on the board. Get in there and get in there early."

I told A.C. and Mychal, "They treated you like a rag doll. That's what you looked like. They sent you flying out of the pack all the time. You've got to stay in there. Don't let anybody leverage you out. Don't be surprised when you get a forearm smash in the back. Don't be surprised when you block somebody out and you're thinking, 'I've got this rebound,' and they come over your back and rake you across the face. We know what they are going to do.

"Our perimeter players have to be more alert, quicker to the spots. The execution has to be better. In the game Golden State beat us, we shot four for fourteen in the last period. Yesterday we shot two for twenty in the last period. Is this a trend? Are we going to let them take us out of our offense?"

Ellis had a horrible first game—3 for 13 from the field, 0 for 2 from 3-point range. Cooper had been on him like a second skin all night. Coop slides through picks better than anyone in the league. He's so slender and elastic. He gets one skinny shoulder into the gap and the rest of him squirts through.

Every time Ellis had a low-scoring game against Dallas or Houston, he came back the next night and scored a bundle. Our concentration had to stay strong against him. Bickerstaff had them back home, looking at game tapes, realizing how hard they made us work to beat them in a close game. I knew he was saying, "We're handling these guys. Give them more pressure. We can beat them."

Earvin picked up the Most Valuable Player trophy at a press conference after Monday's practice. "I should thank Larry Bird for having a slightly off season," he said. "I'll tell him, 'If you want to be slightly off next year, that's okay too.' I want to catch up to him. And when I see Michael Jordan, I'll strangle him for putting all that pressure on me. Because I didn't think I'd ever win it. Dominique Wilkins, Isiah, Barkley . . . I'll kill them too."

Earvin dedicated the award to his father, for working two jobs and sacrificing his own chance to play. Finally, they asked Earvin if his award was the ultimate accomplishment. He shook his head and said, "Diamond rings, that's what I play for. That's all I'm about— winning."

My final comments before Game Two were simple. "This is a key game. We have to match their intensity. Tonight's the night. Tonight's the night you're going to get truly tested. You only become a great team in this league by the number of tests that you can pass. When you pound on gold, when you put gold in the crucible and put it under fire, it only gets purer and stronger. Seattle is trying to pound on us. Make us weaker. Make us afraid. Put us under fire. Wear us out.

"We're a better team. We're experienced. We worked all year for the opportunity to be on top. Now we're moving towards it. We have to keep moving. And you cannot allow a first-time bunch that has not proven itself to talk and bully and maneuver themselves by you."

Game Two was a tough game. We were ahead 56–55 at the half, thanks to a 25-point performance by James. Chambers just couldn't stay with him.

We were up by 6 after three periods, 83–77. We were constantly struggling—taking the ball to the basket, penetrating, blowing by, getting smacked. Going to the free throw line. You have to get a defensively aggressive team into foul trouble right away. Drive the lane, get hammered, punch a hole in their defense like a can opener. The team depends on Earvin for that—a lot.

A.C. Green came alive in the fourth quarter. He finished with 14 rebounds and we overtook them on the boards, 42 to 29. We won the fourth quarter, 29–27, and the game, 112–104.

Reporters got on me in the locker room afterwards. Why weren't we putting them away with big margins? What happened to Show Time basketball? I told them, "This is not ice skating or diving. The idea here is to win, even if it is not pretty. We score two baskets in a row and they call time out. They are going to make us work, to make us grind."

This was now the Western Conference Finals. As you start moving up levels of competition for the biggest prize, every team still standing is there for a reason. Regardless of where they were rated. Regardless of their win-loss record over the regular season. It isn't luck. Seattle was for real.

Back in the summer of 1967, when I was about to start my rookie season for the San Diego Rockets, Bernie Bickerstaff was just out of the University of San Diego basketball program. He had tried out for the Harlem Globetrotters, then returned home. There were games all summer at San Diego Municipal Gym. Bill Walton, who was then a high school kid from La Mesa, would be there sometimes. Elvin Hayes would be there. Bickerstaff used to wear long pants, shoes and socks, and no shirt. I never saw him wear shorts. He was tough—just like he coaches.

It was time to shift the series to their home court. I think the Sonics believed they could win both games up there. The Seattle papers were treating it like a sideshow. After two upsets, Dallas and Houston, after staying close twice in the Forum, they thought the bubble would never burst.

We had a nine o'clock team breakfast on Saturday, May 23rd. Game Three was set for two in the afternoon. We breakfasted together, watched videotapes from the first two games, then got on a bus and headed for the Coliseum. After thirty minutes of shooting, we watched the Pistons and the Celtics on TV. After two Boston Garden losses, the Pistons won their first game at home. The Sonics had to be watching the same game. They had to be thinking, "That's all we have to do. Just like Detroit. Win the home game."

I wrote on the board before the game: "What is hustle? Hustle = Hard work? No! Hustle is a talent." I wanted to break the mind-set of playing not to lose. I wanted them playing to win. Bickerstaff had put five defenders on Earvin trying to wear him down. Every four minutes a fresh player came at him. I said, "Earvin, your attitude has to be: 'Five guys? Bring 'em on!' We've got to break the mind-set of their defense. They want to pressure you into fatigue mistakes. We've got to work against it. There has to be a joy in knowing that we are good, that we are the best team. Let's lift each other up by outworking them on the effort plays. The rest of the game will take care of itself. Let's show them the work ethic today."

Game Three definitely was an effort game. We only won it by a single point, 122–121, but it wasn't really as close as the score makes it seem. We built the lead in each of the first three quarters. We let them back in during the fourth quarter. Xavier McDaniel lifted them with 20 points in the period. Ultimately, we were saved by James Worthy's 39-point performance and by Wes Matthews's great relief minutes late in the second and third quarters.

Coop could have ended up the goat, but he came out as the hero. With about a minute and a half to go, we were up 118–112. Michael controlled the ball in Seattle's court. Instead of patiently running down the clock, he lifted a jumper from the left side. Maurice Lucas blocked it. The Sonics attacked on the other end and Kareem fouled X-Man while he drove. McDaniel made the field goal and the foul. Our lead was three. Bickerstaff called a time-out. They set a play for Dale Ellis to come around a screen by Lucas and pop a jumper. Ellis made his curl and Luke set the screen. Coop was just squeezing by Luke when the ball got delivered to Ellis, who was open about 15 feet away. Ellis sighted the rim and brought the ball up. Michael sprinted and launched himself like a triple jumper. Just as the ball was released, he deflected it with his fingertips.

Everybody slept in Sunday morning. The next game was Monday at two. We watched Detroit thump Boston 145–119. That series now stood at two and two. As usual, Randy had to make two scouting reports, two sets of videotapes.

Practice was late in the afternoon, from three to four-thirty. Bill and I had dinner afterwards with some of the CBS production crew. They like to get a sense of our strategies. It helps the announcers know what to say and helps the camera operators spot the key matchups.

Our Monday morning practice was about two things: airspace and attitude.

Seattle had stayed close because of rebounding. They have brawny frontline players. Chambers weighs 230. Lister is 240. Clemon Johnson is 240. Luke is 238. They were getting four times as many offensive rebounds, which gave them several second attempts to score. They were jostling our guys. The shot would go up and A.C. or Kareem or Earvin would coil themselves to spring. Before they could launch, someone would slam a body on them. They weren't getting off the floor. I said, "We have to control not only the space on the floor. We have to control the airspace. We have to get airborne quicker."

At 3 and 0, we could take the attitude that all we needed to do was win one of the next four. That would be enough to get us past Seattle. But why not take the attitude of going all out to stop them right now? I said, "All year long we've been working on one thing. We've been working to get into position. You're like an army on a campaign. You fight in the valley so you're in a position to attack the ridge. You fight for the ridge so you're in a position to attack the city. You fight for the city so you're in a position to take the capital.

"We're going after them," I said. "We're pushing into the Finals. We've got homecourt advantage because we pushed all season long. If we push today, we'll have the longest rest time, the longest preparation time. We'll have the best position. That's what we're working for."

Our covenant was to play harder. To be the quiet assassins. Not to give them any emotional fuel. To do exactly what we'd done for three games—only harder. Roberto Guerrero had lost the Indy 500 in the final laps that same day. I capitalized on his misfortune with a little exaggeration. I said, "You know what he did, don't you? He took his foot off the gas. By the time they got him started again, the race was lost. We're into the last leg of this series. Don't take your foot off the gas."

The Lakers not only kept their foot on the pedal, they tromped it through the floorboard. Game Four was our best playoff game.

Seattle had a great game plan. It really might have beaten us. But we had adjusted to it so well that they lost confidence. In Game Four they came out and just played. Instead of dictating the tempo with pressure and physical tactics, they tried to run with us. We were alive and tuned. We got the ball to the open man consistently and our defense shut down all three of their big guns. There was still plenty of physical play, but we just collected the free throws and kept pushing. We won every quarter. Converted 44 out of 53 attempts at the line and shot 51% to their 35%. After an ass-kicking series, we turned in a 133–102 blowout performance.

Bernie Bickerstaff had done a hell of a job getting his troops so far. Preseason wisdom had them at the bottom of the totem pole. They mounted a serious challenge for the Conference championship. It was great to see the Seattle players congratulating each other at the end of the game.

For the first time since Ralph Sampson's "funky" shot of May 21st, 1986, we were champions of the Western Conference.

25

Full Circle in Santa Barbara

We almost played the Detroit Pistons. We flew home from Seattle on Monday night. The next Tuesday, Detroit had a 107–106 win sewed up in Boston Garden. All they had to do was inbounds the ball near Boston's basket, then control it for a couple of seconds. The next game would be on their own home court. If they won it, they'd win the Eastern Conference.

Isiah Thomas lofted a pass to Bill Laimbeer, not noticing Larry Bird circling around. Bird snagged the pass. As he fell toward the out-of-bounds line, Dennis Johnson broke for the basket. Bird found him with a pass with one second left and Boston, suddenly, had the series lead at 3–2.

If the Eastern Conference Finals ran to seven games, we'd be out of action until next week. The very soonest we could possibly play was on Sunday.

The Lakers had Tuesday off. Sometime after Bird stole Detroit's game and before the start of our Wednesday practice, Bertka and I made a decision: We had to get the team out of town. We had to create a training camp mentality. There's a fine line between being rested and being slack.

"I'll go crazy," I told Bertka. "Everybody will go crazy if we end up waiting in L.A. for eight days." We had been through almost eight months of playing and traveling together. All of a sudden we were at home in our comfort zones, waiting to play the ultimate series. We were separated. Even though we'd be sharp physically, letting go of our emotional bond might subtract something from the team.

Santa Barbara is less than two hours away from L.A. Mary Lou Liebich is the world's most overworked secretary, answering Mo, Bertka, Pfund, and West. She got on the phone for us. In a few hours, we were tentatively booked into a hotel, the Sheraton, and a practice facility, Santa Barbara City College. An intrasquad game was set for Friday night.

Management was a little upset at first. We needed an okay from Jerry West, but he was on an eastbound flight that Tuesday. We had to move on the arrangements without delay, then clear everything when his jet touched down. The playoffs are the most stressful time of the year for Forum staff. VIPs are demanding tickets and special treatment. The press contingent becomes ten times bigger. We frequently don't know where we'll be playing until seventy-two hours before tip-off. Travel and hotel bookings are insane. Throwing an impromptu training camp into the picture was like adding another sideshow to the circus.

But when we get to this point, there isn't anything that can't and shouldn't be done. Anything. Any request, any plan of action that's going to help get the job done. Or alleviate the pressure on the team. The only thing I care about is giving the players every single thing they need to give them a chance to win.

And this definitely was a need, based on past experience. There was no way we could let the team hang around home for eight days and let everybody pat them on the back and soften them up.

Our Wednesday practice was going to be strictly a blowout. Since no one knew whom we'd be facing, all we could do was work on our game, our basic execution. I walked through the tunnel and into the locker room beforehand. I went through the door and there were Earvin and Michael Cooper, with James over in his corner. Just those three and maybe a couple of others starting to straggle in.

Earvin caught my eye as I walked up to my cubicle. He had this goofy look on his face, as if he was waiting for me to say something. The "Are you thinking what I'm thinking?" look. The wavelength look.

I addressed all three of them. "What do you think if we get out of town?"

Earvin said, "Man, I thought you were thinking that." And I said, "I knew you were thinking the same thing."

He said, "We got to get out of town. We can't stay here with all the wives and friends and parties."

Everybody knew we had a week off. Invitations were starting to pour in. Paramount wanted us to be guests at the opening of *The Witches of Eastwick*, Jack Nicholson's new movie. There was all kinds of hoopla—people wanting to celebrate the team. We wanted to get the players away from that mentality, to be off somewhere where we could hold on to our focus and our commitment and not have to constantly say no. We had to take the attitude that we hadn't won anything yet.

James, Michael, and Earvin agreed. Now we had to sell the Captain on the idea.

When Kareem walked in I said, "Cap, what do you think if we go out of town and go to a little mini-camp?" Now, Kareem has his social world under control. He's been to more Finals and All-Star appearances than anyone in history. I could tell by the look in his eyes that he didn't want to leave L.A. and his kids, his own house, his own bed, his library, and his albums. But I could also see that he knew it was the right thing to do. And he said, "Okay."

After practice the next day, Thursday, we told the team what was up. Everything hinged on the game that night, the sixth Detroit-Boston game. I said, "If Boston wins, we stay right here. If Detroit wins, we go. Just make sure you're in Santa Barbara, checked in and ready to practice by eleven o'clock."

Everybody went home that night and watched. Detroit scored their third win, 113–105, so their series was tied and headed for the deciding match.

Our hotel was on Cabrillo Avenue, right between the beach and Highway 101, not far from the Santa Barbara wharf and only three minutes from the gym. Frank Carbajal is the basketball coach at Santa Barbara City College. I used to work in his summer camps back when I was a player. Frank is a very successful coach. He's a strict disciplinarian, always producing controlled offense and defense-oriented teams. He teaches every single movement of every fundamental basketball skill, broken down into an irreducible, essential action. Whether he has five tremendous players or five of the worst athletes ever, Frank gets them all playing the same kind of low-scoring but fundamentally rock-solid basketball.

At first, Frank was happy to see us there. We had it set up to play a little intrasquad game on Friday. Frank could stir up excitement by handing out tickets around town. He's always looking for ways to promote his program. So he went to the YMCAs and the Boys Clubs and some other youth groups around Santa Barbara. When word got around, suddenly all the boosters and townspeople were intent on seeing this game. Frank didn't realize how many friends he had. The gym only seats about three thousand. On game day he was down to about one hundred tickets and there was a line outside of three or four thousand people. He wasn't ready for that kind of pressure. Bertka knew. He hid out at the hotel instead of going home, where the phone was ringing off the hook.

The game was a total blowout, which was exactly what I wanted. We still had no special direction except to hone basic Laker basketball. We ran and ran.

After the game, Bill and Randy and I went to The Grill in Montecito, five miles south down 101. This was where we had so many dinners back in September, where we plotted out new offensive and defensive directions with our blue, broad-point felt-tip pens all over the big paper place mats. Over spaghetti and meatballs, alderwood-roasted chicken, and Coronas. It was a great feeling—all those sessions, all that work, all those games. Here we were again, full circle, except for a couple of persistent details: the Boston Celtics and the Detroit Pistons. We whipped out our felt-tip pens and wrote in between the spaghetti-sauce spots. This thing wasn't over yet.

We had to give an edge somewhere in our Saturday morning practice. Detroit is a running, perimeter-shooting team. Boston is a power-post team, a lot like us. We gambled on Boston's winning. They held homecourt advantage for the last game. So we prepared for some of the Celtics' tendencies.

Bird always plays a zone defense. He sags in the lane, pretends to cover his man, and keeps an eye peeled to surprise a post-up with a quick double-team. His favorite is to come up blind-side from the baseline. We had to try to keep Bird honest, make the officials see he was playing illegal defense.

McHale is a great shotblocker, the seventh best in the NBA. But he's vulnerable when he's covering a good perimeter player. He has trouble when you drive on him. The biggest weakness of the Celtics is the lack of quickness of their front line. We had to play physical inside and take the ball strong to the basket. We had to run at them, giving the front line no chance to rest.

Boston only gives you one shot. They like to pack the lane and force you to go at them over the top. Their guards are small, but they're extremely aggressive and physical. They always contest your shots. We had to execute our half-court offense very quickly, with precise ball movement.

We didn't emphasize hitting, as we had for Seattle. The whole idea behind our Santa Barbara mini-camp was to maintain conditioning. We had spent so many months, as a team and as individuals, getting our timing and our wind together. We like to play the fastest game possible, within the limits of maintaining control. I said, "We will have nobody to blame but ourselves if we get out of shape this week." So every day we blew out the carbon, worked up a good lather. Whatever drills we did were what we call "contingency motivation drills." That means the drills are controlled and policed by the players. We ran our three-line rush drill a lot. This is a three-man fast break drill. We will set a two-minute time, in which they have to make thirty layups. Two sets of three players are at each end of the floor. One set comes down, a point man and two wing men. They pass, cut, and lay it in. Only three passes are allowed, so they have to run hard. The ball cannot hit the floor. Then another set of three takes it the other way. So you have a continuous fast break, no waiting, and all twelve guys are responsible to make thirty layups with no miss.

I didn't have to demand performance. Anybody who was consistently missing got intense peer pressure from the other eleven guys.

That evening the whole team was invited to a dinner at the home of Barry Berkus. He's an architect and an art collector with a hillside home. Carbajal is one of his best friends.

We rode up together in a small bus. Bertka has lived in Santa Barbara for years and knows everyone in town. There was still some daylight, so he was playing tour guide. "Now, President Reagan's place is down that way. On the other side of this wall is so-and-so's big Italian villa."

All the players started calling him the Land Baron. They said, "We ain't gonna give you any playoff money, Bertka. You live up here? Man, you're already too rich. Hey, driver! Take us by Bertka's house. Let's see the Land Baron's house!"

Dinner was great. There was only the team, the coaches, Barry Berkus, and four or five of his friends. He had a catered buffet laid out. The Mike Tyson/Bonecrusher Smith fight was showing on cable TV. The walls were filled with astounding artwork, paintings by Frank Stella and David Hockney and other great contemporaries, which his whole house was designed to showcase. The view was majestic, just incredible. Several of the houses in that area were designed by him, and they all sort of flow together around the hills. The players were totally amazed. After sundown it was like looking out of an airliner cockpit. There were no streetlights, just the dark hills and the dark sky, the stars and a few lights of Santa Barbara way down below.

The bus ride coming back was even more of a delight. There were very few lights and practically no headlights coming our way. You couldn't see anyone else on the bus, unless they were sitting very close to you. It was like a kids-at-camp setting. I almost expected someone to start telling ghost stories. Instead, they got on poor Mychal Thompson's case.

This was a testing time—good-natured, but with some serious intent behind it. They were wondering if he was going to come through in the playoffs. If Mychal turned out to be a great asset, we had a tremendous chance of winning. If he played halfhearted, Boston's front line could gain ground whenever Kareem was on the bench. The time was now to find out if he had what it takes to join the Laker elite.

Mychal would defend himself against some comment. A voice would say, "Aw, be quiet, Thompson. You've never won anything."

"What do you mean? I won in high school. I won something."

"You won in high school? Hey, Coop! Did you hear that? He won in high school! Tell us what you won in high school. Did you win a class ring?"

"Aw, you guys, I'm a winner, man. I know what it is to win."

Then Kareem said, "Yeah, we're gonna teach you how it really feels to win."

Mychal kept talking, trying to give it back as good as he was getting. He's extremely quick-witted and inventive. But he was out-numbered eleven to one. Kurt said, "We had a guy here last year who used to do a lot of talking, too. But you know, he's playing for the Seattle Supersonics now."

Suddenly, James said, "He's right. He's right." James is usually the last one to participate in any jawing or teasing. "That's right. We don't want to hear any lip service, Thompson. No lip service."

A whole chorus of deep voices went, "Oooooo."

Sunday we had brunch together. We called it a meeting, but the whole purpose was to watch the seventh Boston-Detroit game. There was a big screen set up. There were all the pancakes, all the good French toast and waffles and strawberries they could eat. The attitude was very happy, very light. A couple of television stations from L.A. had sent crews up. They had Michael Cooper wired up for a spot during halftime. Pat O'Brien did the interview. While the rest of the world was in funky, sweaty Boston Garden, the Lakers were all laid back in a sunny Southern California beach outpost. The perfect image. It looked as if we were on vacation. All the guys did their best, off camera, to crack Coop's facade on national TV.

In the second half the players got quiet. They'd groan at a missed shot or a bad play or some failed strategy. It looked as if Detroit were going to win. Then there was a collision between two of the Pistons, Vinnie Johnson and Adrian Dantley. Both of them were shaken up.

With about six minutes left to go, Larry Bird took over. He hit three or four difficult jump shots. Danny Ainge hit a 3-pointer. Everybody in the room was locked into the last few seconds of the telecast, saying things about the players and the action.

When it ended, Boston had won 117–114. Earvin Johnson stood up and said, "Okay. Let's go to work."

Finally,
the Finals

At six o'clock, the evening of Tuesday, June 2nd, Jake O'Donnell dipped the ball down at center court and then tossed it straight up. Kareem Abdul-Jabbar and Robert Parish followed his motions with their eyes. They uncoiled with all their strength, extending their 7-foot bodies and long arms to maximum height. The 1987 NBA Finals were now in action. This was the summit. People had said we couldn't get here—too many obstacles, rising new teams, aging veterans. But we were back.

Santa Barbara had been everything we wanted it to be. It was lively, good for conditioning, good for the team's emotional bonds. Now we needed to face the job ahead. I tried to put the series into perspective in our Monday practice.

"In 1985 we had to win," I said. That was a year of retribution. We lost a championship to the Celtics in 1984, even though we were a stronger team. We were humiliated and mocked. People called us choke artists. The L.A. Fakers. We were driven to reestablish our dignity and our self-respect. In 1986 we wanted to win a repeat championship. But we put limits on ourselves, unconsciously. We boxed ourselves in with the attitude of "How can we top last year?"

I reminded the team about that phrase. I said, "There was truth in that, because there really is no way to top what we did in 1985. It was a forever experience. We don't have to top it.

"This year, 1987, we don't have to win the championship. But we want to. Like a writer who writes a best-seller wants to create another one. Like a painter who creates a masterpiece wants to create another one. Like a lawyer who wins the most prominent case in the nation wants to try another one. It doesn't mean they have to do it. But the great ones want to do it again. So, 1987 isn't about having to win. It isn't about 'How can we top 1985?' It's about wanting to win. That's all there is. That's what declares you to be the very best. It's an athlete's primal instinct."

I had seen a newspaper headline after Boston eliminated Detroit: "Blood, Guts, and Courage Versus Show Time." It set me off.

"Here we go again with the perception that we are less than our opponent. Boston has staved off injuries. Courage has brought them here. Real men, versus you. The superficial, sensitive Lakers. Pampered buddies of the movie stars. Natural athletes, who win because of gifts, not because of years of honing their craft, not because of guts.

"That's what people think. You are less than real. Why are we not called a tactical team, an intelligent team, a team of great strategy? We never hear that. It's always Show Time, it's always flash, it's always style, it's always entertainment. Anything but the truth.

"You and I know, anyone in this league knows, that it's more demanding to play fast break basketball, to make decisions and execute strategy on the run. We all know it's easier to play set-it-up-and-grind-it-out basketball. We know we're a team with great strategy. But the Boston Celtics are always the ones described in that way. Blood and guts and courage. And they are using that perception to minimize your effort. Your tormentor, your opponent, is just reeling with joy over this. It panders to the lowest common denominator—collective jealousy, collective resentment.

"The truth is, there has rarely been a team more dedicated, more passionate, more caring, more together and more real than the Lakers of the 1980s. Especially this year.

"They don't know. They really don't know who the hell we are. Why do we allow the collective psychic energy of the public to hold this image of us?

"Our environment is here on the court. This is where we get the job done. This is our strength. We understand the power of belief. That's the key to our motivation. We all believe in our greatness. This is what we are playing for this year. Not having to win—just wanting to win. Here's what we're up against:

"To begin with, America loves underdogs and heroes. Logic says that the Celtics are the underdog. They're hurt, they're injured, they're broken, they're down. They're tired. They've had two seven-game series. For the Celtics it's been a manly struggle. America loves them more than ever.

"We have 'breezed' through the playoffs. It's as if our wins have had nothing to do with preparation or tactics or execution. The implicit idea is that the Lakers are people of limited or questionable substance.

"No, I am not suggesting that what other people think about the Lakers can deprive us of a championship. Only we can deprive ourselves of a championship. But I'm saying that this collective belief gives us an extra opponent.

"Kareem made a statement during the Golden State series. He said something was coming into the picture that didn't belong there. We caught ourselves and eliminated it. We cannot allow ourselves to be sidetracked by this peripheral opponent: Blood, guts, and courage versus Show Time. Guts versus lack of substance. I want you to think about this.

"If we don't deflect this thinking, it will increase the difficulty of our job. We have to beat everyone then. We've got to beat the Celtics. We've got to beat the media. We've got to beat the officials and we've got to beat the public. That's not our job."

I was really upset about that article and that public attitude. We were supposed to win. If we don't, then blood and guts and injuries beat the superficial team. If we do, we don't deserve any credit. All we beat was an injury-racked underdog. Well, bullshit! The media and the public didn't cry for us when we faced the Philadelphia 76ers in the 1983 Finals. When James Worthy had a broken leg, Bob McAdoo had a torn hamstring, and Norm Nixon had a shoulder separation. And we didn't seek to build any underdog image. We consciously avoided it.

Developing and maintaining a strong bench, preventing all the injuries you can with sufficient rest and advanced medical attention, these are all part of making it in a campaign that can stretch over 100 games. It wasn't chance that gave us terrific chemistry, a deep bench, a healthy squad. The Lakers didn't need to apologize for their excellence. We didn't need to rein it in, either, to subconsciously give our underdog opponent a "fair" chance. At tip-off time you play with what you've got, period.

I told the team, "We cannot tolerate mediocrity in our play. We cannot tolerate mediocrity in our attitude, in our focus, in our game. We cannot tolerate mediocrity in each other. After that game where Sleepy Floyd went crazy, I heard one of you say, 'We played as hard as we can, but we just lost.' If that is going to be your attitude, then you and I are not on the same wavelength at all. You can say, 'We just lost. We got beat. They beat our ass.' But don't rationalize it. Because that is mediocrity. We cannot go in with that attitude at all."

We finished the talk by settling some team business. The league schedule called for two games in L.A. followed by three in Boston, then the last two, if needed, back home again. So we had to make a decision. Would players' wives make the Boston trip? And if so, when? I argued that it was a business trip. I respect the importance of the wives and I understand their wanting to share in the experience. But I was concerned about adding their presence to all the factors of travel and preparation. "It's the same thing as the regular season," I said.

We agreed on a compromise. Game Three was on Sunday. The wives could arrive on Monday, when everyone was settled.

The tip-off went to McHale. Parish attempted a shot and Kareem blocked it. It was the first notch in Kareem's incredible opening-minutes performance, which set the stage for the way we handled the game. Within one minute he had three rebounds. Within two minutes he had three blocked shots.

It was a minute and a half before anyone made a bucket. Both sides turned the ball over with offensive fouls. McHale tried to bodyslam A.C. out of low post position, and James drew an offensive goaltending call trying to tip in a missed shot. We were fresh and excited. Our only problem was containing our electricity. The Celtics looked drained. We were concerned that they might be emotionally intense and well honed after winning the Detroit series. Sometimes it works that way. But they showed the signs of fatigue and of having had no time to prepare. I think they decided to give it a shot in the first two games, but really point toward the ones in their home court.

Kareem opened the scoring with a short hook in the lane. James followed a missed shot for another two. Byron broke loose and went the length of the floor. Bird and McHale were the only defenders who could get back. They didn't even have time to turn around before Byron launched himself and dunked.

K.C. Jones, the Boston coach, called a time-out to regroup. Earvin had missed three attempts in a row, but after the time-out he scored off the fast break and drew a foul off Dennis Johnson. The score had run from twin zeroes to 9–0. We were running and pushing the ball at them, looking for opportunities. We committed some turnovers in the rush, but we were dictating the speed of the game. Of our first 16 possessions, 13 became fast breaks. Boston was struggling. They were 0 for 6 before their first basket.

When their offense finally got going, we matched each point with quick strikes, usually between five and ten seconds after their baskets. Earvin fed Kareem on a dunk and hit three perimeter jump shots in a row. The Celtics never had time to exult.

K.C. called another time-out at the six-minute mark. Coop replaced James. I wanted fresh legs coming in at all times. Two minutes later Kurt entered for A.C., then Mychal for Kareem and James back in for Byron. Boston tried Walton at center and we ran Kareem and Mychal together. Earvin scored the last points of the period on a layup. We were ahead 35–26. We were well balanced. Kareem, James, and Earvin each scored eight.

Boston tried to match our quickness in the second quarter by substituting Darren Daye and Sam Vincent for McHale and DJ— Dennis Johnson. Boston's bench is mistake prone. But you can't sell them short. If you don't pressure them, they can start some momentum. Then the veterans will return and capitalize on it. Daye tries to play aggressive defense. We had to push it at him inside. Vincent has a tremendous first step, almost as explosive as Andrew Toney of the 76ers. We had to contain him.

We traded baskets for the first couple of minutes. Then James drove on Daye and got the hoop plus the foul. Bird and Ainge went to the bench for a breather. Coop stole it from Daye on the other end and James scored on the breakaway. Earvin stole from Daye next time and Coop hit from 24 feet to score three points. The score was 49–30 with eight minutes left in the period.

Bird replaced Daye after less than two minutes of rest. Our lead held steady until the end of the half. We led 69–54 and outrebounded them 27 to 12. At the half we emphasized three things: defense, rebounding, and pushing the ball upcourt quickly.

Bird lifted them in the third period with 14 points and 3 rebounds. But James got 5 rebounds and 8 points, to go with 12 from Earvin. We outscored them by a single point in the third. They fought hard in the fourth and cut 3 off our lead. Ironically, Boston did the most catching up when it was bench against bench in the closing two minutes. But the final was still a Laker blowout, 126–113. James not only led us in scoring with 33, he had 10 assists, the most in his career. Kareem scored 14, with 10 rebounds and 4 blocked shots. We made 55 baskets, and 36 of them were scored inside, on dunks and layups.

In the locker room when we put our hands together, I told the team, "No long interviews. Give Boston their respect. Answer all the questions briefly and politely. Don't give them any fuel."

Down in the locker room, Kareem gave credit to the coaching staff. "No rust," Cap said. "Give credit to Pat, Bill, and Randy. They made us run a lot in the week off. We didn't lose our legs." Mychal extended the same thought beyond the proper boundaries. "Our practices were harder than the game," he said.

He was right, but it was the wrong thing to say.

On top of the press contingent, which was overstocked for the Finals, a passel of TV and movie stars came into the locker room. Celebrities are nothing new in the Lakers' locker room. At different times we've had Ed Asner, Elliot Gould, Gene Kelly, Michael Jackson, and lots of other stars. But this was a flood. All the sports reporters acted as if they had just signed on with the *National Enquirer*. Instant paparazzi. Microphones and cameras were swinging around like berserk compass needles. Down from my cubicle, Don Johnson and Bruce Willis were working their way up to James Worthy's locker. Johnson said, "James Worthy, the baddest dude." I winced.

The locker room is our haven, our place of refuge. I hate to have commotion in there. I'm sure these stars intended to come in and be cool and dignified. I'm sure they want visitors to their sets to hang back, respect their need to concentrate, and stay the hell out of their dressing rooms. But everybody got too jacked up. It was a media moment, a sideshow.

Later, upstairs in the Forum Club, everybody was acting as if it were time to celebrate and they were ready to be the life of the party. Everybody had wanted to party when we were off for eight days. Now everybody was assuming that we were going to be the champions. They were planning the victory parade.

I looked around at the smiling faces and I felt like slapping them all. We had only won one game. As long as the Celtics were still standing, we were still fighting for our lives. We were in a war.

Bertka and Randy and I met in my office. "We were too soft on Bird," Bertka said. "We gave him too many opportunities. We have to deny more of the passes to him. We have to get up in his face. If he doesn't get the ball, he can't score."

The practice on Wednesday was light. When I came in, Kareem was up on the table and Vitti was shaking his head. I asked him what was the matter. "Out for the season," he said. Kareem smiled. "I've just got a twisted ankle," he said. "It's just swollen a little." I made a mental note to have Vitti barred from the Comedy Store.

James had tendinitis in his knees, so two thirds of our front line sat out the practice. Earvin, who probably could have used some rest after playing forty minutes, got out and led the team in layup lines. Our practice was light, mostly concerned with timing. Then we reviewed video and went home.

The next day, prior to Game Two, I said, "We know it's gonna be harder. It's only been one game. In spite of what the press says, we have to think about playing better and improving. The media is doing nothing right now but helping them. I don't know about you guys, but I had a very hard time in this locker room Tuesday night. After we had spent eight months to get where we wanted to be, after playing forty-eight minutes against the Celtics, who are still the world champions, to come in here after winning just one goddamn game and to have a goddamn display. We have to talk about policy!"

They all started nodding in agreement. "You've got to watch about all these people around you. It's that peripheral opponent. I could not get them away from me fast enough. I wanted to smack all of them. And I hope you take the same attitude. Don't allow anybody now to drain you of your energy. Not movie stars, not your wives, your family, your friends. Nobody. Another seven days, fellows. That's it. Seven more days of keeping everybody out.

"We have to keep pounding the ball inside and running it. Rebound, run, post. Our off-guard play is going to be critical because of their double-teaming Kareem, James and Earvin. Float on the perimeter and look for your shot.

"We let Bird take 25 shots. 20 were from outside 18 feet. Let's make him drive. DJ had a horrendous first game. He will be back. We're going to stunt and slide on DJ. We will not rotate on him. We want him to shoot. Stunt back on him, but allow the shot. Rotate to Ainge. He has more depth and range to his shot.

"Kareem was the key for us in the first six minutes of the game. We need the rebounds to create the outlets and start running."

This time we controlled the tip. Byron scored the first points of the game. He came jumping right in between Bird and McHale to grab a rebound and lay it in. It was one of our few bold opening moves. We were very tentative in the first minutes. Boston came back with perimeter shots. Their first four shots went in the hole. They had us down 8 to 4 after two minutes. It took six more minutes to regain the lead.

Worthy scored three straight baskets, then Byron Scott scored three straight. We passed them at 26–25 when Kareem spun right underneath. Parish was expecting a skyhook to the left, so Cap wheeled the other way and scored a layup. Dennis Johnson retook the lead for Boston, but Cooper stung them with a 3-pointer and Byron hit from the perimeter.

Ainge was on Earvin every time the Celtics scored, trying to slow the advance of the ball upcourt. We mixed them up by outletting to Byron and Coop and by sending Earvin up the sideline instead of the middle.

The Celtics came within one point when there was just a minute left in the first quarter. James was testing McHale in the low post. A double team developed, so he kicked the ball out to the point. Earvin initiated a drive and sucked the defense into the lane. Without looking, he flipped the ball back to Cooper. Coop drilled his second 3-pointer.

We started the second quarter with a 38–34 lead. Mychal muscled up through a foul by Bill Walton to score underneath. Mychal is still a finesse player, but he works on his upper-body strength constantly. He can bust through on a physical level whenever it's necessary. In four minutes we had built our lead to seven points, 49–42. Then Cooper attempted another 3-pointer. When it dropped through, the entire crowd jumped to its feet. They stayed up for several minutes, yelling and chanting. They yelled louder when Coop passed to Kareem on the break and Cap dunked. K.C. called a time-out. We had scored 5 straight points in twenty seconds and the lead was now 12.

DJ scored two free throws after the Boston time-out. On our

next possession Cooper attempted another 3-point shot. This one landed on the side of the rim. It rolled from the front to the back, then it kicked up almost as high as the top of the backboard. On the way back down it dropped right through. Michael had just tied the record for most 3-pointers in a Finals game, and we were ahead by 13. With another surge in the last two minutes we pulled to a 75–56 halftime lead. Coop had scored 15 points in 16 minutes. He also accounted for 16 more points, with 8 assists in the quarter, which tied a Finals record held by Robert Reid, Bob Cousy, and Earvin Johnson.

In the halftime talk I just said, "Twenty-four more minutes and we hold serve. Don't let up."

In the second half Bird went to work with a 3-pointer of his own, plus a layup. Kareem and Earvin each got a basket, and James made two free throws. McHale scored a layup. It looked as if they were ready to assert themselves.

Byron blew the confrontation wide open. Bird had the ball down low. We pressured him and he sent it to Danny Ainge near the top of the key. Byron had shifted into the lane as part of our stunting defense, but he never looked directly at Bird. He was watching the situation develop out of the corner of his eye. When the pass was sent up to the top, Byron stepped forward and got a hand on the ball. It hit the floor and he got to it before Ainge could. He started a dribble. Ainge put a body on him. He spun a full 360 degrees counterclockwise off Ainge and outran him to the other end of the court for a slam dunk. McHale turned it over on Boston's next possession, and Kareem scored his 20th point with a short hook in the lane. We were 22 points out in front, with nine and a half minutes left in the period. Boston usually tries to make their strongest statements at the start of each half. We took their best shots each time and came back with something better.

With about four minutes left in the period, McHale started bringing them back offensively with close-range shots. We had just brought Mychal Thompson in for A.C., because Ace has trouble matching up to McHale's longer arms and veteran moves. Mychal has a familiarity with Kevin that goes back to when they played on the same team at Minnesota. But this time it was Mychal's turn to struggle. Bird blocked one of his shot attempts and Parish stole the ball from Coop. McHale dropped in a bank shot and a short baseline jumper. Boston suddenly gained six points on us in about one minute.

I called a time-out with just over two minutes left. We went in to Kareem, but McHale fouled him and he missed both shots. Then, with one and a half to play, Cooper buried his fifth 3-pointer from 25 feet away.

Parish sank two free throws. James Worthy came back and dunked on him, drawing the foul. We had the momentum again. The quarter ended at 107–92.

Boston began the last period with their starting lineup, with the exception of Darren Daye in place of Kevin McHale. James moved against Daye on the baseline. He went into the air and curled the ball up with his left hand. The shot dropped and Daye was called for a foul. On Boston's next possession Mychal rejected Bird's shot attempt. Then James scooped in a shot and drew Ainge into another foul. McHale came in for Daye, but Bird left the game. I wondered if this was a sign that K.C. was conceding the game. Earvin scored from the top of the key and K.C. called a time-out. He ran in Bill Walton and Sam Vincent for DJ and Parish. Earvin stole their next possession from McHale and fed James for another two points on the fast break. Using only two starters, we had run off an 8–0 spurt in one and a half minutes. The crowd began to chant, "Sweep! Sweep!" One minute later, Cooper put in his sixth 3-point bomb. Then Rambis scored two consecutive dunks. K.C. pulled out Danny Ainge, who was the last of the Boston starters still on the court. I brought in Adrian Branch, Mike Smrek, and Wes Matthews. It was subs against subs again for the last six minutes, which is very rare in the Finals. We finished at 141–122. Five Lakers were above 20 points. We had 44 assists, which was a new Finals record and a demonstration of the power of unselfish, single-minded play.

On Friday morning, the local papers were echoing the "Sweep" chant. One of them headlined this story: "Now It's on to Has-Bean Town." We flew out of LAX at half past noon, getting into Logan Airport around eight-thirty, with a day and a half to prepare for Game Three. There were some surprises waiting for us.

27

The Edge

The Friday we spent flying to Boston was our first day off in almost two weeks. We had switched hotels. Buss signed a deal with the Sheraton chain, and so did the NBA. The Boston Sheraton was also where all the official NBA functions and press conferences were going to be held. We figured anything would be better than our experiences at the Marriott in '84 and '85, when we were plagued with constant fire alarms and incredibly slow room service.

The Sheraton turned out to be a zoo: forty-five minutes for room service, lines from the restaurant and the coffee shop out into the lobby. It wasn't the fault of the staff, it was just the sheer numbers of people.

The players were pinned down in their rooms. It's hard for them to go out on the streets in Boston. You never know what kind of harassment will happen. There is always a sense of physical danger when we go to Boston—even for wives and family. There are always threats and crank calls to go along with the fire drills. A couple of years ago, Boston fans threw rocks through the windows of the press contingent's bus. Then they ripped apart a nearby car and set it on fire. Boston is supposed to be the Athens of America, but in our experience it's more like Beirut.

Our first Sheraton false alarm came at three in the morning. At nine we convened for a team breakfast and our first practice session in Boston Garden.

Bertka and I had spent hours talking about what we wanted set up for us at Boston Garden. We had Vitti call and make requests. But you can always bet, no matter what you request of Celtics management, that they will do nothing. They are one of the most uncooperative front offices in the league.

The locker rooms are dirty. Nothing has been done to them in years. We were concerned about heat. We didn't want another locker room steambath, like we had in '85. The windows are high up. When you're playing an afternoon game, the sun pours in. The air becomes stifling. So we wanted to shade the windows. We also contacted an air-conditioning company and rented two portable units. All the details were covered in advance. Everything was supposed to be ready when we arrived for the game on Sunday.

The major part of my job isn't to tell the players what to do. The most important thing I do is to create a great setting for them to work in. I think that's the key to any manager's job—creating an environment that's organized, free of distractions, ready. We were scheduled to practice in the Garden from eleven A.M. to one P.M. I wanted the Lakers to be able to come in, change to their practice clothes in peace, work out effectively, and relax afterwards.

On Sunday, both air conditioners were stacked out in the hall. Our video monitor wasn't set up; neither was the blackboard. No towels. No soft drinks. I yelled, "Bertka!"

He and Gary came down the hall, took a look at all the disorganized crap, and gave me a look that said, "These sonsabitches!"

"That's Boston Garden," Vitti said. "No cooperation. No class." I was furious.

The air-conditioning crew had already showed up. The Boston Garden superintendent sent them home. He said an electrician had to update the circuits first. Of course, no one actually got an electrician on the job until we arrived and pitched a bitch.

We were seeing a little bit of what some people call "the Boston

Mystique" in action. The Boston Mystique isn't leprechauns hiding in the floorboards. It isn't blood and guts. It's a willingness to use any tactic to upset an opponent. Turn up the heat when it's already hot. Shut down the visitor's water heaters. Instigate hard fouls on the court. The General Manager chasing officials all the way to the dressing room to try to intimidate them. To hell with dignity. To hell with fair play.

Boston already has tremendous talent. If you lose there and complain, it sounds as if you're making excuses. You have to win first. The Lakers of the eighties have done that enough by now to speak with authority.

The "Boston Mystique" encourages the lowest common denominator of fan behavior. It grows directly out of the low-rent attitudes of Boston management. They're the Klingons of the NBA. I respect the individual players. Bird will always be one of the legends of the sport. The rest of the starters all have their areas of excellence. Some of the bench people are considerably talented. And K.C. Jones is a class individual. But the organization and its traditions are out-of-date.

Before the game I tried to dispel any "mystique" thinking on the team. I said, "They may be ninety-six and three here for the last two years, but they're one and three against us, the last four times we played here. Block out the Garden. It's just a court. It's ninety-four by fifty. It's the same hardwood, same measurements, same basket, same rim, same net, same everything as any other court you're going to play on. Just put a piece of Plexiglas around it. Block it out.

"Today isn't about playing better. Today is about playing the same way we played all season long.

"Our success so far has been determined by two things: A, advancing the basketball every single time; B, unselfish play.

"Just keep pushing the ball, even when there isn't a break. You're gonna wear them down. Don't think about scoring layups. Don't think about shooting opportunity jumpers off the break. The only thing you can depend on is advancement of the ball. I want you to take it out of the net and across half court in four seconds. Every time. You advance it, you advance it, you advance it. And before you know it, you'll crack their game. You'll get a layup. You'll get a jump shot. You'll get a dunk.

"Our offense has been successful so far because we've been totally unselfish. Everybody shared the ball. We still need that attitude.

"What Boston will want to do is play one great game. We can't let them regain any confidence at all. The first quarter is going to be critical. Whoever comes out and establishes first-quarter dominance will take the game."

I talked a little bit about our defense, about the responsibilities A.C. had to face, and about the fast break. We had allowed them to shoot 55% in Los Angeles. Anything over 50% here, on their home court, would win them the game.

"A.C.," I said, "whoever you played against Denver and against Golden State, you dominated. I think you did a pretty good job against the Seattle Supersonics, but I don't remember right now who you played against. I know who you're playing against in this series because he's kicking your ass." A.C.'s numbers had gone from high to low as the playoffs progressed. The level of competition hadn't changed. He just couldn't handle Kevin McHale in the first two games. Mychal Thompson had to plug the gap.

We were getting lazy on the break. Things had been too easy. Winning sometimes erodes a team's effort.

On breaks, the wing men have to always run out on the edges of the court. It's a discipline thing. Boston wasn't getting anybody back, so we started running direct lines to the basket. That's a bad habit. It allows one defender to counteract two or three guys. But when the wing men stay spread out, the first man down can lure the defender and then kick the ball out to whoever is open.

"You can bet that they're going to get back quicker on defense," I said. "It's not going to be easy like it was at home. They're going to take better shots at the offensive end. They won't be as impatient as they were in Los Angeles.

"Are you ready for them to put more pressure on the ball? Are you prepared to be taken out on drives? Are you prepared for hard fouls? Are you prepared for being clotheslined, like Kurt Rambis was in '84? Are you prepared to be rooted out of the post by McHale and Bird and Parish on offensive rebounds? Are you prepared to play harder than you did in Los Angeles? Are you prepared to be a little more patient on your offense? Are you prepared to do all the little things across the board that will help you win Game Three?

"If you think it's going to be as easy as it was in Los Angeles, then we're going to find ourselves at two and one. Instead of playing to win, we'll be playing to keep them from reaching a tie."

A great team that gets killed in two straight games will usually come back strong in rebounding. It's the first place to invest your effort and rage when you've been frustrated by defeat. Rebounding always makes a statement. Boston made it loud and clear.

For the first quarter of Game Three both teams were matched at 12 rebounds. We took a 29–22 scoring lead. In the second quarter they outboarded us 9 to 3 and outscored us 38 to 27. I thought first-quarter dominance would determine the game, but the turning point came in the middle of the second quarter.

Boston was getting back to protect the basket. Bird hurt us underneath and from the baseline. Ainge got accurate on his long jumpers from the weak side. When Parish picked up his third foul early in the second quarter and Greg Kite came in, it looked like a break for the Lakers. Kite is a 6'11" reserve who averages less than 10 minutes and 2 points a game. He's someone sportswriters pointed to as an example of how the Celtics lack quality bench players. This time, though, Kite was remarkable—an impact player. He was back under our basket anytime we inbounded the ball, containing our fast break. He was their most alert helper on double teams, taking away James Worthy's slashing layups and easy jumpers. He led Boston in pursuit of rebounds and loose balls. His nine boards were a career high. He made the whole team look quicker.

We were ahead 9 points when Kite came in, but we didn't look like the team that ought to be ahead. We looked like a team that was stretched too thin—about to crack.

We were down by 11 when he went out. The Celtics scored on 22 possessions out of 24 while Kite was in the game.

James Worthy had been our deadliest weapon throughout the playoffs. In the first two Boston games, he had scored 56 points in 77 minutes of playing time. He had 7 assists, 6 rebounds, and had shot 68% from the floor, which is supernova territory. He cooled down in the first half of Game Three: 4 for 9 from the field, 1 of 4 at the line, 1 rebound.

Byron Scott attempted two shots and made one. He didn't get to the line at all, didn't have a rebound. A.C. had four boards but no points. Our offensive force was shrinking to Kareem and Earvin. For all their greatness, even those two can't stand off an entire Finals-caliber team.

We were behind 60–56 at the half and 86–78 after three periods. But we gained ground with a run of nine to two, just as the third period ended.

The game came down to the wire. We tried to surge, they tried to hold us off. We'd score from the perimeter, then blow a dunk shot. We'd keep them from shooting for 23 seconds, then they'd force a bad shot and grab their own rebound and drop it in off the glass. Neither team could find a way to dominate the final quarter. No team could score consecutive baskets. We just traded points for the whole period. We lost by six, 109–103. Boston's rebounding edge was 48 to 32—exactly 50% more productivity than us. We just did not have enough passion or fire. Coop said it best: we got outhustled.

Bertka and I sat up until two-thirty in the morning watching the videotape. He said, "Now we'll find out what they're made of." The headline in the L.A. *Times* on June 8th read: "Laker Broom Comes Apart on Parquet Floor."

"Thank God," I thought. "No more talk about sweeps."

When two great teams get to the Finals, it isn't because of their offense or their defense or the cleverness of their coaches. It's because of their effort. Boston knew they had to win. All their effort muscles came into play. They were contesting every shot and pursuing every defensive play. They were patient in their set offense. They waited and kept working for the best shot.

On Monday we held an eleven o'clock practice. I talked about the wives. They didn't want to hear it, but they knew it was true. I said, "I'm not going to make a big deal about it right now. But I want you to think about your total commitment to the Lakers, to me, to each other.

"Last week we made a deal: No wives or friends would come back until Monday. We all agreed that we'd get to Boston, we'd practice, and we'd try to get the third game out of the way. We were unanimous. We would go together as a team and that would be it.

"Today I found out that a number of the wives flew in on their own Friday night. You were supposed to be settling in, resting and preparing mentally for the game, without distractions. I'm not going to fine guys. I'm not going to bench you, or send you home, or yell and scream at you. And I definitely don't want you to go back to your hotel rooms and yell at your wives for getting you in trouble.

"But I want you to think about what happened. We've created a little white lie. We lied to ourselves. There was the same mind-set when we went down to Houston last year and the series was one and one. I know there were a lot of distractions. A lot of partying. I know there were guys not really into the seriousness of our having to win both games. And what happened to us? We weren't ready to play. We weren't ready because we didn't back up our commitment. That's why we didn't get the job done. That's why we spent last summer in misery. It's not the wives' fault we lost. It's our own. But the point is, we broke a covenant.

"Fellas, we played a poor game yesterday. You guys had been flying through the playoffs. We were thirteen and one. We hadn't lost for a long time. Suddenly, we got our ass kicked.

"We've got that beaten feeling today. Sometimes it's hard to deal with. The key is: How do you bounce back from it? Why weren't we focused? We worked, but we did not work intelligently. We were not efficient. We didn't have a total commitment in the game. You could see it in our shot selection. Our selection was frivolous. We were taking early shots. We were taking desperation three-pointers in the last two and a half minutes. We looked like a team ready to crack. We had no balance.

"Our blocking out was totally nonexistent. You're not going to win a jumping contest with Parish and McHale. Hell, they're seven-footers with eight-foot arms. We've got to get good bodies under people. As long as you don't block out, they're going to keep pushing right up to the basket.

"I didn't see any hard fouls, except the ones we got from the Celtics. I saw one immediately from Danny Ainge. He took James out on his first layup attempt. Hard foul, right into the floor. Gave us a message. We didn't contest any of their layups. We just let them waltz in as if we didn't want to risk a foul.

"In the first three minutes of the third period they outscored us ten to two. I had to call time out to remind you, 'Hey, we've got to hustle.' We would call plays, but we wouldn't run them. We'd just get into the set and then do something else. We'd run a strong-side offensive play set and the weak side wouldn't move at all. There was no simultaneous movement. No cohesiveness.

"I think we really became affected by the greatness talk. We started to believe we were so great that we didn't need to worry about effort. They whipped us on the boards in Game Two. Now, in Game Three, the residual of that rebounding effort came back. They whipped us all over the court. We gave them their confidence back.

"Two straight games where we've been dominated on the boards. That's got to stop. We've got to get tough with rebounding. We've got to be more aggressive. We've got to be ready to pound and receive pounding. We've got to take better shots, like we did in Los Angeles.

We've got to run. We didn't use our quickness on Larry Bird until the fourth quarter, when the game was almost lost. For three periods we let Larry Bird throw them in from all over the place. Then, when the game got on the line, Cooper denied him. Bird only scored two free throws in the fourth period. He didn't even catch the basketball.

"Byron and James, you've got to let them know you can do more than just shoot the basketball. You both had great games in Los Angeles. But we're in Boston Garden now and you had horrible shooting games. One for nine and six for eighteen. And you let it affect your whole game. You didn't guard anybody. You didn't rebound the basketball. You didn't make any passes. You just stood around wondering, 'Why isn't my shot going in?'

"Kareem, what we're going to need from you is a fifteen-rebound game. Do you have it in you to get fifteen rebounds? You get four. You get five. You get three. Remember how you got seventeen here in '85? We need a fifteen-rebound game, Cap. This is the time to use all of your gifts in every way. Not just your shooting gifts or your running gifts.

"You've got seven days left. Seven days from today. Are we going to look back like we did in '84 and say, 'I regret I didn't bust my ass to get fifteen boards'? 'I regret that when I was six for eighteen I didn't get thirteen rebounds or make up for it in some other department.'

"Right now, a good performance isn't enough. A great performance isn't enough. What we need from each and every individual at this stage is a superior performance. If you're truly great, like everyone now says you are, you're going to produce superior performances."

I hardly ever talk to Kareem that directly. Only when I know we really need it badly. James seldom needs it, and Byron, since the start of this season, hadn't needed it much either. I was on top of them now because we were annihilated on the boards two games in a row. We had to catch ourselves right away. We were one game away from being tied. And Kareem agreed. The numbers don't lie. The video doesn't lie. The rebound effort charts don't lie.

In my first year of coaching I decided to make Kareem a better defensive player.

I invited him over to the house. We had a few days off, just before a big road swing. He had been playing poorly. He wasn't jumping. There was a lot of criticism of his effort in the press. I got out a tape I edited from twenty or thirty games. Each and every one of them showed him in a defensive position, not blocking out, not jumping, not responding, not pursuing. Just being there. He watched it all and didn't change expression. Then he looked directly at me. He said, "I know in those games that I did some things right."

I said, "Yes, you did. But I want you to see a lot of the things you did wrong first. I'd like you to start really concentrating more defensively. I already know you can score. I want you to take the personal challenge to start reacting better defensively—more rebounding, more shot blocking.

"I want you to forget about offense. Just totally forget about it. Just take the challenge and see if you can dominate a game defensively."

That was the challenge I gave: Try to make the greatest offensive force in the history of the game into a defensive player. My first coaching year.

Kareem was silent for a while. Then he said, "Okay. Whatever you want. But the next time we meet like this, I would rather have to respond to more objective analysis—not just visual. Pat, this is strictly visual and subjective. All you did was pick out the bad things. It's an arbitrary analysis of me not doing well in isolated parts of these games.

"Now, I don't resent it. I understand where you're coming from and I'll do my best to supply you with that. But I want you to supply me with statistical data to corroborate what you've said."

That meeting stimulated our whole program of keeping charts—which later gave us the foundation to build our Career Best Season program. Managers usually get their best ideas from the people they're supposedly in charge of. People think about coaches and managers as running everyone else, making them do what you want them to do. But listening is just as important as giving orders.

What Kareem said opened up my mind. I couldn't be arbitrary with him or Earvin, or any of the other great producers, when they had a bad night. I've got to give them more. Thus was born the rebound effort charts, shot chart analysis, plus and minus ratings. To show them exactly and irrefutably what their production numbers are—just as salespeople always see where they stand, relative to the averages for their district, relative to the other producers in the office. Just as the Goodyear plant knows how many radial tires they've got to turn out in an eight-hour shift.

The first game on our road trip was with the Washington Bullets. Kareem got 39 points, 11 rebounds, and 6 blocked shots.

A great performance occurs when all the factors we believe in as a team happen effortlessly and naturally. You never have to work at a great performance. The effort is academic. When those team factors happen effortlessly and naturally, it's because you're prepared. You're programmed. The self-worth, the knowledge, the skill, the rapport, the sensitivity, the concentration, and the energy all come together. Everything comes out like an instinct. And you gotta play to that.

That was what I wanted the team to find inside themselves for Game Four.

We arrived for our game-day shootaround on Tuesday, June 9th. We ran into some more Boston Mystique. Guys were running power saws. Guys were running vacuum cleaners between the aisles. Noise was coming from all directions. They had scheduled a crew of twenty maintenance workers at the same time as our practice. Conveniently. I had Josh Rosenfeld, our PR director, track down the head of maintenance. He told Josh, "I can't stop them. I'll have to pay overtime!" Josh relayed the message. I said, "Ask him why the hell he doesn't have them working during the Celtics' practice." So Josh was running back and forth like Henry Kissinger, and meanwhile the sweepers were sweeping and the carpenters sawing away. Until I realized the right thing to say.

I told Josh, "Tell him that if Boston ever gets to L.A., they're gonna see five hundred workers in the Forum every time they practice." That cleared the room.

Before the team started shooting I said, "We've got to have a superior performance in Game Four. We're right where we thought we would be. Bucking for a win on the opponent's home floor. It's either going to be three to one and we're playing for a championship, or two to two and a three-game mini-series. If it's two to two, they've got the edge. That's what we're working for. We're playing today for the edge. The psychological edge. To be one game from a championship. That's what today is all about. Let's take it a step forward. Let's do whatever it takes to win.

"Boston is the most dangerous playing from a crippled underdog position. Red Auerbach loves this. He's just thriving on it. Don't fall prey to this. Even after they beat us, they're still talking about all the guys who might not play in the next game. I can just see Auerbach smirking behind the scenes. You can bet that they're all going to be there for Game Four.

"Yes, they do have a mystique, perpetuated by the press. But so do we. We've got a mystique called Show Time. We know what really lies behind it. And the Celtics know that we know. Because we've beaten them with it in the past. We are not just another team. We stand toe-to-toe with them. They've won three championships in the eighties, and so have we. In the last twenty-two games with the Celtics, we're ahead thirteen to nine. That's the difference in the eighties."

We had to make some defensive adjustments for Game Four. Boston set excellent picks in Game Three. Bird is at his best using a pick to get off his shots from the perimeter and the baseline. His timing coming off the screens is extremely important. He needs to catch and shoot off the screen—all in one motion. All he needs is a pocket and a short count. We call it the shooter's pocket. We had to take away the timing. We could not let their passers just find him. We had to adapt to the rhythms in their set.

When Dennis Johnson is setting up a play, he dribbles until everyone is where he wants them to be. Then he shifts his weight when he's ready to deliver the basketball. As soon as he gave that sign, I wanted our guard to belly up on him—tight. We needed more ball pressure. We had to force the point guard back another five feet, so the pass would have to travel more distance. The extra distance would give our defender more time to fight through the pick and recover defensive position.

Double teaming both Parish and McHale was breaking our defense down. "We want to double McHale only," I said. "Everybody else is one on one. We'll double him when the ball is in flight, coming to him. You have to be in his face exactly when he catches the ball."

Boston's "need" play, the one they go to when they've got to get a basket, they call "Hawk." It's an isolation set. DJ and Bird isolated on one side of the court. We decided not to double Bird on the hawk anymore. Larry is the kind of player who looks out at the defense and says, "Okay. C'mon and double-team me. C'mon. I'll let you double-team me. Because I know I'm gonna get a shot for one of my teammates."

He's so good at passing under pressure to the open man that we said, "James, you've got to defend him one on one. When he dribbles and penetrates, then we'll drop the guy down. He won't have the same vision then to see the cutters and open guys."

By restricting the double teams, we could concentrate better on blocking out to rebound. Bertka told them, "This is going to be a game of big-muscle activity. Big muscles, not finesse. Pay attention to shot selection. If we're doubled, pass it out. Repost. Move the ball, swing it. Stop the shooter in the weak-side corner. We have to get to the offensive boards on every shot. We got sixteen offensive boards in two games. That ain't gonna get it done."

What it took was a junior skyhook with two seconds to go; a little luck; and Mychal Thompson.

Game Four started with both teams trying too hard. There was too much pent-up force, like a storm coming in. Shots went up right away, but no one scored for almost two minutes. A.C. did a great job of grabbing offensive rebounds, but he couldn't stop Parish or McHale from setting up wherever they wanted in the low post.

With so many missed shots in the opening minutes, the competition inside was tenacious. Then Ainge started hitting the outside shot. We were winning the rebound battles, but we stayed cold from the floor and from the free throw line. We weren't moving the ball. We shot 28% and made only 2 of 7 foul shots. The Celtics held a 7-point lead at the end of the quarter, 29–22.

Kareem blocked a Robert Parish shot right at the start of the second quarter, then he filled a lane on the fast break. We didn't score on that possession, but the effort level I was seeing made me feel great. If we could sustain our effort, we could find a way to win. We could play through the tightness. In the meantime, Earvin was keeping our offense alive by hitting from all over the court.

James Worthy hadn't scored yet. Our leading playoff scorer was 0 for 5. The Celtics were forcing him to initiate play from farther outside, just as we were trying to do to McHale. With a minute and forty-six seconds left in the second period, James blew past McHale and scored a jumper in the lane while drawing a foul. Half a minute later he faced McHale at the same spot on the court. James stared at him and froze in place for a few seconds, holding the ball down low. McHale took a dozen or so tiny stutter steps, trying to anticipate James's next move. James projected his head and shoulders then took a single dribble to the right. When the defender moved with him, he instantly spun 360 degrees to the left and took a clear path in for a layup. He was like a Porsche that had been out of tune through the first laps of the race. The timing of his offense had suddenly clicked. It was exactly what the Celtics were afraid of.

McHale set up in the low post, going against Kareem. With his back to the basket, McHale held the ball in his left hand. He lashed out a kick with his right leg, and took a backward swing with his right arm at the same time. It wasn't a subtle move. Then he powered in for a short baseline hook.

After losing the ball twice to steals, we were headed for a sure bucket on a fast break attempt. Only fifteen seconds left in the second period. Five on two, with Earvin leading the charge. Kite and DJ had just gotten back underneath when Earvin shoveled a pass to James on the left wing. Worthy made his cut right in front of the Laker bench. He accelerated and launched himself from several feet out. The ball was in both hands above his head. DJ hit James's right wrist as he sailed by. His lower body kept moving forward. Then Kite, coming from James's opposite side, raised a forearm and planted it hard against his rib cage.

His body stretched out parallel to the floor in midair. He dropped hard. The players on the floor clustered around, and the players on the bench stood up and started walking in. For a fraction of a second we didn't know whether to call a medic or a sergeant at arms. James landed on his side and rolled over. He jumped up to his feet and lashed out a fist toward Kite. Missed completely. Earvin grabbed his arms from behind, but he spun counterclockwise out of Earvin's grip and clipped Kite on the chin with a second jab. I ran out and got between them just as Kite was pulling back his arm to retaliate. Kurt Rambis, meanwhile, took DJ for a nonvoluntary backward walk to the sidelines.

The situation came back under control pretty quickly, but you could tell that a storm was getting ready to break.

I had to wait for a ruling. Kite made the dirty move, but Worthy took the first swing. They could both be ejected. Sometimes lesser players bait the great ones into fights just to make something like this happen. In the Finals of 1986, Ralph Sampson was thrown out after tangling with Jerry Sichting. It's like trading a knight for a pawn on the chessboard—a lousy deal. I remembered the incident in the 1984 Finals, when Kurt was coming in fast for a layup and McHale clubbed him in the throat. It sent him crashing out of control and could have very easily ended his career. We were ahead and we blew our lead because we were fixated on paying them back. It was an ugly example of how a ruthless team can take a stylish team out of its game.

Earl Strom, one of the officials, went over to the scorer's table. They conferred for a half minute, then they nodded to each other. DJ was guilty of a two-shot foul, Kite and Worthy each got technical fouls. They could both remain in the game, but on probation. One more "T" and they'd be out.

James made both free throws, then McHale put through a baseline fallaway with one second remaining in the first half. Earvin took the inbounds pass. With one foot on the Celtics' free throw line, he threw it to our goal like a quarterback trying to hit a flanker going deep. The ball landed inside the hoop and rumbled back and forth one time before it fell out. It summed up our whole first half: not connecting, but beginning to look dangerous.

The Celtics led at the half 55 to 47. Our shooting percentage was 39%, climbing slowly out of the basement. We held a small edge on the boards, 30 to 25. James had revived for 7 points in under two minutes. Meanwhile, Bird was unusually silent so far: three shot attempts and no makes. I sensed that the second half was going to be hellacious.

Both teams came out firing. DJ hit first, then Worthy, then McHale, then Scott. At about one and a half minutes in, Larry Bird scored his first basket—a 20-footer from the sideline. It was the first of 21 points that he would score in the half. It put the Celtics 10 points ahead. In roughly five minutes Bird had 10 points and we were behind by 16.

As soon as Bird lit up, Earvin took the Laker offense onto his own shoulders. He scored 8 straight. But he was tired and we would need him fresh in the fourth quarter. And we needed to try to take control of the game. We needed team offense. To create our opportunities, we had to apply more intense defensive pressure. The Celtics were playing their own game, ripping shot after shot. If we slipped any further behind, this would turn into another ass-kicking like the Memorial Day Massacre.

I called time out. I said, "We have one shot at this thing. From looking at your faces and seeing your body language, we're on the way to getting beat by twenty-five points. Unless we do something to change the tempo of the game defensively. We're going with the 'fist' defense." I inserted A.C. and Byron to run with James, Mychal, and Coop. Throwing heavy defensive pressure at a great team is the most physically demanding job in basketball. We had to have fresh legs.

The fist defense involves quick traps at half court or in the box where the half-court line and the sideline come together. It made the Celtics struggle more to initiate their offense. They had to scramble to get open for passes. So they started to take the first shot they could take, instead of working it into the low post or over to the weak side. They lost their poise and their patience.

That was what we wanted them to do. K.C. called a time-out with less than three minutes left in the period. I told the team, "Let's get it inside ten. That's all we want. Get their lead inside ten points for the fourth quarter."

We got it down to seven. We didn't execute the defense perfectly, but Boston took horrendous shots. From their time-out to the end of the period, we outscored them 11 to 4.

In terms of mental toughness, Bird is one of the greatest athletes in the world. But the Achilles' heel of the Celtics, all season long, had been a tendency to give away leads in the fourth quarter. Their bench had only been trusted with 13 minutes of first-half playing time. Darren Daye's 38 seconds was the only reserve play in the whole third period. We had them on the ropes. The question was: How tough would they be in that position?

Earl Strom warned both benches before the fourth quarter: Any more scuffles and players would be ejected. K.C. opened with Bird and DJ plus three reserves—Darren Daye, Kite, and Sichting. After half a minute he plugged McHale back in. Pretty soon he had returned the whole starting five. Earvin replaced Byron on the speedy pressing team.

The teams kept answering each other, basket for basket. Kareem returned. Two and a half minutes into the period, Bird and Earvin collided under the basket. The point of Bird's right knee banged the inside of Earvin's right knee. Earvin got up and hobbled around, trying to shake off the pain and stiffness. After less than a minute he was saying, "Send me back in, Riles."

We pushed the ball into the low post. Our offense started to look functional again, but the Boston low post defenders fouled us every time we got the ball inside. Kareem and Mychal drew fouls on Bird and Parish, converting three of four shots at the line. Our defense forced Boston into a 24-second-clock violation. Kareem drew Parish's fifth foul and made both shots. Then Mychal drew McHale's fourth foul and made both shots. With half a period left to play, we had tied the score at 93.

Boston came back with intensity. Ainge got out on two consecutive fast breaks. In the next three minutes they built a 10–2 scoring lead. There were three and a half minutes to play. Our defense tightened up again. We held them scoreless for the next three and a quarter minutes. We chipped on their lead with free throws. Kareem stripped the ball out of Parish's hands. Cooper scavenged it off the floor and started a Laker fast break. While the Celtics rushed to get underneath, he stopped at the 3-point line and nailed it.

When James dropped in a shot from the middle of the lane half a minute later, we were down by one point, 103–102, less than a minute to play. Boston called time out and went to Larry Bird. He missed a baseline shot under heavy pressure from Kareem. Mychal Thompson rebounded and got the ball out to Earvin on the break. Now was the time for poise and control. We ran our automatic, a play we've used over and over again in the eighties. It's a Show Time play starring our mainstays, Earvin and Kareem. Earvin dribbles up the right side. Ainge is applying extreme pressure all the way. Michael Cooper posts up down low. Coop pivots and sets a pick on DJ. Kareem, watching Earvin's eyes, receives his signal. He makes a V cut, as if he's headed for the top of the free throw line. Parish goes over the top of Cooper to follow, which is the signal for Earvin to put the ball in flight. With no one but a 6'2" guard between himself and the basket, Kareem jumps to full height. In one motion at the top of his jump he catches Earvin's lob pass with both hands and jams it through the hoop. Now Boston was down by one, 104–103. Twenty-nine seconds were left to play.

This time Bird caught us with a 3-pointer from the weak-side corner. We were 2 points down with twelve seconds to play, 106–104.

It was our turn to call time out. We had to get off a quick shot. If it missed, we had to commit a foul. When play resumed, Kareem planted himself underneath and took a pass. He launched a right-handed hook shot with seven seconds left. McHale hacked his arm. Kareem could tie the game at the line. If we could withstand their offense, the game would go into overtime.

Kareem sank the first shot. He lined up the second one. Several fans in his line of vision had pulled off their shirts. They were waving them like maniacs. The blubber on their stomachs shook. They screamed at the tops of their lungs.

Kareem's second foul shot nicked the front of the rim on the inside, then hit the back, then looped out to the right. McHale jumped for it, with Mychal Thompson right behind him. McHale grabbed the ball just as Thompson hit it off his hands. It flew out of bounds. McHale believed—or acted as if he believed—that it had gone out off Mychal. Earvin was clapping his hands at our good luck and smiling. McHale, looking in the opposite direction, was signaling his teammates to head downcourt for a Boston possession. Danny Ainge was literally jumping for joy at midcourt. Then they heard the official's call and reality set in. We called time out and set up the "Kentucky" play, a forced switch.

On our inbounds play, Worthy drew defenders to the right while Earvin rolled left. In the switch, McHale was left guarding Earvin—a Buick versus a Lamborghini. Earvin took the pass and faced McHale. Faking a pass to Kareem, Earvin put his head down and dribbled once. Making a deceptive shuffle step, he shifted gears and broke laterally across the court. McHale hustled to catch up. Bird and Parish converged toward Earvin as he picked up the ball in the middle of the lane. McHale jumped sideways and extended his left arm to full reach. Earvin flipped a 12-foot running hook shot over all three of them. Kareem was alone underneath. He jumped up when Earvin released, ready to tip in or to rebound a miss. The shot went in perfectly.

Two seconds remained in the game. Boston called their seventh and last time-out. Bird attempted another 3-pointer out of his catch-and-shoot motion in the left corner, but he had to rush it. The ball banged off the rim. The buzzer went off. We had our win on the enemy's home court.

Now we were truly poised. Mychal Thompson, alone, had as many fourth-quarter rebounds as the entire Celtics team. We won the quarter, 29–21. The one-point victory margin was enough to get the job done. We hadn't won the championship, but we had won the edge. Everything we had been fighting for for over 100 plus games in exhibition, regular season, and playoffs we unlocked in Game Four. It was the most important game of the year.

Red Auerbach dogged Earl Strom's footsteps all the way back to the changing rooms, yelling obscenities. Just before he closed the door in Auerbach's face, Strom said, "Arnold, you're showing the class you've shown your entire life."

There was a great celebration dinner that night. Afterwards, Bertka and I watched the Game Four video over and over at the hotel. We heard a reference on the tape to the legendary leprechaun who lives in Boston Garden and helps the Celtics. Bertka stopped the tape and cracked a smile. He said, "The leprechaun bounced off Mychal Thompson."

28

Victory

Boston kicked us from pillar to post in Game Five. Both teams were cold in the first quarter. The scoring came slow. We were tied at the end of the period, 25–25. We stayed cold in the second quarter and the Celtics didn't. Scott and Worthy had one basket each. All the Boston starters scored between 5 and 9 points apiece. They outrebounded us 26 to 19. They made the hard effort plays. Bird scored at one end, then blocked a shot five seconds later at the other end. Other players were watching a ball go out of bounds. Bird dove for it, hit the ground like a hay bale, and saved it to a teammate. Boston was ahead by 12 as the half wound down. Danny Ainge tossed in a running, 45-foot 3-pointer with no time left. We were down 63–48.

Ainge must have thought he was Michael Cooper. He made four more 3-pointers in the third period. Boston increased its lead to 96–77. Mychal Thompson brought us back slightly in the fourth with 11 points, but the Celtics preserved their margin to the end of the game, winning it 123–108.

Afterwards, some people speculated that Boston could have won all three at home, that one more Celtic basket in Game Four could have swung the whole series. That's a crock. We busted them open in Four. Even though the margin was only one point, we effectively unlocked their techniques. If they had won, we would have come out twice as tough in Five. But because we were ahead 3–1 for Game Five, we experienced a natural letdown. We had been cooped up in a crowded hotel for a week. We had built ourselves a large comfort zone. People were thinking about getting back to L.A.

That's why I don't like the 2-3-2 schedule for the Finals. Under the former plan, which was 2-2-1-1-1, the team with homecourt advantage played at home in the fifth game. You never got trapped in the opponent's city for a week.

Don't misunderstand. The Lakers came out to win Game Five, but we were only fighting for a quick finish. Boston was fighting for its life. If the Celtics had crumbled, we probably would have kicked into top gear and created a rout. Because they were staunch and determined, some of our guys subconsciously pulled in their horns and said, "If they want it that bad, hell, we'll save our energy for playing at home." Kareem, Earvin, Coop, and Mychal each delivered a strong effort. They're the most toughened players on the team. This was Mychal's first championship series, but he experienced seven seasons of carrying championship dreams on his shoulders in Portland. He had learned to deal with harsh times. Worthy was average. The pounding he absorbed in Game Four took its toll.

James did not arrive in Boston as totally toughened as some of the other players. I believe he is at that plateau now. The Celtics have always believed in hammering James to undercut his game. He has had to learn that the best way to deal with intimidation is to go right into its face.

Byron was subpar for the third game in a row. Of all our players, he had done the most all season long to meet the Career Best challenge. He improved in 17 out of 19 of the areas we measured. He shot 53%, most of it from outside, in the blowouts in Los Angeles. Then he hit 2 for 9 from the floor and 0 for 5 from 3-point range in our first Boston loss. The media heaped blame on him. He didn't snap back in the next game. Pressure increased. His confidence became a little fragile again. It started to play with his mind and undermined his game even more. He was slightly out of control in Game Five—too tight. You could see it in several ways. He had the ball knocked out of his hands when he tried to dribble past a defender. He drew a foul when he tried to retaliate for some rough play, getting a technical when he argued the call. He missed a scoop shot because he held the ball a tenth of a second too long.

Every mistake made him strain and struggle harder against the frustration, which just made the rhythms of his game become more elusive.

A.C. played a fair game, but he was still a gifted youngster facing taller, more resourceful opponents. In the dialect of the NBA, McHale and Parish took him to school.

We didn't move the ball well as a team. Our typical number of assists in a game is over 30. In Game Five we had only 16. That meant we didn't get many easy shots and we didn't control the tempo—no flow, too much isolation. We only scored 19 of 52 on the fast break. So be it.

Chris and I went straight to the hotel and packed our bags. We sat on the bed until four in the morning, watching the video of that game over and over. Finally I lay down, but I never slept that night. I didn't sleep the next night, either—or the one after that.

We caught an early flight for Los Angeles. It was Friday, June 12th. The bus ride to Logan Airport was like a death march—almost total silence. We had one day to fly, one day to practice, and Game Six on Sunday. Bertka slept a little. I kept watching the tape on a portable monitor. I thought about the conversation I had had with Coop and Earvin at the airport. We had talked about Byron and how much we needed him. They're a tight trio. They always socialize together on the road and at home. I asked them: "What's wrong with Byron? How're we gonna get him back? We're running out of time. We need him now."

Coop said, "Wanda and I stayed up all night with Byron and Anita. Just talking about the game and what we had to do to win. He said he was really down and he thought he was being blamed for the losses in Boston."

There was never a single word from any of our players in the press about him. I went out of my way to deflect questions about his performance. I said, "Byron's tough. He's had a great season. He'll come back." And I believed what I was saying. Byron was part of the combination that had gotten us into the Finals. He had my confidence. All he lacked was his own.

Before Game Five, when there was a possibility of leaving Boston with a championship, we arranged for security and for a team bus to meet our plane. We decided to hold steady with those arrangements. We would board the bus and take everyone to the Forum for a team meeting, instead of dispersing. We felt comfortable and confident. We could envision how different everything would be playing in the Forum, but we didn't want to send the team away without a message.

We got off the plane around noon. The bus took us to the Forum and down the tunnel into the lower level. Vitti sent everyone to the locker room. I took Kareem to one side and asked him to be ready to address his team. Kareem is still the most profoundly respected of the Lakers. Every word he says has impact.

My message was only five minutes long. I said we had to put ourselves right back where the season began, with attitude. How we had worked, dedicated ourselves, pushed for Career Best efforts. Now we had just one thing left: to win one game. I said, "For the next forty-eight hours, just focus on this game. Don't allow anything else to come into your life. And focus on the attitude that you're going to bring to practice tomorrow—a work-oriented attitude. We're going to go hard. We're going to hit.

"I didn't prepare you right for Game Five. I didn't push you in practice after you won Game Four because I thought you were tired. It was my fault we didn't give Game Five a championship effort. And we got caught.

"When we come to work tomorrow, we come in with an attitude to kick ass. We're going to scrimmage. We ain't coming in here to shoot layups and go home. Byron, you know you've got to come. James, A.C., you've got to be ready to go hard for forty-eight minutes. Forget about what happened in Boston. Forget about peripheral opponents. Forget the criticism and just get with the program. We're at home, where our record is 37 and 4, in front of our city, our fans, and our families. And we will get it done on Sunday. You can bet on it."

I looked around. Then I said, "Cap, you got anything to say?"

Kareem looked at everyone for a moment, then said, "I didn't come all this way to lose. We didn't work this hard and do all the things we did this year to give it away. I'm coming to play on Sunday, and I expect everyone else to, too."

Earvin erupted. "Yeah! Let's bring it in, man. Let's do it!"

When the meeting broke up, I called Byron up to my office. Everyone else went home. Byron came in with a very defensive air, sat down, and stared like a face carved inside an Egyptian tomb. He waited for me to begin.

I said, "What's wrong? What's going on with you?"

"I'll be okay. There ain't nothing wrong."

"I talked to your compadres and they are concerned. They asked me to talk to you. The two guys that you care the most about. We've talked. They're concerned about you, and that makes me concerned. Because I'm starting you on Sunday and we're playing for a world championship and you're not in the right frame of mind. Not now. It's not the time to withdraw."

I didn't yell, but I was almost beside myself. "You've got one thing in front of you. You've got a chance to win a world championship. You think your teammates and coaches are blaming you?

"Go back, Byron. Read the press. The writers are hammering you. They're saying you're weak and you can't play in Boston Garden and all this shit. That's them writing about your performance. Now you're taking their opinion and transferring it. You're putting it on me and your teammates. That isn't fair. You aren't performing, Byron. When you're a starter on the Los Angeles Lakers and you're playing for a world championship, criticism comes with the territory.

"Go back and talk to Earvin. Go back and talk to Kareem. Talk to those guys about getting criticized when you don't perform. If you want to be great, if you want to walk with those guys and be a part of them, you've got to handle that bullshit. Nobody can handle it for you."

He listened. He didn't acknowledge anything, but I could see that it hit home. I said, "Byron, if I was down on you, I'd sit you on the bench. If I thought you were making us lose, I don't care who you are, I'd sit you down. But I don't believe that. I believe that you're a part of this team and you're going to help us win it. That's why I haven't said a word to you about your game. I haven't jerked you out, other than our normal rotation.

"The people who are criticizing you are not part of the inner workings of this team. They have nothing to do with the character or the play sets or the attitude. I want you to come back tomorrow with a different attitude. I want you to think about your teammates and Buck and Coop depending on you, depending on you to play hard and play defense. Are we on the right wavelength?"

Byron nodded. "I'll be okay." I believed him.

Our practice on Saturday was like a training camp. They poured out the effort like guys trying to break into the league. We ran three-line fast break drills, sprinting. Then we went three on three full court, four on four full court, and five on five half court with live blocking-out. We were purely physical for half an hour, then we sent everyone back home to rest.

Reporters were waiting outside. I asked the team to keep their comments short. Talk about being ready. Talk about wanting to see the fans come out. Get the crowds excited. We want them to come in and yell for the first fifteen minutes. We want to hear everybody singing, "I Love L.A."

I went home and read through the mail that had piled up during our week in Boston. I wrote notes to people. I lay in the hammock out under the eucalyptus trees. I shot some hoops. James wrestled with me on the lawn.

I left the house on a compact discs expedition. I found an oldies collection with "Yes I'm Ready" by Barbara Mason and "Since I Don't Have You" by the Skyliners. My favorite song of theirs is "This I Swear Is True." I went to five different stores trying to find a CD with "This I Swear." Finally, after buying about thirty other discs, I gave up the search.

I came home, ate dinner with my family, and played with James awhile. Then I went back out to the office until three-thirty in the morning. I watched more videotape and wrote up my pregame talk. I started thinking about what I'd say if we won, what I'd say if we lost—but I didn't figure to lose. I worked out my thoughts on guaranteeing a repeat title. I wanted to be totally prepared.

Around three-thirty I went upstairs to bed. Though I hadn't slept since Wednesday, I still couldn't sleep. I went back to my office and read. Then I took a sauna and steam, listened to the oldies disc over and over. Around nine on Sunday morning I finally got into my car and drove to the Forum to wait. I was carrying a clean shirt, tie, and slacks in my briefcase. I expected to run into some champagne.

Earvin was waiting alone. He had his shoes and his uniform sitting out, ready. I said, "What are you doing here at this hour?" He looked at me and said, "I haven't slept in three days." He had gotten in by banging on a door until one of the janitors heard him. I told him how I hadn't slept either. We laughed at each other. It was a great moment. While I was stirring around my home, not able to stay in one spot for more than a few minutes at a time, not able to sleep, Earvin was shooting baskets alone in his home, playing records, being restless. Two people, one mind.

When the guys came in, there was a freshness to everyone's aspect. Their eyes were clear and alert. Byron was loose, gabbing with everybody.

Everybody took a seat in front of his locker. I told them, "Let's just go out and run, pass and catch. That's all we want to do—run, pass and catch. Do you know what that is, fellas?" They smiled, shifted around a little, and gave each other looks. This sounded like fun.

I wanted to take the heaviness off the game. It wasn't going to be an intellectual exercise. We just had to take all the things we had drilled on all season long and perform them right. I said, "But while you're running, you're thinking. And when you're catching, you're going to drive right down their throats. We're going to show them aggressive communication and wild rebounding. We're going to be tough. We're going in with the disposition of dominating the court. We're going to control them with our defense. Intensity and emotion with poise and control. We won't try to win it in the first six minutes. Control." They were ready . . . Too ready.

The tip went up at 2:14, Sunday afternoon, June 14th. Kareem directed the ball to James, then headed for the low post position. After a great screen on James, Kareem hooked back to the post. Earvin made a perfect pass, directly under the basket. He dropped the ball in easily.

At the other end, Dennis Johnson came driving around a screen by Larry Bird, having a clear path to the basket. Kareem crossed over from the far side and blocked the shot to Earvin exactly as it left DJ's shooting hand. Earvin sent the rebound up the sideline. James was flying. He caught the ball, made his cut, and rode it in for a slam.

Kareem kept his promise. In the first 20 seconds I knew he had come to play one of the best games of his life. James was right there with him. He scored inside twice more. At just over two minutes played, ahead 8–2, I was certain that we would win.

Boston called a time-out to adjust, and then everything began to go downhill.

The Celtics started doing what they do best. They pounded it inside to McHale, and he scored a hook. Byron came back with a beautiful fast break layup, a delayed release after a long jump with DJ alongside him all the way. Then McHale scored again inside, drawing a foul on A.C. this time.

That was the start of a 15–2 scoring streak: 4 for Parish, 6 for DJ, 2 for Bird, and 3 for McHale.

It reminded me of 1982, the sixth game of the Finals, versus Philadelphia. The players were fired up. They came out charging. We got off a nine to nothing spurt. The fans were going crazy. Then Philly took a time-out. They started to get back in the game, kept chipping away at our lead until a shot block by Bob McAdoo turned the game back in our favor, late in the fourth quarter.

Boston all of a sudden looked like the masters of the situation. They were penetrating on drives and working over our low post defenders. They were moving the ball fluidly. We looked frustrated and inefficient. Our anticipation had gone up too many notches. We were hyper, playing past the level of control. We started taking quick shots, trying to crack the game instead of patiently working our offense and defense. Coop couldn't hit. Earvin couldn't hit. Mychal and Kareem kept us in the game, but the Celtics held a 32–25 margin at the end of the first quarter.

The second quarter looked the same. We pulled closer on Kareem's and Worthy's scoring, but the guards couldn't catch fire. Our passing was badly timed. Larry Bird single-handedly derailed a four-on-two fast break because we didn't spread out the attack with smart ball movement. Three minutes later, Bird stole the ball from Cooper and started a three-on-one. Kareem blocked it all alone, but he drew his third foul. Still, we pulled within one point when Cooper finally threw in a bank shot off the fast break. Earvin got his second bucket as the period wound down. Bird began to get hot at the same time, though. They kept the lead. It was 56–51 at the half. I thought it was a blessing to be that close.

We were so off-balance. Kareem and Worthy together had made 35 points; the other six players had only made 16. Even with Kareem's going 9 for 11 and James's going 7 for 10, our field goal percentage was only 48. Coop and A.C. were both 1 for 5. Byron was 1 for 4, Earvin 2 for 9. We were 5 for 11 at the line, versus the Celtics' 11 for 11.

At halftime, Coop and Earvin were sitting side by side in the locker room. Earvin asked him, "Hey, are you rushing?"

Coop said, "Yeah. Are you?"

"Yeah. I'm rushing too."

I didn't show any video footage. I didn't put any X's and O's on the blackboard. I just wrote: Defense, Control, Execution, Shot Selection. It's our day. I said, "We want this so much that we're playing beyond ourselves. All we have to do is get back to playing our game. We're going to win it or lose it in the first three minutes of the third period. After three minutes, either the score will be tied, or we'll be down by twelve. And if we go down twelve to this team, it's probably going to be over with. We'll be playing a seventh game. If we can get this thing tied in the first three minutes, we're going to win today."

I wanted to make them focus strictly on the present moment. I didn't want them thinking about letting it get down to the wire.

Somehow, we entered the third period unbelievably ready and Boston came out flat. It was still hard to score. Earvin finished a drive with a little three-foot scoop shot. Score: 56–53. Then we traded possessions without making baskets. There were a lot of great-effort plays that didn't accomplish much. Our defense was tough, but somehow the shots on the other end eluded us. A.C. missed a driving layup by forcing too hard, but he put in a pair of free throws. I kept thinking, "We're not going to get any better opportunity than this."

At a minute and forty-five seconds into the period, Kareem was called for his fourth foul. I had to bring him off the floor—the guy who had done the most to keep us competitive.

Something great happened. With Kareem on the bench, the rest of the guys knew that they had to settle down, pull together, and play great defense. Otherwise we were dead.

DJ set up on the right side of the key to pass to McHale in the low post. Byron Scott shifted over for a double team, which meant that James had to come over too. But playing possum a little, he just came partway over. He let McHale and DJ have a clear line of sight to each other.

DJ made the pass into the low post and we double-teamed McHale. On McHale's pass back to DJ on the perimeter, James made a lunge for the ball, catching it with his fingertips. He deflected the ball at a slight backward angle toward the sideline, out of bounds. Instead of watching it go on out, he raced over. Earvin saw him go. He started loping downcourt, toward our basket. He wasn't sure James could make it, but he had to take the chance.

James was on the outer edge of control, but he knew he could reach that ball. He had to launch himself face first to make it happen. At the moment his left hand made contact, he looked like a sprinter blasting out of the starting blocks. Then Earvin saw James twist his neck to look for a teammate downcourt. That was the confirmation. James was flattened out in midair, full extension thrust. His left hand smacked the ball sideways, angling toward Earvin and toward our basket.

Earvin had to slow his stride a half step. He gathered the ball in. As he did, James made a half turn in the air. He landed full length on the hardwood on his back. His momentum created a slide about two body lengths long. At the end of it, he had regained enough control to sit halfway up, twist his neck, and take a look. He saw Earvin stuffing the ball in the hole. Score: 57–56, our first lead since the opening minutes.

Worthy's dive was the play of the year. It was the classic tenet of Laker basketball once again—our defense igniting our offense, a stick of dynamite in a logjam. Half a minute later he scored a dunk off a fast break. Earvin connected on a 20-footer from the left. James stuffed off an assist from Earvin. Byron surprised them with an 18-footer. A.C. tipped in one of his own missed shots. Mychal got rebounds in bunches. One of them he put back up for a score. James, the silent one all season long, was yelling encouragement, calling for the ball in the post, carrying on like a frontline soldier in a holy war.

In about seven and a half minutes we ran up an 18 to 2 barrage. We forced four Celtic turnovers and only committed one. By the end of the period our lead was 81–68. The Celtics got only 12 points, one of the lowest scoring quarters in playoff history. We put in 30. Our defense went from tough to successful.

Earvin, A.C., Byron, Mychal, and Coop started the fourth period. Usually, when we're blowing a team out, Kareem stays on the bench. This time he tapped me on the shoulder and said, "Who do I take?"

Kareem wanted another piece of this action. Forty years old. The guy who was supposed to be over the hill and dragging the team down with him. I sent him in, along with James, for Earvin and A.C. Mychal stayed. He scored a layup and Coop hit a long one. Our lead was 19 points. After Boston scored a couple of their own, Kareem dropped in a short hook and drew Parish into his sixth foul at the same time. Three points.

Kareem went on to make 14. The last three involved a 12-foot hook and foul number five on Kevin McHale.

I wanted to bring each of the starters out one at a time—letting them get their applause. The display Kareem was putting on messed up my timing. The greatest player in the history of the game was doing his thing. I had to watch.

With a minute and a half left, the score at 106–91, I substituted

Mike Smrek, Adrian Branch, and Wes Matthews for Kareem, Earvin, and Coop. Worthy had fouled out, one of the few times in his whole career. I embraced Earvin as he got to the sideline. Kareem took the long route down to the Celtics bench, where he shook hands with their coaches. Earvin stepped up to the bench and Billy Thompson hugged him. Then Kareem arrived. He, Billy, and Earvin held on to each other.

When play resumed, Darren Daye got two free throws for Boston. They were the last points of the '86–'87 NBA season. A.C. went in for Byron, who collected a round of applause. Wes Matthews dribbled the ball in a weave around the midcourt line while 17,505 fans counted off the last seconds. Then they rushed the floor.

We had done it. In our city, on our court, in front of our friends and our families. Undefeated at home throughout the playoffs. The World Champions.

I could hear the announcer giving individual scoring figures as I made for the tunnel. Each name set off a big roar. "Kurt Rambis —one. A.C. Green—six. Michael Cooper—six. Byron Scott— eight. Mychal Thompson—fifteen. Magic Johnson—sixteen. James Worthy—twenty-two. And the Captain. Kareem Abdul-Jabbar. Thirty-two points!"

Earvin walked in and took the first bottle of champagne. He put his thumb over the mouth of the bottle and shook it up. Making a whooping noise that echoed off the walls, he sprayed everything and everybody in a fifteen-foot radius.

Keith Erickson tried to interview some of the players. A.C., who doesn't drink for religious reasons, accepted his champagne and quietly put it aside. He said he was thankful, that it was a blessing to be on such a team. Wes carried on about the greatness of Earvin. Adrian yelled, "Pour some champagne on me!"

I told Keith, "I'm gonna become a regular person again. I'm gonna enjoy my life!"

Kareem and the other starters were up on a wooden platform, getting ready for presentation of the championship trophy.

Then all the people watching on television saw something that I don't think has ever been seen before. The wives of the players and coaches came in to share the moment: Linda Rambis, Wanda Cooper, Angela Worthy, Pam Matthews, Solveig Bertka, Anita Scott. Up there on the platform with their husbands were the women who kept everything together through the constant road trips, the constant practices, and the emotional ups and downs in this nomadic warrior NBA life. They deserved the joy. Chris Riley was there, too. As she always is for me.

The joy continued for nearly two hours. I heard Earvin tell a group of reporters, "It's the greatest championship by far. Because last year nobody thought we could win anything." Jerry Buss talked about how important it was to listen to Jerry West, how keeping James Worthy and adding Mychal Thompson made us great. He stepped over and hugged Mychal. He said, "What a game you played! Jerry and Pat told me what you'd mean, but I had no idea! You were just great."

Mychal told his boss, "We can do it again."

Those were my sentiments, too. I had spent a lot of time thinking about the question of repeating. I knew it was going to be asked. I didn't want to stumble over it and make a qualified statement. I didn't want to feel as if I were preparing an excuse for a letdown in the coming year. So I said, "I'm going to guarantee to everyone we're going to repeat." People looked at me like I was a lunatic.

After two hours of effusion and champagne, Earvin stood up on a chair and told everyone, "That's it. It's time for the team to be alone. Thanks, everybody."

The thing about winning the title is that it takes so long. You have to climb a mountain to get there. When you win it's instantaneous euphoria. The scene on the court, with all our fans pouring onto the floor, seemed like fifteen seconds. The two hours in the locker room seemed like a few minutes. After that, it's all afterglow, total satisfaction.

There were so many parties and special moments in the next several days, before we took off for the Bahamas. I remember Kareem addressing the parade crowd on the steps of City Hall, saying how he loved seeing the banner that read "Saludas Lakers, Campeónes Mundial." I remember Earvin taking the podium and shouting, "We're the number one team. You're the number one sports fans. We're in the number one city, and we've got the number one mayor. So, hey, have a good time."

The greatest memory is our team party. This is what we do, every time we win a championship. There's no other party that can ever compare. Our victory parties are celebration in the purest sense of the word. We celebrate each other. Everyone is a star, everyone gets the message that they are loved.

We met at On The Rocks, a small private club on Sunset Strip. There was no one there except people from the inner circle. Players, their families, the publicity staff, managers, coaches, all the people who keep the Laker machinery turning.

Everyone was dancing. Chris danced with Coop while I danced with Wanda. Then we'd split up and draw other people onto the floor. Earvin became the center of the fun, just as he does on a basketball court. He had a song played over and over again. He sang it and brought everybody in. Then he would call one person at a time, calling out names to the rhythm of the music. Each person came into the center. They each had to dance alone, improvising, while everyone formed a circle around them. I never saw James so loose and relaxed in the five years I've known him. All his intense, serious demeanor was lifted off like a veil. All the pressure was gone and his smile never left his face. Everybody applauded him like crazy when his turn came to dance in the center. It was the ultimate acknowledgment: He had arrived as a leader and as a player.

Bahamas
Farewell

Matthew came down with one last tray of drinks. He said, "Forget about the chairs. I'll get 'em tomorrow." We looked around. There was nobody else left on the beach. The sun was low over the water. Matthew and his partner had already stashed every bit of cabana equipment except the chairs we were using. Chris had left to get herself ready for dinner.

I said, "Buck, this is where we're always going to be. If you want to come walking down this way, we're going to be propped up here. Just being lazy, enjoying the moment. So don't ever feel like you're infringing. It's wide open."

He said, "Okay, Riles." He straightened up and rolled one shoulder back and then the other, loosening up. He gave me a smile. Then he said good-bye and sauntered down the beach toward his hotel.

I started picking up our towels and our books and our cassettes.

I looked around. Earvin was thirty or forty yards away, getting to be farther in the distance. I looked down to the cabana, fifty yards away in the opposite direction, and I wondered whether I should lug the chairs down. Then I thought, "Nobody's gonna steal 'em here." The sun was just on top of the water. The sky was orange and the water wasn't green anymore but steel gray. The beach sand was rose colored, the Moorish roofs of the villas had a pink blush. And there was this one guy walking away from me with a gray T-shirt that was flopping with the breeze.

I got a shudder. I thought, "You know, one day he's going to be gone forever. He's gonna walk right out of my life, and the Lakers' lives, and the fans' lives. And that's gonna be it."

The same thing happened when Jerry West told me he was quitting the game. We had played together for five years. I always used to say I lived on parasitic value. I knew how to complement and support the play of the best guard in the NBA. We had just gotten beat by the Milwaukee Bucks, eliminated in the first round of playoff competition on April 7th, 1974. It was two years after achieving a championship on the winningest team in league history. Jerry had a muscle tear that would never get better. Nowadays, Vitti could probably fix it without a problem, but sports medicine was fairly primitive then. Jerry was soaping up in the shower when he turned to me and said, "This is my last game." Jerry didn't want any big deal made over him. He doesn't enjoy the limelight. He was the greatest guard that the game had known, a complex personality and a loyal friend. When we won this championship, he came into the locker room, had a sip of champagne, shook a few hands, and left. I've never been around anyone who wanted to win more than him.

Watching Earvin go down the beach gave me the same mixture of feelings. It was part insecurity, wondering if I could ever be as successful without his presence, and part wondering if the simple pleasure that we experience with each other, the sensations of thinking the same thoughts at the same time, could ever happen again.

Just after we finished with Boston, Kareem, Jerry West and Jerry Buss came to terms on a contract extension. The greatest player in basketball history would be with us two more years. Then I'd see him walk away, too. Earvin walked farther down the beach and the sun went into the Atlantic Ocean and that was it.

I picked up my stuff and walked up the hill, looking for the path to our rooms. All of a sudden the hill looked like just any hill, anywhere. My focus was sharp. I saw the weeds and the sticks and the dirt, things that I hadn't noticed for hours. When I got to the top of the hill, I looked one more time and he was gone.

I felt alone.

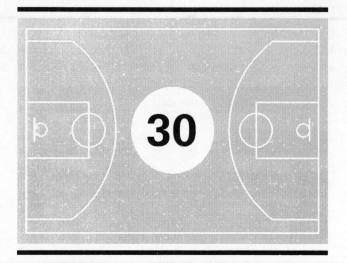

30

The Future
Is Now

All summer long I wondered exactly what attitude we should take into the new season. Plenty has been said about how it's impossible to repeat in the NBA. I didn't want to reinforce that thinking.

Just before training camp, I sent each of the players a personal letter. This is part of it:

"I don't know about you, but I need a game to coach. I hope you need a game to play, a real competitive one.

"Next year is not about winning another championship or having one more ring or developing bigger reputations. It's about leaving footprints.

"After four championships in eight years, we have arrived at a point in this team's history where there is just one thing left for us to accomplish. That is to become a team for all ages and eras, the greatest basketball team ever. We do not merely want to be considered the best of the best. It is time to truly separate ourselves from the pack and become the only ones who do what we do. Unique. That is the essence of Show Time.

"The future is now, fellas."